WRONG
WOMEN

WRONG WOMEN

SELLING SEX IN MONTO, DUBLIN'S FORGOTTEN RED LIGHT DISTRICT

CAROLINE WEST

First published in the UK by Eriu
An imprint of Bonnier Books UK

5th Floor, HYLO
103–105 Bunhill Row
London, EC1Y 8LZ

Owned by Bonnier Books
Sveavägen 56, Stockholm, Sweden

𝕏 – @eriu_books

⬛ – @eriubooks

Trade Paperback – 978-1-80418-441-7
Ebook – 978-1-80418-718-0

A CIP catalogue of this book is available from the British Library.

Typeset by IDSUK (Data Connection) Ltd
Printed and bound by Clays Ltd, Elcograf S.p.A.

1 3 5 7 9 10 8 6 4 2

Copyright © Dr Caroline West 2025
Map copyright © Lou Walker 2025

www.bonnierbooks.co.uk

For the women and girls of Monto

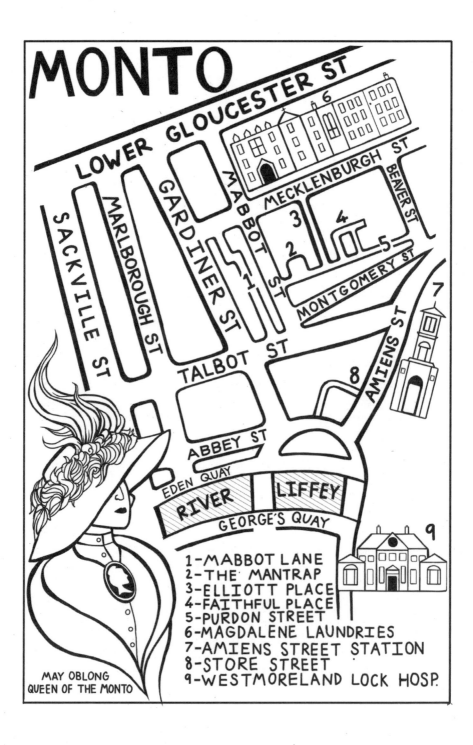

CONTENTS

INTRODUCTION

'There's too much madness that went through Monto for that energy to go. It lives on in the air still.'

– Gemma Dunleavy, great-granddaughter of the
Granny Dunleavy, the midwife of Monto

On Sean McDermott Street in the north inner city of Dublin, the Magdalene Laundry building looms empty, having survived attempts from a Japanese hotel chain to turn it into a boutique hotel in 2018. Plans are now under way to turn the site into a memorial centre for the thousands of women confined in the laundry system, but a more forgotten part of Irish women's history lies on the streets behind its flaking red-brick facade. A site of extremes, this neighbourhood was where many women changed their fortunes for better or worse in one of the most legendary red-light districts of the British Empire – Monto.

A mere dot on the landscape, Monto's geographical location was far exceeded by its reputation, and its notoriety travelled far across Europe and America. From around 1860 to 1925, thousands of women sold sex in Monto, an essentially tolerated red-light district that operated with ruthlessness from top to bottom. In this urban space less than a square mile big, women could accumulate wealth, sending their children to private schools and affording the finest fashions and attending high-society gatherings, or they could find themselves on the streets, struggling to survive and ravaged by syphilis. Brothels sat side by side with family homes, and visitors from across the globe enjoyed evenings of carousing in its brothels, pubs and streets. Monto was a landscape with layers; not only did it have physical boundaries, but it also had moral and class boundaries, with opulent establishments for the wealthy and rotting tenements or the streets for those with pennies. Violence was common, life was short, and the thousands of women who passed through Monto were mostly forgotten. Unlike many similar red-light areas, Monto has an official date of closure – 12 March 1925, when Frank Duff and his volunteers from the Legion of Mary marched in to close it down. With all of its undesirable residents turfed out, a crucifix was hung publicly to reclaim the area. Monto was cleansed.

However, nowadays Monto is mostly forgotten by the general public and its wild stories silenced. It was a relic of British colonialism, according to some, and not a fitting part of the new Irish Free State and the architecture of confinement that the Catholic Church championed. Women who sold sex were not allowed to be a visible part of this new era, and so their stories were erased and the buildings were demolished. However, like the sale of sex itself, Monto has been preserved in pockets of knowledge, paragraphs here and there, newspaper reports, oral folklore and family history.

This book is the result of a chance encounter with a singular sentence that struck me and stayed with me for years. In 2011, I went back to university to complete an MA and PhD in sexuality studies at DCU, as I was fascinated with how sex can tell us so much about humans, from behaviour to attitudes, to technology and theories of pleasure and violence. I had briefly heard of Monto and thought of it from time to time but hadn't fully explored it yet. Everything changed in 2015 after a random glance while passing a dusty bookshop on Parnell Street that I hadn't known to ever be open. This warm summer's afternoon, its door was ajar, and in the window was Maurice Curtis's book *To Hell or Monto*. I snatched it up and devoured it, but a brief sentence stopped me in my tracks. Curtis wrote that the women of Monto were often smothered with pillows when they went into hospital to be treated for syphilis. I had to reread that as goosebumps rippled up my arms, and this statement, informed by local Monto historian Terry Fagan, stayed with me as I finished my studies, waiting to be explored further.

This new connection with Monto allowed me to see a surprisingly large number of parallels with the women in my PhD – female porn performers in America in the 21st century. I'd never have thought the women walking the cobblestones of Monto would have had so much in common with porn stars having sex on screen an ocean away and centuries later.

My PhD research involved going to Vegas to attend the Adult Entertainment Expo and AVN awards show in January 2016. This event is known as the Oscars of porn, where performers meet with fans and have a glitzy awards ceremony with performers winning trophies for 'best ass' or 'best gangbang'. It was a surreal and overwhelming space, in both positive and negative ways. The environment felt like a pop-up red-light district, and while this was 2016, it had striking similarities with Monto a century earlier. Just as Monto had 'flash houses', which were brothels where the upper classes frolicked, the porn expo had different packages for different clients. This ranged from premium access to the most popular performers for high-paying clients to free autographs, photos and time with stars who commanded lower status for those who couldn't afford luxury access to more famous celebrity performers. In both spaces, fashion was used as advertising, with some outfits more outrageous than others and some dressed in a modest fashion, conveying an appearance of wealth and class. Money, power and precarity were similarly in flux, as both spaces resisted attempts at closure from state and religious groups.

Both spaces were populated by voyeurs, tourists, entrepreneurs, predators, hustlers, opportunists, disrupters, partiers, substance users, independent workers, victims, stigmatised women, mothers, daughters, exploiters, fans, thrivers, capitalists, celebrities, families, security staff, survivors, managers, students, the rich, the poor, the exploited, entertainers, business owners, feminists, resistors, creators, protesters, writers and religious saviours. All interacted with each other through differing levels of power and access.

Despite seeming radically different at first, being aware of these similarities is important if we want to learn about the sale of sex in the context of other locations, demographics and eras. They help us see what has changed, for better or worse, and what *hasn't* changed in this aspect of human life, particularly in women's lived experiences – and for *which* women. We can also compare the experiences of women in other locations in the same time frame, who often saw the same clients and operated in similar power structures. While Monto was unique in having the Catholic Church play such a substantial role in closing it down, commonalities in the sex trade existed then and now, and they can help fill in gaps in knowledge and, in some cases, uncover the voices of the women in these circumstances. Each chapter of this book paints a picture of an aspect of Monto that was transformed by class, money and time, including the type of client, decor and working conditions.

The reader may notice that the terms 'sex worker' and 'prostitute' are both used in the text. Language is a site of struggle, according to feminist revolutionary thinker bell hooks, as it is a space where we can name ourselves. It's therefore also a controversial space when it comes to sex and those who sell or trade it.

The term 'sex work' was coined by an American woman named Carol Leigh in 1979. She felt the term used by feminists at the time, 'sex use industry', did not reflect her personal experiences of selling sex and so she came up with the phrase 'sex work' to centre her experience rather than the clients', and to frame her selling of sex as work. She was a proudly self-declared sex worker and rejected the label of 'prostitute'. Carol's advocacy ushered in a new age of analysis for the sex trade, connecting sex work with labour rights, safety, autonomy and feminism while centring the voices of those who had lived experience.

Today, many feminists who reject the term 'sex worker' prefer to use the term 'prostituted woman' to highlight their view that selling sex is an act of violence against women from the men who buy it. Some women in the industry, like many in Amsterdam today, prefer to call themselves prostitutes and believe 'sex worker' is too broad a term as it refers to many kinds of sexual services, not just penetrative sex. The terms used to talk about selling sex have remained controversial in different feminist camps and are still hotly debated today.

Since we do not know what the women of Monto would have preferred, this book uses the term 'prostitute' for the women and girls of Monto who were involved in the sale of sex. In its original usage in Victorian Britain, it was a neutral term that did not take sides on agency and consent because that was not a part of the conversation back then. It was also a word the women of Monto were familiar with as sex worker would not be invented until decades later. When present-day women were interviewed for this book, they wanted to use the term 'sex worker' to reflect their job and beliefs, and so both terms are used here.

This is not a book that aims to provide a comprehensive guide to every aspect of sex work, prostitution and trafficking in history or the current era. That would be a mammoth encyclopaedia that would date rapidly in terms of technology, money, violence, stigma, demographics and forms of sex work. And it *still* wouldn't cover everything. This is also *not* a book that is here to debate the rightness or wrongness of different approaches to the sex trade. Instead, it focuses on the stories of the people behind the ideologies. I do, however, encourage you to access more information on these topics, particularly from the perspectives of people with lived experiences of all kinds.

A few years ago, when I interviewed a UK porn performer with Irish heritage named Blath, she highlighted how a focus on a simple 'good or bad' approach to selling sex means missing out on so much rich knowledge and understanding:

> I don't like the empowerment narrative. I just think it's not useful because I think it's just not the most important conversation to be having about sex work – we need to be having conversations about safety, about workers' rights, about payment, about diversity. I think empowerment is just way down on the list, to be honest. It's great if people do find that, but other workers don't and it's not okay to say 'oh it's okay if you do this work but only if you feel this certain emotion about it'. And it seems to be [it's] only [in] those types of work that people are asked that question. People don't ask other labourers if they feel empowered by their work. Usually journalists have this kind of pre-notion in their head of whether they are going to go with 'empowerment' or 'exploitation'. You need to go in without those preconceptions and actually listen.

Beyond the simple binary of exploitation or empowerment, this book is a study into the history of the unrecognised, the voice that other people would prefer not to hear, and the spectrum of violence against women, particularly marginalised women. Decolonising your bookshelf is a fantastic idea, but so is declassifying it. So often the stories that we hear are of privileged women, but what about the working-class woman? The single mother? The sex worker? The migrant woman? The homeless woman? Working-class histories have been forgotten about, with many now lost to the passing of time and memory. The women of Monto are remembered as the 'poor unfortunates', but what were their stories? How did they support each other and form a sense of community? How did they end up in Monto, and how did they leave? Did they leave?

These stories are important because the way that the 'wrong' kind of woman has been treated in Ireland has resulted in intergenerational trauma and violence on a personal, societal and state level.

What we are unfortunately missing from the women of Monto is an insight into the kind of language they used to describe their work, themselves or their clients. We know local people referred to the women as 'doxies' or 'spunkers', which is British slang for a promiscuous woman, but how did the women feel about that word or being called a 'poor unfortunate'? The term 'sex work' wasn't invented then, and the age of consent was 13, so terms such as 'child prostitution' or 'sex trafficking' were not part of Monto descriptions. Did the women see their activities as work, exploitation or some other point along that spectrum?

While we can't directly interview the women and girls of Monto, this book strives to promote their voices as much as possible and support them with the voices of their descendants. In this book you will hear from a great-great-granddaughter and a great-granddaughter of madam Annie Meehan, Paula Meehan and Pearl Brock. Paula is a poet and playwright born in Monto who grew up hearing whispers and snippets about what her great-granny had been up to and has used Annie's experiences in her work, which focuses on women's experiences of loss, trauma and love. Pearl is a therapist who works with many types of clients, including sex workers, and she lives with some of her great-great-grandmother Annie's remaining belongings in her house. Both Paula and Pearl trace Annie's impact through their families and their work, highlighting the intergenerational impact of trauma, poverty, sexual violence and violence.

A great-grandson to madam and convicted murderer Margaret Carroll, whose sister Nannie McLoughlin was also a madam, Martin Coffey is an author of books such as *What's Your Name Again?* who has sifted through his family history to discover how their connections to Monto have shaped his family since Margaret was convicted. His grandmother Annie Carroll also spent time in Monto, and his family stories and artefacts from Monto are essential items to help us understand Monto on a personal level – Martin happily spoke for hours about his family history for this book, and his published works on Monto are well worth reading.

Folklorist, and son of the last tenant of Foley street in Monto, Terry Fagan is an invaluable source of material for this book and for Monto life in general. Born in Monto himself, he was wise enough to record the stories of the elderly Monto residents he assisted, which we can be immensely grateful for, and through his interviews here we can hear a visceral account of life in the tenements. Published in his book *Monto: Madams, Murder and Black Coddle*, he also plays these recordings on his weekly Monto tour, a must-do activity for those wanting to learn more about Monto from its former residents, as well as reading his books on north-inner-city Dublin life.

Women working in the sex trade today and those who work with them were also interviewed at a banner-making event for the International Day to End Violence Against Sex Workers, which was hosted by Sex Workers Alliance Ireland in 2023. Coordinator Mardi Kennedy, spokesperson Linda Kavanagh and those present generously shared their understandings of their lived experiences and their thoughts on Monto and its inhabitants. Present-day sex worker Sophie also kindly shares her personal experiences of selling sex by the canal in Dublin, allowing us to compare modern-day experiences with those of the past. Another person with lived sex-work experience who shares their thoughts on their experience is Izzy Tiernan, former Students' Union Vice President and Welfare and Equality at University of Galway, who experienced stigma and minimisation due to their involvement in sex work.

Journalist Sarah McInerney has spent a large part of her career in Irish media covering the murders of women, some of whom were involved in the sex trade. She shares her thoughts here on how the media addresses sex work or prostitution and how reporting can impact how we see victims. Parallels between Monto and the present day are sadly far too common, and Sarah discusses some approaches to how we can disrupt unethical reporting that causes harm and stigma to vulnerable people.

Someone unfortunately familiar with the impact of the media's sensationalising of the murder of a woman selling sex is Hirantha Pereira, brother of Belinda Pereira. Belinda was murdered in Dublin in 1996 and her murder remains unsolved. Hirantha talks to us about his family finding out that Belinda was a sex worker through newspaper headlines about her murder when they flew to Ireland to identify her body. Hirantha discusses the trauma of this dehumanisation and stigma. Counsellor Elisa Donovan also discusses how she organised a vigil for Geila Ibram, a woman murdered while working as a sex worker in Limerick in 2023 and she kindly shares her speech with us here.

Aileen Quigley also graciously shared her experiences of living with the experience of her daughter dying by suicide a few days after a Guard released images of her naked when she was at a vulnerable moment. Aileen's heartbreak shows us the continuation of violence against women even if the means have changed since the days of Monto.

How we tell these stories and remember the humanity of the people we talk about has to be considered as part of ethical remembrance, and activist Jennifer Cooper shares how she works towards this through her work in the Crossbones graveyard in London, a unique space of celebration, kindness and empathy.

A serendipitous moment brought this book to a close. Just as I was ready to hit 'send' on the final edits I discovered that the singular sentence about the women being smothered that had spurred me to write this book turned out to be spoken by Dublin-based singer Gemma Dunleavy's great-uncle, Billy. Gemma is also the great-granddaughter of the Granny Dunleavy (who was born Theresa Doyle), the midwife of Monto. A whole new family chapter unfolded before us in real time as we connected the dots, shared tears and goosebumps, excitable voice notes, and a whirlwind 24 hours of Gemma uncovering family history for the first time and me frantically adding this magic to these pages in the moments before the deadline. Monto's spirit, that Gemma speaks about here, had continued to be a disruptive, mischievous force and had made sure this book would include these stories. I'll be forever indebted to Gemma for harnessing that spirit to include this new knowledge.

The stories from my interviews with Terry, Martin, Paula, Pearl, Gemma, Sarah, Hirantha, Izzy, Jennifer, Sophie, Mardi, Linda, Aileen, Elisa and the sex workers from SWAI are woven through medical records, memories of local residents, official documents, academic theories, folklore, scraps of words and sentences, and the experiences of those in similar situations at the same time as Monto's existence. The photos in this book are all of women who worked selling sex in Monto, and are thankfully preserved by Martin, Terry and Pearl, giving us a real glimpse of the women of Monto. This way, we can build a picture of what life was really like for these women and girls of Monto, leading us to reflect on how we can learn from them to support people in similar situations today. When we want to learn about a subject, it's a good idea to look for the gaps. It's important to ask what is missing and whose voices are missing. Using a range of resources beyond academia, we can peer through cracks into the lives of those living long ago, those women whose names were taken from them. These cracks, found in the lyrics of a song, whispered family history or scraps of fabric, allow us to envision the women's lives and situate them in the context of the choices available to them and how other women in similar red-light districts felt. They are peepholes into the past that have evaded the erasure of Church and state, allowing us a glimpse at the *real* lives of those who were reduced to the status of the Wrong Women.

CHAPTER 1

DILEMMAS OF SURVIVAL

The majority of the women of Monto did not wake up one day and decide to head to a brothel; there are numerous factors which shaped their sense of choice and lifestyle options. The Ireland of the late 19th and 20th century was a difficult place to be a woman, especially when she was also working class, with only a few options for a safe and secure living. The more vulnerable she was, the more at risk of violence she became, and the less likely it was that she had income outside of selling sex to survive or to escape to a new life. Understanding the roots of these nuanced experiences can help us understand how Monto came to be.

National schools were established in 1831, but girls were often kept out of school to help at home, especially in rural Ireland. Mainly educating girls on how to be housewives, some schools for girls refused to participate in exams until the end of the 19th century. Schooling also became a way to cement cultural ideals of femininity and promote what a 'good' religious Irish woman should be, whether that was through a Protestant or Catholic education.

After the 1870s, women were more likely to be educated, becoming fluent in English as well as Irish, which increased both employment prospects and their ability to emigrate. Being able to emigrate to America, England or Australia meant the possibility of escaping a life of poverty and a lack of marriage options. However, women were not allowed to go to university until 1879, and those who did manage to go were mainly from wealthier backgrounds. Other options included Protestant and Catholic colleges, but these were also predominantly for middle-class women. Schools and colleges not only increased a woman's chance of employment, but also offered support through social clubs and college societies, providing more access to a comfortable life than those without these networks could obtain.

Class also played a role when it came to children who needed extra support but instead found more suffering. While orphans from middle-class families mainly went to orphanages, poorer orphans and children under 14 that had been abandoned or neglected by parents more often than not ended up in industrial schools. Children aged 12 to 16 who had committed crimes or were absent from school could find themselves placed in reformatory schools, charged as criminals and sentenced to what would turn out to be a hellscape for the thousands of children who were abused behind those doors.

With a majority unable to read or write upon entry, the children in these institutions also faced a restricted diet so they would have just enough energy for work and none for challenging the violence they were subjected to. Coming into effect in 1868 under the Industrial Schools Act, these schools grew rapidly. By 1900 there were 71 schools with tens of thousands of children forced to be there, often having already experienced mother and baby homes, children's homes and fostering.

Testimonies from living survivors of these places detailed how abuse of all kinds was rampant, and children were traumatised instead of being cared for. It is entirely possible that victims from this punitive system ended up in Monto after they were released at the age of 16 with few alternatives available to them, still barely literate, malnourished and without a support system to go back to. Monto was a means to survive and to stay out of another state institution, although Monto itself would become an institution of sorts that confined many to its streets in need of survival.

Many women turned to begging during the Great Famine, from 1845–50, and its aftermath. Some found seasonal retail work or agricultural work; others were able to find seamstress jobs. Factory work offered some independence for women, but most jobs were in Dublin. In many workplaces, women were absent from positions of power, such as governing and policing positions. Conditions in the factories were often brutal, with workers dealing with locked windows, filthy workspaces, withheld wages, rats, verbal abuse and sexual violence from employers. The nature of gender discrimination and precarious employment meant that it was common for many women to supplement their wages through selling sex.

Able-bodied girls could be taken on by wealthier families as domestic servants, with the prettiest girls more successful at securing this kind of employment. Middle-class women who did not have to work outside the home often spent their time concerned with philanthropic activities, delegating the responsibility for high-standard housework to their servants. Most girls who survived the industrial schools found work as domestic servants after they were released. However, this was hard work with a high turnover that was sometimes accompanied by abuse from the family, including sexual abuse. Their background and lack of power or choice made such workers especially vulnerable to exploitation and unwanted pregnancy as a result of rape. If the girls had come from the workhouse, their housekeeping skills were less refined and could result in their being fired for poor results.

For some women, the nunnery was a pathway to escape unwanted marriage, poverty and violence and to have a roof over their head. Convents spread rapidly at the end of the 19th century, and by 1901 there were over 8,000 nuns across Ireland.

Some nuns became nurses for the poor; others set up charities and orphanages to look after those in need. They also managed refuges and industrial schools, with the vast majority of Irish convents focusing on education. Historian and author of *Women Surviving*, Maria Luddy suggests that the convent offered an alternative to the limited choices available for lower-class women, and therefore represented a way to live without the challenges of survival on the street or in an abusive marriage, or one that demanded many children. Becoming a nun also meant a rise in class status as nuns were afforded more respectability in Irish society, above lay Catholic women. Similarly, historian Myrtle Hill notes that the convent offered a way to access travel, education, female friendships and perhaps covert lesbian relationships that would not have been socially acceptable at the time. One could speculate that Monto offered similar opportunities within its borders.

Thousands of young people orphaned by the Famine went to the US, Britain or Australia and ended up working in the red-light districts there. This is hardly surprising as their options often remained the same even if the location had changed. Utilising paid emigration schemes, the women often left their children in the workhouse, many later sending money for their children to join them if their fortunes had improved.

The devastation of the Famine left farmers trying to keep land in their families, resulting in daughters being left out of inheritances in favour of brothers. If they could afford it, the parents might stretch to one dowry for one daughter, with the others left with no option but to seek support elsewhere. Some women experienced violence by in-laws or siblings who wanted the land for themselves. Even if they were able to secure the land, it was not plain sailing from then on. There were fights with neighbours, trespassers or officials trying to evict them. Institutions had already come to be seen as a tool of control – a daughter or widow could find herself at risk of being committed to an asylum to be kept out of the way of an inheritance.

Not all women wanted to stay with their families either. Violence was not restricted to fights or murder, with incest and sexual violence present in many families, evidenced by court records. In court, perpetrators were often unrepentant, seeing their daughters as stand-ins for their wives and expecting to freely rape their children when they wanted to. Incest was common enough to be a regular feature of court life, but proceedings were conducted in secret. Priests supported this move as they wished to promote the virtuous family ideal rather than talk about the reality. This secrecy, combined with a lack of convictions, was a situation of 'double powerlessness' for women as they were not protected in their families or by the state. They were subject to stigma and blamed for being tainted, while the men remained silent and generally safe from consequences. In some cases of rape, women were forced to marry their rapists to save face and the family name.

Some women fled their families, who were pressuring them to enter arranged marriages in order to marry into land, money or the emerging middle classes. Families could also work together to stop a woman marrying whom she wanted to, and the threat of violence made staying locally with their intended husband too dangerous.

Fleeing the threat of violence is an unwanted part of life that many women in Ireland have faced over millennia, and sadly continues to this day. Murder and domestic abuse in marriage was common, with newspapers noting daily court sessions for domestic violence towards wives and mothers. While divorce was legal, poverty made escape difficult. Without her husband's income, a wife found herself in a precarious situation. Reporting to the police was an unappealing option for women because of fear of repercussions, both financial and physical. Society's view that domestic violence was simply part of working-class life made it even more difficult for a woman to find support.

Perhaps the least desirable option for survival amongst women who found themselves with few options was the workhouse. Created in 1838 with the Act for the Relief of the Destitute Poor, the workhouse was a support for those in desperate need. However, far from being a sanctuary, it was a site of violence in multiple forms.

The poor relief system grew rapidly with the Great Famine, eventually numbering 163 workhouses across the island of Ireland, with the last workhouse in operation until 1948 in Northern Ireland. The Famine saw intense overcrowding, with over 140,000 people residing in workhouses in 1848. Single mothers and children composed the majority of workhouse inmates. In 1851, 59.5 per cent of workhouse residents were women, and in 1858, only 6 per cent of the South Dublin workhouse inmates were able-bodied men, while 34 per cent were children.

Even after securing entry to a workhouse, survival was far from guaranteed. Instead, residents faced overcrowding, viral diseases, violence and only minor reprieve from hunger. A quarter of a million people died in Irish workhouse institutions between 1846 and 1851 and were buried in unconsecrated graves in the workhouse grounds, an element designed to deter through stigma.

Another grim factor that deterred people from entering the workhouse was the 1832 Anatomy Act, which permitted unclaimed bodies from the workhouse to be given to anatomy schools for dissection, supplying the rapidly expanding organised medical system. Historian Cormac Ó Gráda says that this fear was a 'punishment for the sin of pauperism', where even in death the person was considered a burden on society.

The resident's diet was extremely poor in the workhouse. Records from a Donegal workhouse show a typical day's food:

Working Men and Women and Children above 13:
Breakfast: 7oz. Oatmeal 1/2 pt. Buttermilk 1/2 pt. Mixed
Sweet Milk
Dinner: 3 1/2 lbs. Potatoes 1pt. Buttermilk
Supper: 4oz. Oatmeal 1/3 qt. Buttermilk

Those who engaged in the hard physical labour expected in the workhouses were often denied extra rations in order to stimulate their desire to better their lives. Unsurprisingly, the effort needed to survive is hard to find when on the brink of death through starvation. Skeletons recovered from workhouse graveyards and analysed by academic Linda G. Lynch reflected poor living conditions, with many showing poor bone condition due to malnutrition, broken bones and trauma from violence, and lots of evidence of infections. Lynch also suggests they also experienced 'psychological distress' from their time before entering the workhouse, which is unsurprising given the horrors experienced during the Famine. These traumas were cemented further through seeing children (theirs and others) dying on a frequent basis, in addition to a poor diet, overcrowding, stigma and violence from their peers.

Violence also came in the form of systematic separation. Men, women and children over the age of two were separated and slept in different buildings. 'Legitimate' and 'illegitimate' families were further separated from the general population, eating meals in their own area. Single mothers were viewed as 'dissolute females' and were to be kept away from other women in case they led them astray. Women who sold sex were treated as outcasts by both Church and society and had to endure a status in the workhouse below that of pauper. These women were not accommodated within the main buildings but in roughly built sheds cut off from the other inmates. These facilities were also overcrowded and had poor sanitation.

Mothers struggled with the balance of employment and child-care as some workhouses would not permit a child to stay in the workhouse while their mother was at work, and some employers would not permit a mother to bring her child with her. Wealthier families could pay for childcare, but this was not an option for those in the workhouse; at best, they could hope to be supported by a local charity. Many mothers died in the workhouses, leaving their children totally dependent on the system for survival. If their child made it to adulthood, life would not get much easier.

Sexual violence was also a feature of life in the workhouse. In 1844, 16 girls accused the master of Tralee Union workhouse of 'most improper conduct'. In the Dublin South Union workhouse, the girls protested about male officials searching them, often stripping them naked in view of the other residents. Men in positions of power were dismissed for fathering children with residents or sexually abusing young boys. Verbal abuse was rife too; the children were called the 'lowest of God's creation', 'fiends', 'baboons', 'uncultivated brutes', 'devils', 'paupers fed on public bounty' and 'worse than the lower regions'. Workhouse children were expected to be independent at 13, but many were left institutionalised and undoubtedly traumatised. They were poorly educated, had prison records and were vulnerable to exploitation in servant jobs, leaving them struggling to find safe employment. Some also disappeared, an occurrence that has persisted to this day, with 52 children going missing without a trace from state care from 2017 to 2023.

Back in Monto, the platform at nearby Connolly train station became symbolic in many ways. The moment the young girl's toes made contact with the concrete, she simultaneously became more vulnerable to violence while her opportunities to escape poverty or get married increased. Freshly arrived women in need of money were met at the train stations by good-looking men, who promised them a job in a factory or as a domestic servant. In reality, these men were not Good Samaritans – they were enforcers for the madams, and the women they targeted ended up in the brothels. The madams selected their best-looking men for this role, who would be more likely to charm the girls into compliance. Some were happy to go; others were threatened with violence if they didn't go. Also known as fancy men or bully boys, they were sometimes family or the husbands of the madams, but they were always willing to use violence to achieve the goals of the madams. They also kept an eye on the interactions between the women and the clients, and evicted those who didn't pay up or who got too rowdy. Bully boy side hustles included shaking down the clients and the women for protection money, and sexual violence was an acceptable tool in their arsenal.

Considering these factors, the question of the level of choice, agency and bodily autonomy experienced by the women of Monto is a complex one with multiple conflicting and changing truths. We often think of selling sex in black-and-white terms of 'exploitation' or 'empowerment', when it can be both, neither or somewhere in the middle. Here, former University of Galway Student Union officer Izzy Tiernan shares their experience of being reduced to 'just' a sex worker:

> I was very fortunate that those two aspects of enjoying the work and needing the work did overlap for me in sex work, and many women don't have that opportunity and many sex workers don't have that opportunity. But because sex work is work you still have to remember you are taking into account both of those aspects, that not all sex work is just out of necessity. Yes the majority of it will be, because it is still crim-inalised and still stigmatised, still hard to be a sex worker. But there are people who do enjoy what they do for work and sex workers are not different from that. There will be

people who have to do it, there'll be people who have to do it *and* enjoy it, and I was one of those. It's not spoken about because it's so easy to demonise and pity sex workers, so easy to pity. Pity was one of the emotions that I would come in contact with, with people saying, 'Oh, I'm sorry you had to do that.' And I say, 'Thank you, fine, I appreciate that. Yes, I did have to do it, but I did enjoy it and I would appreciate it if you didn't pity my choice in that.' You know, my choice to do that was influenced but that doesn't mean that I need pity from someone who doesn't understand the situation.

Historian Maria Luddy states that it is 'naive' to think that all the women in Monto were just victims: 'Though their lives were harsh they did make choices even if those choices were limited by the lack of other economically viable means of livelihood.' Women did not passively accept their fate during the Famine – they protested, petitioned and formed communities to support each other, often when their husbands had died or refused to contribute to the survival of the family. They played an active role in shaping their own lives and deciding their own futures. Many women went into the sex trade with a set time and goal, with some lasting a few weeks and retiring with enough money to get them out of their previous situation.

Some women found that the lifestyle worked for them and chose their path forward in the sex trade even if they knew the hardships involved, such as this woman in London who worked at the same time as her Monto counterparts:

I carried on with these fellows all the time we were there, and made a lot of money, and bought better dresses and some jewellery, that altered me wonderful. One officer offered to keep me if I liked to come and live with him. He said he would take a house for me in the town, and keep a pony carriage if I would consent; but although I saw it would make me rise in the world, I refused. I was fond of my old associates, and did not like the society of gentlemen. [. . .] Some of the girls here live in houses. I don't; I never could abear it. You ain't your own master, and I always liked my freedom. I'm not comfortable exactly; it's a brutal sort of life this.

Monto was a way for many of its inhabitants to escape oppressive or violent family life, challenge social and gender norms, make some money, survive, dress better, live better, find a partner or find a pathway to a new life in America or England. These were all choices that may not have been available to them had they stayed at home. They were competent at using the resources available to them and building community. Financial benefit was not the only benefit from selling sex. It could give women access to the upper classes, with whom they could negotiate an exclusive contract, securing lodgings and status, as infamous Irish madam Peg Plunkett demonstrated in the 18th century.

However, to access these perks, the women had no shortage of hurdles in their way. They had to entertain clients in the parlour and the bedroom, learn how to rob the men without being caught, survive sexual violence, manage their interactions with madams, manageresses and bully boys, and keep the police sweet. They also had to maintain their appearance and physical, mental and sexual health. Ticking all these boxes became harder the more the women were exposed to violence and trauma, and their choice, agency and survival became even more complicated and difficult the longer they stayed in Monto.

Luddy insists that the choices of the women must be respected:

Commentators on prostitution portrayed prostitutes as women whose lives were destroyed by sexual experience. Rescuers never accepted that, in a country which provided few employment opportunities for women, women could choose prostitution as a viable means of earning or supplementing an income.

We can't ask the women of Monto about their understanding of consent, and we also have to recognise that the culture of the time saw 13-year-olds as legally capable of giving consent. What we now term 'child marriage' was simply marriage for much of society then, and teenage girls marrying older men was common across the country. Our 21st-century understandings of sex, consent, abuse and sexual violence are leaps and bounds ahead of the Victorian era, and they also exist today in a very different context and country from both the Irish Free State and Ireland under British colonisation. However, we can learn about so many more aspects of the lives of the women who were shaped by Monto and, in return, left their own mark on Irish history.

CHAPTER 2

MORAL MAPPING

Despite its notoriety, Monto occupied a physically meagre area. Tucked away in a roughly one-square-mile block, the era of Monto was a product of being the right place at the right time.

Stepping out of Connolly train station and walking down Talbot Street towards the bustle of O'Connell Street, a visitor to Dublin's fair city could easily stroll past the entrance to the most concentrated zone of sexual pleasure and sexual violence in Irish history.

This entrance to Monto is now renamed and flanked by a convenience shop on one side and an apartment block on the other. Another entrance lies a few feet away – once a pathway to a world that thrived in the night-time economy of alcohol, sex and violence, now a neglected laneway that barely warrants a passing glance.

Monto's name derived from Montgomery Street, which had previously been named World's End. It is now Foley Street, hosting an exhibition space, apartments and the remaining cobblestones from Monto's heyday. Sean McDermott Street Lower and its laundry is now bookended by a student accommodation block and a charity shop. On James Joyce Street, madam May Oblong's shop has been reborn as a block of flats and an exhibition space. Gardiner Street and its army of bed and breakfasts is the barrier between Monto and O'Connell Street. Reflected in the cheap lodging houses of Monto's era, these B&Bs are now frequently used as accommodation for the homeless and a no-frills bed for the night. At its southern end, Foley Street finishes at the intersection of Amiens Street and Buckingham Street. From this neighbourhood, a visitor could merrily wander into Monto after a few scoops in nearby Mullet's bar, still in operation today on Amiens Street.

Once they slipped into one of the numerous entrances to Monto, a plucky visitor could venture down Railway Street in the shadow of the laundry, or a myriad of laneways, cul-de-sacs, outhouses and a maze of alleyways which criss-crossed the centre of Monto in ways that visitors found impossible to navigate. Eileen McLoughlin Park now occupies the heart of the old Monto. Also known as Liberty Park, this leafy space is a refuge from the noisy streets, providing the calmness that was often sorely missing in Monto's time. Beaver Street is still there, the site of the last house of Monto. Operating as the James J. Daly (Ltd) brush manufacturing factory in its later years, its painted sign is flaking away as the years pass since its abandonment in the 1980s.

At the intersection of Foley Street and James Joyce Street, one direction leads past the site of May Oblong's shop, where she kept an eye on her fiefdom; in the other direction the cobblestones suffer the weight of heavy vehicles today, but over 150 years ago, the same stones were trodden on by madams on their way to collect money or slash faces, and urinated on by drunken British sailors. Blood was splashed, tears trickled their way down, and vomit and faeces were liberally distributed across the stones.

Monto was a multilevel, multisensory environment. There was a corn mill and printing works on Sean McDermott Street, and Purdon Street hosted another corn mill, a sawmill, a sugar bakery and a forge, with neighbouring Summerhill being the site of a coach factory and a dairy on Buckingham Street. One Monto resident's complaint, discovered by historian Maria Luddy, paints a picture of how this blending of activities worked on a day-to-day basis:

On one side of these houses are the catholic schools with about 300 pupils. Opposite are tenement houses whose rooms are occupied by respectable tradesmen and their families who live here owing to their proximity to the factories, etc. These five houses of ill fame stand out in bold relief, their outward respectability being of itself an attraction. By day you will see these handsome balconied windows all open and young women of abandoned life, fashionably attired, smoking cigarettes and cracking audibly their obscene jests. At night these houses are illuminated and cars conveying tipsy young gentlemen rolling to the door which are thrown open no privacy being observed. The children and their teachers cannot avoid these sights.

Four-storey Georgian houses loomed over two-storey terraced houses around Elliott Place and smaller whitewashed cottages on Purdon Street. When Monto was crumbling, its skyline changed again with the demolishing of the tenement slums and the completion of the six-storey-tall St Mary's Mansions, which filled the space when Gloucester Street was wiped off the map through decay and demolition.

Monto's brothels operated alongside class lines too – at least in the early days before the area's total descent into decaying tenements. Upper-class clients of madam Lizzie Arnold enjoyed quite sumptuous surroundings in her establishments at 83 and 111 Lower Mecklenburgh Street. The higher the number, the more flash the brothel. Some madams such as Annie Mack essentially established a fiefdom of property, businesses and control. So extensive was her empire that Monto was sometimes called Macktown – she could be spotted in her premises at numbers 20, 85, 86 and 87, which were later taken over by Annie Meehan. The madams moved around just as much as the women that worked for them as they acquired more property to turn into brothels and wealth.

As Monto's sparkle and glamour began to diminish, its descent into decay was rapid. A house on nearby Upper Buckingham Street cost £8,000 in 1791 but had fallen to £500 less than 50 years later. Monto and its surrounds were in freefall into a slumland where houses were sold for a few pounds yet were still unaffordable to most of their tenants, who lived off handfuls of shillings. Georgian buildings had high ceilings and large windows to let light in, but those relegated to the basements had poor light, contributing to mould problems. In the lower-class tenements there was often even less light as some of the windows were boarded up. This was a combination of efforts to protect children from seeing the nightly goings-on, negligent landlords who didn't care about repairs or mould, attempts at keeping the heat in, and efforts to avoid the tax on windows.

As time passed, Monto's brothels became concentrated in the lower numbers of Mecklenburgh Street and the half-dozen alleys and lanes around Faithful Place and Elliott Place, which consisted of terraced houses with four rooms and was where Martin Coffey's great-grandmother Margaret Carroll lived. Madams also rented rooms from other landlords or owned single rooms in tenements that they rented by the hour or the night. These were situated in crumbling buildings with families for neighbours.

Further down in Monto's spatial and class hierarchy, some women had no access to an indoor space of any kind. These were normally women who were older, had lost their looks, had been kicked out of the flash houses, were harmed or disabled, or more desperate for clients due to addiction or ill health. They met clients in laneways and doorways and did not have the luxury of shelter from the elements. Hoping the darkness would be forgiving, these women selling sex in the shadows had less power and control over whom they saw and for how much, often receiving just a bottle of beer as payment. Recessed coach houses provided a brief aspect of cover but were extremely dangerous spaces for the women, with no witnesses or help if the men chose to be violent. These women could be found around Mabbot Street, Faithful Place and Purdon Street, with its maze of alleys; before Plunket became Annie Meehan upon marriage, she lived in 10 Purdon Street.

What a red-light district also needs is timing and opportunity, and Monto had that in spades with the combination of the descent into slums, making property cheap, and a steady influx of clientele due to the expansion of the British Empire and rapid industrialisation. A stream of new women and girls arrived thanks to the Famine and the lack of opportunities elsewhere for them. With such a transitory population and a discreet location, Monto had the perfect recipe for success as it was able to provide anonymity for its clients, another essential ingredient of a thriving red-light district.

Monto wasn't just a geographically hidden area – its confinement was also a moral one. In the Victorian era, prostitution came to be viewed as a necessary evil, tolerated but only if it was hidden, and so the Victorians became masters of creating centres of mass entertainment that included red-light districts. This zoning of illicit pleasures led to the establishment of immoral districts, where the wrong women could be isolated out of sight of respectable women. Women who sold sex were associated with 'irrepressible evil', which had the potential to physically and morally contaminate others, so they were confined to vice districts, geographically and morally different to the rest of society.

Male visitors to Monto found its borders porous, slipping in and out of its streets at their leisure. However, some women of Monto did not have this freedom and were confined indoors by their madams. We are left with chilling notions about what this confinement meant for how much consent they had, how and when they managed to leave this situation if they wanted to, and what happened if they did try to leave. In small acts of rebellion and resistance, the women found ways to challenge this control by paying local children to help them smuggle in alcohol or cigarettes through buckets they lowered down from their windows.

Ireland's societal structures and traditions thus contained well-tested social, moral and physical mechanisms for controlling and containing women, particularly young, sexually active women. Recently, scholars such as James Smith have analysed the ways in which the 20th-century Irish state and Church controlled sexually deviant women. Smith suggests that an 'architecture of containment' was developed to control them, and this system was developed to target women who sold sex. This containment was both physical and figurative as women were locked up in laundries and their potentially dangerous bodies kept away from good women and good men. In these places, women had to reject their prior lives and be reformed from their fallen ways of having extramarital sex or selling sex, even if it was for survival. The tool of corruption was sex, whether it was sex outside of marriage for procreation or it was for sale, for any reason.

Prostitutes were not considered respectable women, unless they were high-class courtesans with access to wealth, status and blackmailable clients. This dehumanisation has historically led to physical violence, stigma and a multitude of health problems through their framing as the wrong kind of women that should not be part of society, never mind a *listened to* part of society. What Monto shows us is how the physical location of sex, power and violence overlaps with social, moral and cultural norms about who the ideal woman is.

While we can debate how much today's cultural norms reflect the same attitudes to those in the sex trade of Monto's time, Monto itself has now been physically contained in the past. All but one of its buildings are demolished, and its cobblestones where people lived and died connect the past with the present. Lower Gloucester Street was renamed Sean McDermott Street, and Mecklenburgh Street Upper had a brief stint as Tyrone Street but has been renamed Railway Street since 1911. The land that once hosted the flash houses of Mecklenburgh Street was given to the nuns and became part of the laundry grounds, where women faced a different kind of confinement. Mabbot Street spent some time as Corporation Street but is now named James Joyce Street. Much of this renaming was done to erase the past connections to Monto and to gentrify the area – an issue that continues even today, with locals often priced out of living in the space their families had lived in for generations.

CHAPTER 3

BIG AND BOLD

Monto has been called Europe's 'biggest and boldest red-light district', 'the biggest epicentre of prostitution in the then British Empire' and 'reputedly the largest in Europe at the time'. But is this claim to fame (or infamy) as the largest vice centre in Europe actually true?

To examine this assertion, we can first look at the numbers reported to be working in the sex trade. The Dublin Metropolitan Police reported 1,630 women to be selling sex in Dublin in 1838. On his visit to red-light districts around the UK and Ireland, religious reformer William Logan claimed to be reliably informed that there were 1,700 women selling sex in Dublin in 1842, but reports seeing only 200 near the barracks in Dublin. In 1842 there were 1,287 known brothels in Dublin; if they had an average of three to five women working in them, the number of women could be 3,800–6,400.

The year 1850 saw 4,650 arrests for prostitution, which fell to 3,846 in 1866, falling further in 1870 with 3,255 women being arrested for prostitution in Dublin. By 1901, the Dublin Metropolitan Police were aware of over 1,500 women selling sex, dropping further back to 1,067 arrests in 1912.

The census of 1861 saw 134 self-declared brothel-keepers listed, with 131 of these being women, and by 1868, there were 132 brothels across Dublin. The number of known prostitutes fell further in 1890 to 436 and brothel numbers fell further still in 1894 to 74 brothels, mostly in Monto with an average of three women working from each one, making the number of women around 222.

Are these numbers trustworthy? In a word, no.

There are too many sinkholes in this numerical swamp. Not all arrested were actually selling sex; some were arrested because they 'looked' like a woman who sold sex. Martin's personal story highlights how arrest records and labels are problematic:

After my great-grandmother was involved in the murder, there was a woman arrested and put in prison with her, but all she did was bring a candle to the door so that my great-grandmother could pick the man's pockets. That woman had nothing to do with the murder, but she got five years in prison. She wasn't a prostitute, she was a nurse from Dun Laoghaire, and was most probably taking care of abortions. She died in prison.

Annie Higgins, whose candlelight got her five years in prison alongside Margaret and Nannie.

Addresses transformed quickly – from flash house to crumbling tenement room, to family accommodation, to short-term lodgings. If a woman was living in a house where sex was or had been sold, it was no guarantee that she herself was involved, yet she could be recorded as a prostitute on official documents, sometimes without her knowledge or consent, since the women were often illiterate.

The numbers of women passing through rescue centres is also not a reflection of the true situation. If a woman found herself begging for admittance to an asylum, she could be refused entry if she was too 'hardened' as the asylum wanted to claim high numbers of 'reformed' women and that was easier with those who were 'newly fallen' than those who had been traumatised for years.

Another group of women provides clarity for us as to why official records are not always trustworthy when it comes to women, particularly women who sell sex. In Kildare, the British Army maintained a barracks at the Curragh. Today a popular racecourse, in the early and mid-19th century it was considered a red-light district because of the women who lived in the town and worked as prostitutes for the British soldiers. Given the nickname the 'Curragh Wrens', these women lived in the hedges and bush near the barracks, in dire circumstances but with a communal approach to survival as they formed a community of mutual aid. They endured incredibly difficult conditions and faced violence from individuals and state bodies, along with extreme poverty. Some of the women found amongst the Curragh Wrens were married, either officially or unofficially, to their army husbands, but due to a shortage of space in the barracks they had to live outside the camp next to the Wrens or in the town if they could afford it. They were mostly dismissed as prostitutes by outsiders. The same happened in Dublin barracks as the British Army had thousands of Irish soldiers whose wives tried to live as close to the barracks as possible. In Dublin, this was Monto. These women were also at risk of being labelled prostitutes and judged by the company they kept. Single female lodgers were a big part of Monto too and may sometimes have been considered prostitutes but were not.

The word 'prostitute' was weaponised against women who didn't look or behave the way they 'should'. If a woman resisted the social pressure to be a good woman, she was to be taught a lesson by being labelled as a prostitute, regardless of whether she was one. As a social reformer of the time remarked, 'literally every woman who yields to her passion and loses her virtue is a prostitute'. The men who did this – for it was men in state institutions such as the police and hospitals who had this power – knew the harm it would cause, and the instant a woman was labelled a prostitute, she joined the ranks of the wrong kind of women. Many nuns happily followed this example of stigmatisation. The rebels, the troublemakers, the queer women, the sexually adventurous, the victims, the survivors, those who sought birth control – all were viewed as a challenge to the ideal woman who stayed at home making babies and obeying her husband.

There was also a backlash against women's groups speaking up for the rights of women, especially working-class women. Women began to frequent pubs in the 1880s – traditionally spaces for men who initially didn't take kindly to having their environment intruded upon. These women were often labelled as prostitutes to get them out of such spaces when the men decided they were too troublesome. And with that label, they often sentenced them to years of institutionalisation. Did they know what they were doing, that they were condemning those women for the rest of their lives? Given the collaboration between various state institutions across countries and eras, it's hard to fathom how they could *not* know.

When a demographic is always in flux, accurate numbers are hard to establish. The numbers and cases of the sex trade often came from second-hand information or were inflated to secure

Woman sleeping on the street; like many women of Monto, home was often the streets or a hallway if they were lucky.

funding or public support to tackle the issue. These numbers become more complicated because many of the women did not live in brothels. Some women rented a room from a madam or landlady but were independent workers, known as 'privateers'. Many women slept in doorways or on the street, never gracing the census reports.

An arriving ship could swell the population of Monto by thousands for a short period of time, with a flood of men with money ready to party, gamble, drink, have sex or rape. Privateers would no doubt try to maximise this swell as much as they could without facing a challenge from Monto's residents. They came into Monto from elsewhere, did what they needed to do and went back to their homes outside of Monto, making accurate numbers impossible.

The 'social evil' of prostitution was also played up to an almost hysterical level by religious reformers, resulting in the intrigue and taboo of a red-light district and the wildness of its reputation. Scandal meant attention, and sex scandals resulted in outrage and money to fix the issue. Additionally, historians and reformers have offered different time frames for how long women stayed in the trade. According to the Westmoreland Lock Hospital, the average time was nine years, but Irish historian John Finnegan suggests it was five years, while British reformer William Logan pins the average time as four months. The impact of class also has to be taken into account, as those in lower-class brothels or on the streets saw more clients for less money and spent longer in the trade due to a lack of other options.

Complete census records before 1901 don't exist, but prostitution and brothel-keeping are also occupations that not everyone would disclose on a census, although some did. To illustrate this, Maria Luddy shows that one census return saw only six prostitutes listed for the whole of Cobh, which is far from the reality of the much higher numbers of women selling sex. Women do not self-identify in the 1901 or the 1911 census as prostitutes – rather, they are described as such by Dublin Metropolitan Police officers. While the release of the 1926 census in 2026 will bring more information to light, these are all bits and pieces of the puzzle of Monto and can never provide full answers.

With the passing of various laws, more women came before the courts, but some used different names or took the rap for others, which hopelessly skews the statistics into the realm of the unreliable. Changing their names was also a fast solution to hiding from landlords they owed rent to or to avoid clients they didn't want to see. Martin Coffey's great-grandmother went by several names, such as Margaret Carroll, Margaret Finn (which was her maiden name), Bridie Finn, Margaret McLoughlin or Maggie. Madam Maggie Arnold also went by Mrs Arnott, Meg Arnott,

Margaret Carroll, Martin Coffey's great-grandmother.

Eliza Arnold, Lizzie Arnold, Maggie Noble or Margaret Noble. May Roberts became May Oblong upon marriage. One woman from Elliott Place was known by Olive Hills, Lily Byrne, Lily Keefe or Lily Campbell. This was often a tactic to try to trick judges and escape trouble. For many, Monto became a place to reinvent themselves, change their name and identity, and survive, and sometimes thrive.

Some of the madams were not newcomers to Monto and had started off selling sex then moved up the ladder. Prostitutes were predominantly working class, although they also operated in a system stratified by class, from street worker to high-class courtesan. Those from wealthier backgrounds could access higher classes of clientele who provided luxury accommodation for them, leaving brothel and street prostitution to the lower classes. Monto also hosted families working in the same trade. Sisters Bella and Mary Hutchinson from Belfast lived together in Elliott Place in 1921, following in the footsteps of Peg Plunkett and her sister. This may seem shocking on the surface, but if one daughter was experiencing hardship in the family home, they may have been only too eager to flee with their sister in the hopes of a better life.

We can't pin down all the women in Monto that sold sex, but we can look at similar districts and try to compare. In 1878 there were up to 50,000 women selling sex across the whole of Paris, and 50,000–60,000 in London. Liverpool was reported to have 1,000 brothels in 1860, and since most brothels had five or six women selling sex, this is 5,000–6,000 at any one time.

Clearly, Monto pales in comparison to these vast numbers. But what made Monto otherwise big and bold was its longevity combined with its infamy. For its 60 to 70 years of existence, the number of prostitutes was higher at Monto's start and dropped off towards its end. With a conservative estimate of an average of 500 women and girls selling sex there each year, there were tens of thousands of women passing through Monto over its lifespan. Whether or not the real number is higher or lower, it is safe to say that tens of thousands of women in Ireland and abroad experienced Monto through its sex trade. The many thousands of clients carried the legendary tales of Monto with them as material for songs and lad banter, while many women in Monto buried their experiences in the backs of their minds for fear of institutionalisation and stigma.

Arrest records give us some data but can't tell us everything, and certainly can't tell us how the woman herself felt about it. More important than the futile task of proving the exact numbers of women present in Monto are the women's stories and learning from them to make life safer for those in the sex trade today. This means looking at the *culture* of prostitution rather than a sole focus on statistics which can never show us the full story. Whatever the true figure is, life selling sex in Monto involved multiple impacts on the women's sexual, physical and mental health.

The women of Monto are one part of the picture. But who were they selling sex to? If we were to believe the Dubliners, the tsar of Russia was partial to a visit. The song 'Take Me up to Monto' has the lyrics:

When the Tzar of Russia
And the King of Prussia
Landed in the Phoenix Park in a big balloon
They asked the Police band to play
The Wearing of the Green
But the buggers in the Depot
Didn't know that tune
So they both went up to Monto, Monto, Monto
They both went up to Monto, langeroo, to you

Alas, as astonishing a vision as this sounds, it is simply artistic licence. Known visitors who *did* happily sample the offerings of Monto included writer, medical student and Senator Oliver St John Gogarty and James Joyce, who used Monto as the setting for his red-light-district scenes in *Ulysses*. The upper-class brothels, known as flash houses, were frequented by nobility, the wealthy, politicians, military officers and sea captains. Clients who needed discretion came into the area after dark in hackneys with the curtains drawn. Other headline-grabbing visitors to Monto include the Prince of Wales, who was partial to an evening at Annie Mack's establishment. Later known as King Edward VII, he was said to be a regular visitor when he did his military training in Ireland.

Backing on to Monto were the army barracks at Aldborough House. Together with other barracks around Dublin, they allowed for the passage of thousands of soldiers on their way to barracks around the country or waiting to be deployed abroad in times of war. Carousing with women was an experience much anticipated, and the men shared true stories and tall tales and gave their personal recommendations, as this soldier recalls:

> On arrival at a new station we pre-War soldiers always made enquiries as to what sort of a place it was for booze and fillies. If both were in abundance it was a glorious place from our point of view . . . Each man had been issued with a pamphlet signed by Lord Kitchener warning him about the dangers of French wine and women; they may as well have not been issued for all the notice we took of them.

The clients of second-class brothels were not as wealthy as those in the flash houses. They were mainly manual workers who came through Monto due to their work on the docks or the railways, both fast-growing industries depositing tens of thousands of workers on the streets of Dublin every year. They passed clerks and shop assistants on their way in and out of the brothels and hurried past those on the street headed to third-class brothels. This class of clients were farmers up in Dublin for livestock markets, students with a bit of spare cash, and priests trying to go unnoticed.

But no matter the class of brothel, a service was expected in exchange for money, and clients wanted a sensory adventure. They got their wish, on all fronts.

CHAPTER 4

COBBLESTONE SYMPHONIES

Monto put a uniquely Irish stamp on the soundscape of the sex trade, ensuring that the infamy of the area lives on. While written records may be in short supply, oral traditions have preserved some sex-trade and working-class history. One sensory element intrinsically entwined with life in Monto was sound. For centuries, Irish people had understood the emotional impact of music, filtered into three main categories: music for weeping (*goltraige*), music for laughing (*geanntraige*) and music for sleeping (*suantraige*). All three categories fit neatly into the rhythm of the brothel alongside the orchestra of daily city life.

Monto was not a place where slumber was peaceful; rather, the noise was overwhelming for many and an uncomfortable acoustic environment to survive in. Catholic campaigner Frank Duff was certainly appalled at the assault on the senses in Monto:

That Saturday afternoon was indescribably shocking and depressing. Even that early, the business side of the place was in full swing. The men had poured down in great numbers, and the general orgy aspect was sickening in evidence. The atmosphere reeked with evil.

As well as regular hooleys and the sounds of brothel entertainment, the tenements were noisy places due to the sheer volume of inhabitants. At night-time the population of this square mile rapidly inflated with hundreds of women, clients, independent workers, voyeurs, drinkers, revolutionaries, madams, vigilantes, students, saviours, bully boys, police and those looking for a place to sleep. The wheels of the jarveys ferrying passengers to the flash houses clacked along on the cobblestones, the clip-clop of the horses' hooves announcing the presence of wealthy clients entering the area. The cadence of the cobblestones' rhythm was interspersed with the tinkling of glasses smashing, fights, laughing, vomiting and whistles to give warning of incoming police. Groups of drunken sailors and soldiers loudly talked, sang and fought on the streets as they went from pub to brothel to lodgings; voices and accents were in daily flux as strangers mixed with residents and regulars.

The lure of a boisterous, fast-paced soundscape produced by the mishmash of sex and taboo was an obvious appeal to men after weeks or months at sea or at war, emboldened by money in their pockets and respite from watchful eyes. To help with the smooth extraction of this disposable income, the flash houses curated a raucous atmosphere to encourage clients to linger, allowing their bills to creep up as they became drunker and bolder. The front parlour was a social space, while the upper floors were quieter and the sounds more sexual. Noise wasn't just created by the couples, it also came from the frequent orgies that were part of the experience of communal enjoyment amongst sailors and soldiers, who revelled in the sounds of multiple bodies having sex at the same time.

Monto's unique rhythm of sex and speech persevered to the time of Paula Meehan's childhood in the 20th century, a few generations after her great-grandmother's voice echoed along the very same streets:

I grew up in an oral tradition: the stories, the singers, the old people, the lore, the sometimes very empowering lore. I soon developed, I believe, a hunger for ritualized sound, in and of itself. [. . .] The old whores were still around when I was a child, it had the lore of the docks and the dockland community. It was a vivid, interesting, and textured world for me with a lot of song, a lot of music, not least the music of the city itself, the steel hoop rims on cobbles, the horses' hooves. There was an abattoir near us. I remember the squealing of pigs and the cries of sheep waiting to be slaughtered. The music of the Latin, of the bells of the church, all of that – a fantastically rich childhood in sonic terms.

A soundscape provokes emotional and physical responses of all kinds because of how the inhabitants and architecture combine to create a sound unique to each location and moment in time. Music arouses not just the physical and emotional senses, but the sexual ones too, and when connected to selling sex, it creates a world of permission to explore desire. Society adds music to all important moments; the Victorian brothel was no different.

The symphony of Monto was made up of an eclectic medley of music. Hustling for clients, the chirps and squeals of live animals, lewd language and singing at top volume all seamlessly blended with melodies from pianos, fiddles, harmoniums, melodeons, tin whistles and mouth organs. For those who couldn't afford tickets to the National Concert Hall or didn't want to be in an environment where they felt like outsiders, the brothel offered a sensual space for working-class enjoyment and a more daring exploration of desire beyond watchful Victorian eyes.

Monto curated its own melody to accompany its goings-on, with its rhythm fluctuation from morning to night and by proximity to poverty. The piano and pianola were staples in some upper-class brothels. Joyce writes about the delights of the melodies from Bella

Cohen's pianola in *Ulysses*, and his naming of the character Professor Godwin may be a nod to the piano men of the brothels of Storyville, a similar red-light district in New Orleans, who were nicknamed 'professors'. His use of this name is a sign that people in Dublin were aware of the delights of the New Orleans red-light district and took inspiration from each other. Other instruments such as the harmonium and tin whistle were also commonplace at the time, easy to store and to replace when they were inevitably lost or stolen.

Invented in the 1890s, the gramophone democratised access to music and allowed lower-class brothels to dispense with the need for a piano man. Not just a part of a brothel's appeal, the gramophone was also useful in times of police raids, when they were used to conceal bottles of whiskey. Sailors brought the latest records into Monto, and the madams heartily welcomed new songs in their quest to provide the most alluring atmosphere for people to part with their money. Those who couldn't afford instruments or gramophones settled for old valve radios, recognising the need for music of some kind. The result of this cross-cultural influence transformed the brothel into a melting pot of culture, sound and demographics, making Monto not a cultural ghetto but a space of creativity.

While the popularity of the song 'Take Me up to Monto' has helped keep the memory of Monto alive, songs were a feature of Monto itself when it was alive and kicking in the streets of inner-city Dublin, offering us an opportunity to uncover it further. We can thank sailors for providing a key insight into the attitudes and activities of the red-light districts they visited, as they memorialised their exploits in sea shanties. Their songs contained advice about quack treatments for venereal disease and provided an emotional release valve to get the men through their harsh voyages. The frequency of robbery warnings in shanties and ballads suggests they were a known and acceptable risk. Shanties also teased the erotic possibilities awaiting the sailors, as seen in 'The Fire Ship', which uses sailing terminology to describe the action to be had on land:

So up the stairs and into bed I took that maiden fair.
I fired off my cannon into her thatch of hair.
I fired off a broadside until my shot was spent,
Then rammed that fire ship's waterline until my ram was bent.

From 1913 the Guinness brewers became ship owners and used their own cross-channel fleet to serve Liverpool, Manchester, London and Bristol, employing many Irish sailors who mixed with their British and American counterparts to create shanties sung with a mixture of Irish, Scottish and English accents. We can see the Irish influence on shanties such as 'The Drunken Sailor', sung to the tune of the 18th-century shanty 'Oró Sé Do Bheatha Bhaile', and in the creation of mixed-language songs.

The Dublin medical students who frequented Monto learned from the soldiers and sailors they bumped into and took inspiration from them to create their own bawdy songs about Monto:

O there goes Mrs. Mack;
She keeps a house of imprudence,
She keeps an old back parlour
For us poxy medical students.

The last madam of Monto, Becky Cooper, also featured in a not-so-flattering song:

Italy's maids are fair to see
And France's maids are willing
But less expensive 'tis to me
Becky's for a shilling.

These local and international songs were the soundtracks to Joyce and St John Gogarty's visits to Monto. They heard these joyous, indulgent songs, but perhaps they also heard the laments of the women whose voices carried on the wind from brothel to bedroom, and legends about visits from the banshee, a female character from Irish folklore who appears wailing and howling when someone is about to die. Monto resident Elizabeth Dillon, who grew up with this soundtrack, heard the women at night while she lay in bed:

> They were lovely singers. They would sing sad songs. You could hear them from a long way off up Corporation Street. One girl would start to sing first, then after a while they all joined in.

This feminine soulful synergy is today reflected in the soft lyrical storytelling music of Gemma Dunleavy, whose 2020 EP *Up De Flats* features the voices of her family, friends and neighbours

Pets were a common part of the soundscape of Monto.

coming together to create music that is uniquely their sound, their world and their lives.

Music also came in the form of birdsong, a common soundtrack for both brothels and family homes in Monto, as it was for many of the women of other red-light districts around the world. Mary Waldron, who grew up on Gloucester Street in the 1910s, remembers the joy that birds brought to their owners: 'and the birds would be chirping. And they'd talk to their birds. Oh, yes!' In the red-light districts of Boston and New Orleans, pets were common in brothels for both entertainment and companionship, with birds, dogs and even monkeys contributing to the brothel symphony. Parrots in New Orleans entertained guests by screeching insults at them as they passed by, and in Monto, Becky Cooper's talking parrot would squawk, '*Becky not here! Becky not here!*' Living in Monto since childhood, Mary Murphy remembers sneaking over to Becky's house to peer in the window and provoke the parrot for fun, but this came with high risk:

> Sometimes we sneaked up to look in the window at it. We would all be laughing when, all of a sudden, Becky would come from nowhere. She would let a scream at us and then chase us down Railway Street, shouting, 'I will tell your mothers you were down at my house, you little bastards!'

Life was also precarious for a bird if a woman lost her job, lodgings or couldn't afford to feed it or keep it safely. In some Dublin tenements it was a common occurrence to wake up to the carcass of the bird, left by rats who scurried through the holes in the walls.

Monto's inhabitants also contributed to the soundscape of the street as they used the space to socialise, play, settle arguments and support each other through difficult times. Resident Aggie Coffey describes the summer sounds of Monto streets from her childhood:

The kids would be gone up to bed and the men would be playing cards and the women would be out skipping. Jemmy West would come down with his ould melodeon and he'd start playing that. Somebody else would play the mouth organ or maybe someone would play on a comb. [. . .] They'd be all out dancing and singing there down in Railway Street.

Families, neighbours, madams and the women would gather to watch the goings-on as a form of entertainment and used it as a temporary escape from their cramped and uncomfortable living spaces. In the lower-class brothels, the women would stand at the doorway or on the street to attract passing trade and talk with their neighbours.

Outdoor socialising was an integral part of Monto Life.

While on the surface Monto may have appeared to be a hedonistic world of partying, underneath its brash exterior the sounds of sadness resulting from violence echoed across its cobblestones. The raucous clash of curses, excited talk, laughter, moans and groans lessened as the class of the brothel went down, until the brothel became a bare, rotting space to quickly do the deed in sombre surroundings, instead of relaxing all night in opulent, warm, softly lit spaces with food, alcohol and groups of glamorous women. If the women had no access to a brothel, they had to resort to the streets and alleyways, adding their touts for business to the rest of the street sounds.

As the night grew darker and the alcohol flowed, courage grew and tempers flared. While children played outside during the day, they were called in at dusk to avoid seeing the events of the night.

Women braving the elements in their shawls and coats, looking for business in Elliott Place. Note the boarded up windows to block out the sights and sounds of the sex trade for the families who lived side by side with the women.

Some women without access to brothels resorted to tenement hallways, but these were not always accessible. Chrissie Ryan lived in Monto and recalls her father having to put an iron bar up against the front door at night to try to keep the women out of the hallways as the children couldn't sleep with the noise.

Another former resident recounts the unwelcome noise pollution that seeped into her room at night as she tried to fall asleep:

> I used to lie there on the floor on straw and I'd hear the screams and many times I used to think it was the cats, but it wasn't. It was women in the back lanes getting beaten and gang raped and what not.

Screams fading to silence were a soundtrack to many red-light districts. Women with less access to support have historically been extremely vulnerable, and the more muted they were, the more at risk they became. To manage the negative effects of these disruptive acoustics, the residents of Monto adopted some unhealthy coping mechanisms. Pearl recalls her grandfather telling her that the women of Monto often resorted to sleeping medications such as laudanum to find some reprieve, silencing their minds for a short time at least.

Monto was not just a geographical space; it was also a linguistic space with its own unique slang and terminology shaping Monto's sounds. Upper-class brothels in other red-light districts were often called parlours, bordellos, whorehouses or bawdy houses; in Monto they were known as flash houses. The brothels in general were also called the 'bad houses' or 'kip houses', although resident Tommy 'Duckegg' Kirwan called them 'red-light houses'. Another former Monto resident, Mary Corbally, shares some more local descriptions:

> In them years they was called 'unfortunate girls'. We never heard the word 'whores', never heard 'prostitute'. Very rarely

you'd hear of a brothel, it was a 'kip' and the madams we called them kip-keepers.

Unique slang originating in working-class areas, like Cockney rhyming slang, gives us an insight into how local communities devise their own ways to make sense of their experiences. Shared creation of language is part of being in a community, especially a marginalised community thrown together by difficult circumstances. Talking to each other was a way to process their experiences and bond over the shared hardship of life in poverty. The women in Monto were also exposed to clients who may have shared words used in other red-light districts and adopted or adapted them.

In the 18th century, women selling sex in Ireland were referred to as 'whores', 'harlots', 'strolling women' or 'lewd women', but by the time Monto emerged the tone had changed from salacious to pitiful, with terms such as 'poor unfortunate' or 'unhappy creature' or 'nightwalker'. Across the Irish Sea, a 'bat' was English slang for an inexpensive prostitute, while 'Madge' referred to a woman's genitals. Words created in London's red-light district, such as 'flabbergast', 'cock and bull story', 'bamboozle', 'catcall' and 'gibberish', are still used today. We can only lament the loss of the full vocabulary Monto might claim to have contributed to the English and Irish languages.

Pubs were a big part of socialising in Monto and it's easy to picture the women meeting there on their time off, as well as while recruiting and touting for business. Did they console each other, slag off each other's clothes, settle grievances, complain about their madams? How did they talk about their clients, and were some clients off limits for public discussion? Did the women make fun of them or share tips for tricking them? In *Ulysses*, Molly Bloom gives us a hint of how the women of Monto might have gossiped about their clients:

What does a man look like – standing there with his two bags full and the other thing sticking up at you – like a hat rack? Sure it's no wonder they hide it under a cabbage leaf.

Interestingly, we do know some of what the women of Monto talked about. Terry, the residents he interviewed, Pearl, Paula and Martin all have family stories and local knowledge and folklore about the hidden role that Irish women played in the fight for independence, hidden due to its 'unsavoury' nature and connection to 'British sin' and not Irish purity. Scandalous or not, the women of Monto played an important role in the Easter Rising by informing the Irish rebels of the plans of the British Army that they expertly gleaned from the soldiers in their drunken post-orgasmic bliss. This information about enemy plans had to be extracted with the skill of a bomb technician, as a drunken soldier could turn from happy to violent far too rapidly. If he realised what she was doing and how much trouble he was going to be in, she was at extreme risk of violence. If she didn't get the information needed, she may have also been vulnerable at the hands of those who requested it politely or otherwise. Soft, gentle, probing questions mixed with the seduction tools of a brothel therefore made many British men unwittingly help the Irish nationalist cause thanks to the women's mastery of combining their words of seduction with their manipulation of men.

This feminised weaponisation of words and sounds for survival follows generations of Irish women using their voices in any way they could to make their presence felt, including the act of cursing someone to bad luck. Curses are recognised now as a 'potent art' that required knowledge, composure, practice and wit, all factors present in varying forms in a red-light district. Irish women were well known for being excellent wordsmiths and coming up with creative ways to curse those who wronged them. During the Famine, female beggars would take advantage of the fear of being cursed to ask for food as they were unlikely to be turned down. These beggars and other Famine survivors often found their way into Monto, bringing their curses with them. Post Famine, women were not allowed to hold positions of power in groups such as the Land League, but curses gave women a way to resist male power. Rural Irish women used their words, often imaginatively, to rework and resist patriarchy. Their unique use of language also allowed women to express their anger and make sense of their situations and experience a sense of power – 'a gruesome therapy and misanthropic coping strategy in fraught times', which was common at the time of Monto. Their words and curses were a way to resist societal pressures and to find a sense of power when often there wasn't much to be had. They cursed the madams as they kicked them out, cursed the bully boys for their extortion and violence, and cursed their clients for not treating them properly. As the English language and culture spread across Ireland and the rest of the British Empire, cursing gave way to swear words like 'fuck'.

'Fuck' dominated vulgar vocabulary at the time of Monto, but it was absolutely not welcome in polite society. 'Fuck' was reserved for the lower classes as this 'vulgar' language was perceived by the middle and upper classes as disgusting and far too explicit. They preferred euphemisms or medical terms if they absolutely *had* to speak about sex or the body publicly, since they viewed swear words as a form of contamination by the perverted lower classes. Such language made sex too visible, too present, too *loud*. Foul language was a sign the person had succumbed to deviant pleasures, far outside the realm of acceptable sexuality, and complaints from the residents of a street just next to Monto give us an insight into the kind of language heard in the area:

We, the inhabitants of the above-mentioned streets, are unable to open our back windows on account of the filthy and blasphemous language which would then become audible, and pollute the ears of our wives and families. This annoyance is worse on Saturday when the drunken inhabitants of the Court are allowed to issue from it to the adjacent Streets, and disturb the neighbourhood until a very late hour without interference from the Police.

Monto inhabitants and visitors might have been heard using terms such as 'prick', 'frig', 'bugger' and 'cunt', which were in popular usage in Victorian England. Monto visitor James Joyce used these terms in his love letters to Nora Barnacle, where he excitedly shares his sexual arousal thinking about Nora's farts. He refers to orgasming as 'coming off' while St John Gogarthy referred to sperm as 'gravy'.

As well as their bawdy songs being infamous, sailors and soldiers have long had a reputation too for using swear words, often called 'flash' language. Similarly, if the local jarveys were anything like their English counterparts, swearing was part of the job. Such words had been used for centuries, particularly amongst the working classes, including women. The swear words of Monto also likely included Irish terms such as 'pit' (vulva) and 'bod' (penis), or perhaps one of Joyce's favourites, 'prick' 'middle leg' or 'mickey', and Paula Meehan attests to some Irish speakers known to have lived in Monto.

Monto put a uniquely Irish stamp on the soundscape of the sex trade, ensuring that the infamy of the area lives on. While written records may be in short supply, oral traditions have preserved some sex-trade and working-class history. The voices that uttered or sang these words had a large variety of accents – authors Tadhg O'Keeffe and Patrick Ryan note that Monto was simultaneously extremely local and extremely global. The mix of soldiers, sailors and tourists visiting and staying in the area, even in the dosshouses, lent the area an international feel, a variety of accents and languages mixing within the soundscape. Religious campaigner Frank Duff describes this aural blend:

> [It] was like being in another country. That 'exotic' flavour did not arise from (although it was intensified by) the sort of visitors you would encounter – such for instance as the big party of Turks, complete with red fezzes, just come straight from the boat.

Monto was a melting pot of different demographics and cultures, reflected in the skin tone of the Monto babies often left behind as a result of an entanglement with a soldier or sailor. Paula feels that this international influence is in her blood:

> If you had done DNA tests in the 1930s, you would find a huge number of people with African blood, with eastern Mediterranean blood, absolutely. Soldiers came in from all over the world, they were not just English, they were coming in from across the empire. I saw this myself in my school mates, how much melanin they would have, how tanned they got. I would get very, very dark in the summer, and my father would pass as North African, no problem. My hair was black when I was young. Genetically, that area was a very diffuse place, and a diverse culture is also a healthier culture.

Martin Coffey's grandmother Annie Carroll's Tipperary accent blended with the inner-city accent of Monto, which in turn mixed with accents from across the British Empire. After Dublin and foreign-born women, Wicklow women comprised the third highest demographic of patients admitted to Westmoreland Lock Hospital from 1860 to 1910, many having spent time in Monto. The blending of their accents with the inner city and foreign tones

Annie Carroll with her friend Mary Vincent. Mary was found abandoned on a road in Phibsborough as a baby, and later sold sex in Monto to survive. Annie supported her to leave.

created a medley of Monto's own. This exposure lives on in Paula's life today:

> I had a direct plumb line into a very vital and lively oral culture. Story telling, songs, the actual language of the people themselves, the pure Dublin accent. Even today if I've been away a few weeks the minute I come back to the city and hear the rich Dublin accent, something visceral happens in my stomach.

However, just as Monto was shut down, its music was silenced too. In the establishment of the Irish state, the popularity of jazz and other high-energy music that contributed to an atmosphere of permissiveness was seen as a threat to the purity of Irish women. It began to be targeted in the push for Catholic sexual-morality teachings, as this 1930s newspaper letter shows:

Dear Irish colleens, hasten ye and crush
Jazz dancing, for it makes the Virgin Mary blush.
Root out such vile creations from our sod,
Come, banish these modes, so displeasing to God.
Patriotic daughters, it's up to you
To cease jazz dancing for the sake of Róisín Dhu.

Bawdy songs began to be censored at the end of the 19th century, minimising our chance to learn about Monto through song. They were changed over time to be less vulgar and more cryptic to hide the overt sexual elements. For example, the lyric 'get your oatcakes done' was sanitised from its original 'keep your cunthole warm'. The women were stripped of personality and power through the enforcement of silence via institutionalisation, physically and emotionally removing them from the community they once had. Conversely, those who were able to use those spaces to build a better life for themselves may have seen silence as a refuge. Silence can provide a space to think and heal and is a moment of pause for figuring out the next steps. Silence could be a respite from the sensory overwhelm of their lives – if they were free to make that choice, of course.

Demonstrated in recent times on social media, ballads and shanties are working-class products that are collaborative, adaptable and open to new additions, a result of their melting pot of performers. Their very structure is suited to the topic of sex as the structure of the ballad 'lends itself to the repetitive pulls and thrusts of a masturbatory cadence', according to academic Tom Joudrey. This makes them perfectly suited to flourish in a red-light district and transform across time and location. However, their erotic nature made them vulnerable to censorship and so we have lost another pathway to knowing more about how the historical sex trade worked.

Irish women's use of song when going through hard times was a way to process their experiences and grew in popularity during the Famine. Topics such as intimacy and sexual and domestic violence are often excluded from historical records for a variety of reasons, but folklore and music allowed women to tell their stories of survival when they weren't going to be listened to by the rest of society. The songs were a means of contribution to history and community, even if the women were illiterate.

Gemma Dunleavy's creative approach to her music reflects Monto's unique use of collaborative sound and storytelling through using a wide range of musicians. This method also reflects the transitory nature of Monto, and the mishmash of different stories and understandings of how sex was sold there reminds us of how Monto was many things to many people at many different times of its existence. Monto was never one thing – it was a manifestation of every aspect of the human experience. Gemma brings this multifaceted energy to life in her music, granting us another glimpse into how the spirit of Monto lives on in the moxie of its descendants:

> I had different stories, images and scenes in me that I was drawn to, and I would just start writing music around them, but with no lyrics because I didn't want it to be literal. Different musicians would come in and out. I would briefly explain very loosely the terms, the different levels of the brothels, and I would get their interpretation of what's playing if they're in the kip house, or if they're in a flash house. We made music with that concept for a while; it was just like a nice kind of loose direction.

The relationship between music and selling sex has also continued to this day, with the creation of the *Sex Workers' Opera*. Written by sex workers and performed across the world, this musical is an excellent example of peer support and intersectionality in addressing 'controversial' topics and providing a space for those selling sex to tell their stories themselves. The closing song of the performance is entitled 'Listen to Me' and includes the lyrics

I am so many things you cannot see,
Listen to me, Listen to me.
Mother and brother and daughter and lover,
Listen to me, Listen to me.

This production is both a community-building event and an awareness-raising initiative and holds the potential to have a greater social impact on a wider audience than academia or the media.

Sound is a tool to preserve memory and foster community, but it is vulnerable to censorship, and the forces of Irish nationalism inextricably connected with Catholicism meant knowledge and language about 'bawdy' topics were less desirable to preserve amongst the middle classes, institutions and official bodies. The sad result of this hierarchy of 'worthy' subjects is the loss of many aspects of working-class knowledge, especially that of women or marginalised groups.

CHAPTER 5

SPECTACLE AND LIBERTY

The lure of the brothel was an obvious one.

Not only were clients looking forward to time away from work, but they also had an expectation of having sex with women as part of their experience, alongside alcohol, drugs and a party vibe. This expectation was evident in the 1860s when sailors were coming into the dock: they would sing 'Early in the Morning', which includes the line 'Now my boys we're in the docks / The pretty girls come out in flocks'.

Faced with the knowledge of a hard life of labouring, war and poverty, the brothel functioned as a refuge for its clients. While they may not have considered paying for sex before they'd joined the army or navy, the threat of death paved a pathway to the brothel door. Some were barely out of their teens, forced into joining up due to a lack of other options or conscription. As one soldier explained, the visit to a brothel seemed like a no-brainer:

We were constantly in the presence of death, and no man knew when his turn might come. I suppose that subconsciously we wanted as much of life as we could get while we still had life, and if bought love is no substitute for the real thing, it at any rate seemed better than nothing.

The men sought to quell their sense of looming mortality by throwing caution and their wages to the wind and satisfying every sense they had. The madams were only too happy to indulge and create a space of reprieve for their clients – for the right price, of course. Viewed this way, the clients were seeking an experience that was life-affirming and comforting for them. However, we do not know if the women felt the same about the interactions with the men. They may indeed have, if they were able to use their time in Monto to create a better life for themselves, but some also suffered and died as a result of their experiences with these thrill-seeking men.

In the Georgian buildings of the more well-off part of Monto, the doors were kept closed, with the bully boys on guard for unruly or unwelcome potential clients. The madams here had their names displayed in the half-circular fanlights over the front doors. While none of these seem to have survived to this day, we can see similar examples in the red-light district of Storyville, New Orleans. Inside, the front parlour was used for entertaining men with food, drink and music, before being led upstairs to the bedrooms for entertainment of the carnal kind. The women also lived in these upper-floor rooms and paid rent to the madams, creating a space that worked for both business and living. More esteemed establishments used soft lighting provided by paraffin oil lamps, gas lamps and candles for a forgiving atmosphere. The flash houses of Monto had fireplaces, fresh flowers, good furnishings, a variety of glasses for expensive alcohol such as champagne, mirrors, canopied beds, cushions, pianos and lace curtains in the window for discretion.

The walls often had patterned wallpaper and gold-framed paintings and etchings of nude women on the wall, and clients dined on fine china if food was on offer. Upper-class madams aimed to provide a multisensory experience for their clients, including building an air of decadence. The atmosphere was

*Monto homes were decorated from floor to ceiling
as a point of pride.*

designed to assist with the smooth separation of the man from
his money, and each madam aimed for the best reputation. Monto
resident Kathleen Cummins remembers sneaking a look into
madam May Oblong's house and seeing such extravagant
furniture that she thought she 'must be a very rich woman';
Kathleen was correct, as May certainly had the money to splash
out on opulent surroundings. Mrs Mack's brothel offered a similar
state of luxury to clients:

> Every portion of the House is in the most thorough state
> of repair, and nicely painted and decorated, and comprises
> two parlours, two drawing rooms, several bedrooms, a good
> basement storey, and a small yard, &c. [The lease includes]
> the entire excellent Household Furniture, comprising a

capital square London-made piano, mahogany, loo, card, dinner, breakfast and work tables; a prime spring stuffed sofa in haircloth; carved and gilt chimney and pier glasses; chimney ornaments, a nice lot of framed and glazed engravings; Brussels and Kidderminster carpets and hearth rugs; a capital speaking parrot and cage [etc.].

If the madam couldn't afford it, there were other ways to present a veneer of luxury. Madam Annie Meehan, also known as Anne or Anna Meehan, was part of a gang that robbed depots and warehouses for tea, fine wines, brandy, carpets and textiles and were happy to display their spoils across her network of brothels.

Annie Meehan – married at 13, a mother at 14, a madam and the great-great-grandmother to Pearl and great-grandmother to Paula.

Charles Meehan, notorious gangster and husband of Annie Meehan, and great-great-grandfather to Pearl and great-grandfather to Paula.

In the 1880s and 1890s, erotic postcards were commonly associated with sailors and soldiers, acquired and distributed on their travels around the British Empire. If a madam did not have access to a camera, she could frame these postcards that were gifted by clients or stolen from them. In places like San Francisco, the brothels had their own mottoes framed in every room, with one being 'What Is Home Without Mother?'. With the love of Irish sayings as decorations in Irish homes, we can only speculate what slogans the women of Monto were amused by on their walls.

In other red-light districts, many upper-class brothels had themed rooms, from Asian-themed to European-themed. At least one Irish migrant woman selling sex in New York preserved a sense of home through her use of Irish decor, which was a comfort to both her and her clients. Monto may very well have followed this example to appeal to returning Irish men desperate for a feeling of 'home'. The smell of turf would have assisted with this, and the presence of Irish songs and instruments would have been soothing and appealing to those young men returning from difficult conditions.

The decor set an alluring stage for the main draw of the brothel – the entertainment. An enormous and essential part of the offerings in a brothel, clients could enjoy gambling, stripteases, food, drinking, music, singing, dancing Irish jigs and reels, and a jovial ambience where a man with money and time could freely explore his desires. An atmosphere like that can be intoxicating for those wanting an escape from restrictive social norms or the hard life ahead of them, alongside those whose desires were more violent. Most casual labourers worked long days every day, with no such things as sick pay or annual leave, so it's no wonder that they wanted to party and make the most of this combination of free time, money and anonymity when they could get it. The madams of Monto were ready to meet their needs for the right fee.

Excavations at other red-light districts have revealed that food was immensely important in better-class establishments. Unearthing the brothel of madam Mary Ann Hall in Washington DC revealed a luxury menu of wild birds, turtles, fish, fruit and expensive cuts of beef. We know dinners were provided in madam Becky Cooper's brothel in Monto, but we can only wonder about what could have been excavated under her floorboards to paint a picture of a wild night in her establishment.

In the American West, at least one saloon was known to serve Christmas dinner, and the Meehans of Monto were no strangers to luxury festive shindigs, according to their great-great-granddaughter Pearl:

Christmas was huge and it would be celebrated for the whole month and New Year's Eve was as well. The parties were ridiculous. They used to rent rooms out to their party guests. They would invite people over and it would be a showcase of the girls who would be done up and put on show. My great-grandfather used to tell me these stories of famous people coming to the parties, like James Joyce.

In a brothel in Australia where many Irish women worked and lived at the same time as their peers in Monto, large amounts of oyster shells, absinthe bottles and 77 champagne bottles were discovered during archaeological excavations, hinting at a decadent experience provided to clients. Oysters were also found in lower-class brothels, albeit a lesser amount. In Dublin, oysters were easily purchased from travelling street hawkers. If shellfish was a major draw in Australian brothels, perhaps clients in Monto enjoyed local specialities such as cockles and mussels, as the infamous Molly Malone was purported to sell as she wheeled her wheelbarrow around Dublin. Shellfish was a common dish in Dublin at this time, and some widows and their children had survived the Famine by gathering cockles at the beach to boil and eat with milk and oatmeal, showing their creativity with few resources.

Keeping the alcohol flowing meant keeping the money flowing, as drunken sailors made riskier decisions and were easier to separate from their cash, by consent or by force. Upper-class brothels provided champagne, wine and fine glassware to consume it from; some also provided absinthe. Beer was more commonly consumed at lower-class establishments. While the Scottish red-light districts offered clients their local whisky, in Monto they could enjoy a variety of Dublin whiskey brands such as Roe & Co., while the guidebook *Thom's Directory* records the rapid development of 23 distilleries and 32 breweries in Dublin alone in the 1860s. The stratospheric rise of Guinness at the same time as Monto meant that the black stuff was a firm part of Monto's appeal for its international clientele. Poitín was also a feature of many a raucous night, with braver clients requesting Penny Dreadfuls. Costing the aforementioned penny, this was a mixture of poitín, sulphuric acid and water. The harshness of poitín also helped keep the women who worked on the streets warm as they stood outside in all weathers, often with just the flimsiest of clothes to keep out the elements.

Also an integral part of the brothel, smoking was a common feature of working-class life in Dublin, with men using a pipe known as a 'duidin', and women smoking a more delicate pipe known as a 'yard of clay'. Irish-made cigarettes that may have been found in Monto at the time include brands such as Lambkins Navy Cut and Lily of Killarney, with pouches of tobacco cheaper than cigarettes. Smoking was another way to police the working class, especially women, as seen by historian Holly Dunbar, who traces a raging argument in the letters pages of the *Irish Independent* from 1919 to 1921. These rants from the public showed the disgust held for female smokers, who were accused of betraying their soft Irish Catholic femininity through smoking. This disgust didn't seem to deter the soldiers and sailors buying tins of snuff on nearby O'Connell Street, who were also not opposed to receiving business cards from the Monto women they bumped into there. Some of them quite happily followed them back to the brothels.

In red-light districts around the world, gambling was a firm part of the entertainment on offer, from marbles to cards, and Monto was no different. In Ireland, horse racing, card games and gambling had been popular since the start of the 18th century, and sailors would often bring their own gambling dice, known as a sailor's ivory and crown. Card tables for both fun parlour games and serious gambling were provided, and games were universally understood by the international guests in the brothel.

The madams and women worked hard as a unit to provide a vibrant atmosphere where the clients relaxed enough to spend money and remain in a good mood. This teamwork was essential for the extraction of maximum money with minimal risk of violence.

However, the spectacle could not last forever, and the splendour of the flash houses quickly turned to squalor as Monto declined. The once lavish patterned wallpaper was now in varying degrees of peeling decay. Those in worse conditions also had mould on the walls, impacting the health of the inhabitants further. Lower-class brothels and single rooms were often missing pieces of floorboard and bannisters as they were ripped up for firewood in hard times.

A former resident describes the inside of the tenements in the 1930s, which gives us a clue as to the conditions of some of the lower-class brothels towards the end of Monto:

Rooms were typically spartan in appearance. Furniture usually consisted of a few chairs, stools or wooden boxes, a dresser or sideboard, one or two beds made of iron or brass, straw mattresses for the floor, and a wooden tea chest for coal. Beside the open fireplace with metal grill were a water bucket, cooking kettle, and metal washing vat. On the mantelboard stood religious statues, candles, a paraffin oil lamp, and assorted small artefacts. Walls held religious pictures, family photos, and perhaps a calendar. The setting could be embellished by nice curtains, a window flower box, and a singing bird in a cage which added a bit of colour and cheer to the otherwise drab atmosphere.

In the lower-class brothels, poor ventilation resulted in cold, damp rooms that smelled of decay, mould and mildew. Horsehair and straw mattresses also contributed to the unpleasant smell, and the straw harboured bugs and lice. If the inhabitants were unlucky enough to also have cockroaches present, the air was tainted by an oily, musty tint that lingered in a hellish manner. The tallow candles used to provide light gave the rooms a foul meaty smell, and if the paraffin oil lamps of the flash houses went bad, the oil could smell like gasoline and produce sooty smoke that coated the walls, floors and surfaces. In less fortunate locations, this coating was left to build up over time, contributing to the health problems of the inhabitants who had few alternatives to move to.

Strong smells also came from the humans of Monto, who often battled bad breath due to a lack of dental care or DIY dentistry that resulted in infections. If the women had no access to soap, cleaning facilities or clean clothes, their personal hygiene suffered greatly; even more so when they had their periods. Combined with stomach-churning smells from gangrene from untreated syphilis, thrush and bacterial vaginosis, the women experienced a lack of dignity, comfort and personal care. Despite suffering in this way, they often had no other option for survival but to continue selling sex. The impact on their sexual, physical and emotional health was multifaceted and contributed to their slide towards a painful death that could have been prevented if they had had access to support and safety from violence.

Elizabeth Dillon, a resident of Corporation Street, grew up witnessing her mother constantly fighting a losing battle to keep their living space clean and fresh-smelling after their overnight guests had left:

My mother used to scrub the clothes in a big tin bath on the table. She always had her sleeves rolled up. She was a clean woman and old before her time. God help her, always scrubbing the floor and out on the lobby of the house. That was because people used to sleep on the lobbies in the night-time and there would be a bit of a smell after they had gone in the morning.

Adding to the kaleidoscope of smells from unwashed clothes and bodies, many of the women also struggled with alcohol use. Often described as a pungent, foul odour, the smell of methylated spirits lingered long after the women left to conduct their business. If they smoked opium, which was rare but still present in Dublin, a sickly sweet smell would be added to the stench.

Mixing brothels with overcrowded family rooms resulted in an assault on a person's sense of smell. In 1885, the report of the Royal Commission on Sewerage and Drainage found 93 people in one house on Upper Gloucester Street in Monto. In the nearby tenements of Henrietta Street, 104 people were registered as living in one house in the 1911 census. Since most tenements had no running water, we can (thankfully) only imagine the smell emanating from the mound of a hundred people's excrement left in the summer sun to be eaten by rats and enveloped by swarms of bluebottles. Most families had a slop bucket that they kept in their room for night-time, dragging it down to the yard in the morning, since going barefoot down flights of stairs in the dark was a risky journey, with rats and strangers for company. If it was raining, they faced the possibility of standing in puddles leaking from the heap of decaying and fresh sewage near the outhouse; the bucket was viewed as a better option. The morning aroma must have been an unpleasant way to start the day, to understate the obvious.

Despite these challenges, what the women could clean they did and did so with pride. Many oral testimonies show how the women of Monto spent time scrubbing, inside and outside, and filling window boxes with colourful flowers. But things grew worse as extreme poverty seeped in and claimed more victims. Some families had up to 20 children, all in one or two rooms, and the bare rooms rented by the women became even more of a health hazard, crumbling by the day. By the end of Monto, the tenements had become an extreme health hazard, with sewage traps regularly spilling open after rainfall and 30 rats found in one kitchen in one week.

With the smells of the tenements, backyard livestock, horse waste, sewage from the overly polluted Liffey, malted barley and hops from the numerous breweries, local factories and the Sean McDermott Street Laundry, Monto was not for the faint of heart or delicate of nose. The slums were viewed as 'human piggeries', inhabited by people who needed to be inspected, controlled, sanitised and gawked at. Martin reflects on how his grandmother Annie Carroll could have felt living in these conditions after moving to Dublin to reunite with her mother after growing up separately from her in Tipperary:

> The tenement houses in the area where her mother lived out her life must have been very strange indeed for this young country woman, with the smell of boiled cabbage, bodies washed and unwashed, hallways marked with years of blood, sweat and tears, stairways drenched and stained from all sorts of human waste that was carried out in buckets to the one and only toilet in the backyard. Did she perhaps at any time long for the fresh, clean air of Thomastown in County Tipperary?

As the women swapped the streets of Monto for the hospital, marriage or emigration, we can only hope they were able to settle in a more pleasant-smelling environment.

CHAPTER 6

TRICKS OF THE TRADE

Women working in the sex trade have long been used to finding ways to advertise their services and stand out from their competitors. Prostitutes in ancient Greece wore sandals that imprinted the words 'follow me' in the dirt, while those selling sex in the red-light district of Hell's Half Acre in California stood on wooden platforms outside their homes to attract clients, which appeared to be a successful tactic as they could see up to 30 men a day. Madams in Paris threw extravagant parties that were the talk of the town, while in Dublin, madam and courtesan Peg Plunkett's parties at her brothel on what is now Balfe Street, near St Stephen's Green, were the stuff of legend. The women of Monto did not slack when it came to being just as creative as their contemporaries.

Simply put, the men wanted women, as good-looking as they could get them. Sometimes they wanted the same woman; other times they wanted someone new or someone who specialised in a particular service. When money and status permitted them to access the higher-class brothels, they were promised the best women available. For the choosier clients of Monto, that meant clean, fresh-faced, well-dressed and soft-skinned young women and young teenagers.

To meet this demand, the madams capitalised on the constant influx of new women, since their reputations for having the newest and most beautiful women as star attractions had to be consistently maintained. The women acted as walking advertisements for the brothel by dressing up in fine clothes and attending high-society events, giving their targets a glimpse of what delights could be on the menu. They were often to be found at horse-racing events such as the Dublin Horse Show, Fairyhouse and Punchestown, since a day at the races was an indulgent pastime for the wealthy. They were also present at the theatres and society balls in glamorous hotels such as the Shelbourne and the Gresham and went shopping on Grafton Street alongside the upper-class shoppers who were there to see and be seen. They may also have attended the numerous bazaars and charity fairs in Dublin, which had much social prestige and attracted wealthy clientele for the women to entice.

Using clothing like chameleons, the women expertly blended into these circles to seduce the men and their money. Social reformer Robert Wilson describes how they secured their targets in these situations:

> They dress as ordinary well behaved women do – they do not openly stare at passers by – they will gently, almost accidentally, as it were, jostle against the person they wish to solicit – modestly wait in a retired spot – attend public meetings, concerts, soirees, and churches, and, by a look or smile significant, draw away the unheeding youth or man who does not suspect that beneath that decent garb there can lurk habitual prostitution and its dangers.

One could also suggest that many men knew *exactly* what that smile meant and were more than happy to follow and add an extra layer of pleasure to their day out.

Paddy McCormack, born in 1916 in Monto, tells us how the madams also used the landscape as a marketing tool to showcase their most alluring commodities:

I remember May Oblong, the madam. She used to drive the best looking girls around the streets on horse and cart. They used to be sitting on both sides of it and she would be sitting on the top seat all dressed up, driving the horse. May Oblong was advertising for the men to come down to her house and what a way to do it!

May Dunne, born on Railway Street, is the niece of May Oblong's driver and describes this same horse and cart:

It was a beautiful pony and trap, all decked out with leather and arm rests. The horse had all these beautiful brass badges on the harness. Even the horse's head was decked out in shining brass.

The spectacle of May's procession easily stood out amongst both the run-down streets and the affluent ones, showing that May had a firm grasp on the concept of optics and knew how to maximise her assets – human and otherwise. This business acumen may have been morally distasteful to some, but it allowed May to build substantial wealth that enabled her to dismiss these attitudes from the comfort of a luxurious house. Many of the young women working for her were able to monetise their experiences and leave for new lives; others succumbed to her violence which included being slashed across the face. Her presence was therefore not only a display of unapologetic wealth, but also a visible reminder of the violence that could, and often did, accompany the clip-clop of her horses on the cobblestones as she collected her dues. Across the Atlantic Ocean, her peer Pearl De Vere used the same tactic in Colorado in the 1890s. Pearl used her glamorous horse-drawn carriage to make a bold statement: she had power, style, money and her girls were the finest in town. Both May and Pearl showed how skilled they were at seduction through bold statements for maximum profit and power, and how appearance was a tool to manipulate in order to succeed.

The high-class madams of Monto followed the examples set by their peers and hand-selected each woman that worked for them and provided them with the latest fashions to wear. Appearance was very important, and to be well dressed meant not only higher status, but perhaps a higher chance to attract rich clients who could provide stability. To afford these clothes, the madams charged higher rates from their clients, who wanted classy, well-presented women. Entry applications had to be completed before a client could step foot inside, and these applications were used to weed out the cheaper men who couldn't play their parts in keeping up appearances.

Parties and social gatherings were an important way to curate a glamorous reputation. Today, Pearl remembers hearing stories of the legendary parties her great-great-grandmother Annie Meehan threw to showcase their inventory of women, fine surroundings and finesse:

> They had so many houses that they would rotate them, clean them up, then have a grand reopening party. The houses would be lovely; the girls would be all there dressed up and it was a big advertisement for the business.

Many of the women of Dublin worked locally in factories, in the markets or as dressmakers, supplementing their wages through selling sex as their incomes fluctuated or expensive bills landed at their doors. These particular women were especially valuable to the madams, who viewed them as a source of new workplace arrivals that might be lured to Monto. Whether this recruitment was freely done by the women or under duress from the madams, or if they got a cut of profits for their service, we might never know.

Also recognised as essential by the madams was the power of scent to seduce a man and separate him from his cash. The aroma of a business can be key to its financial success, and modern-day casinos have recognised this connection. Research has shown that when Vegas casinos pump perfume around certain machines, the profits at those machines almost double. The soft, feminine smells of the brothel were a respite from the ships, barracks, farms and factories that the clients toiled all day in with other men. Scent is intimately connected with our emotions and desires, and if they can be manipulated, it maximises profit. The madams understood that an easy way to do that was to connect sex and smell, as the multi-billion-dollar perfume industry also demonstrates in most of its adverts.

Some brothels fared better than others when it came to providing a pleasant-smelling environment for their workers and customers. The well-off madams could afford to hire women from the local community to clean the brothels and keep their girls clean and fresh-smelling. Smell was so important in the seduction of clients that excavations of Victorian American brothels have revealed a large volume of perfume bottles, lotions, douches and dental products. In Ireland, women used perfumes to varying degrees of success:

> 'The girls do be puttin it on their handkerchers . . . if they're gain' walking out with the police . . . [I]t takes the smell of the turf out of their hair and clothes and gives them a great charrum.' The official had a sniff of the 'White Rose' and found that it had a 'rank powerful odour of shaving-soap and hair oil', hardly the most attractive of perfumes!

A more appealing smell came from the delicate herbal scent of lavender, which has been associated with selling sex since the ancient Romans. The tenement floors of Monto and Henrietta Street were waxed with Malone's lavender polish, which is still used today and one of Ireland's longest-selling products. Henrietta Street tenement museum has an example of the purple and white tin that was a staple in many homes after 1902. Madams who bought flowers may have picked up some bunches of lavender for their establishments while shopping on Sackville Street and at local markets such as Moore Street, where May Oblong met her husband. In the 1860s, they also had access to lavender via the street sellers on the corner of Wicklow Street and Grafton Street, whose cry of 'Sweet lavender' was heard as the women shopped and strolled. Finding lavender in the miasma of Monto therefore situates it within the global history of sex work, prostitution and trafficking, showing the importance of viewing the sex trade in context.

Lavender was a common smell across Victorian brothels, its association with the sex trade recognised in the original version of the ballad 'The Unfortunate Rake'. Later covered by Irish singer Christy Moore, the unfortunate rake (a slang term for a soldier up to no good) asked for his coffin to be covered in lavender to cover the smell from his syphilis-riddled corpse:

Over my coffin put handfuls of lavender
Handfuls of lavender on every side
Bunches of roses all over my coffin
Saying there goes a young man cut down in his prime.

Lavender is apparently worn in the afterlife too. The ghost of brothel owner Madame Katherine in Washington DC is said to not only wear a lavender-coloured dress with purple bows when she appears, but also leaves a trail of lavender perfume lingering behind her as she floats through the site of her former premises on her other-worldly adventures.

Another important service provided was discretion, with upper-class clients fearing social ruin more than violence or robbery. These clients could avail of a hackney cab to deliver them anonymously to the steps of the finer establishments. This perk was paid for by the madams, but the drivers would be sure to *kindly* suggest a tip from clients to ensure maximum discretion. Some brothels were rumoured to have tunnels whereby those who didn't want to be seen entering or leaving could secretly slip in and out. Madams were not shy about capitalising on this fear of social ruin and employed blackmail where they could in order to increase their wealth or status. This tactic came in handy before Monto when high-society madam Peg Plunkett found that the IOUs she had been given were in fact worthless. She navigated her way out of debt by telling former clients that unless they paid up sharpish they would be exposed in her memoirs. Her strategy paid off as she became wealthy again for a time, making 600 guineas from her blackmailing, going to her grave with some of the more salacious details concerning her customers. We can only wonder what secrets the clients of Monto preferred to keep quiet too.

In New Orleans, madams were just as aware of the power of blackmail over men who very much wanted their predilections kept quiet. Legendary Storyville madam Norma Wallace was meticulous in her blackmailing of high-class clientele:

> Norma liked to keep an eye out when they were undressing and note anything unusual: a birthmark; or a phallus of an unusual shape. She kept abundant records in a little black book, and if politicians made nasty noises, she was not above telling them what she knew, and advising them that their best option was to let sleeping dogs lie.

Many madams were experienced negotiators and highly skilled at networking. They put these skills to use in cultivating relationships with those who could direct clients their way. Being ahead of the curve is important in many aspects of life, and the madams of Monto knew this was especially true for proactively sourcing clients. Society balls were one place where they cultivated relationships with commanding officers, who could supply a discerning madam with a steady stream of clients in exchange for a promise to keep them safe from syphilis. Students also proved to be key for the smooth running of the brothels, and local medical students enjoyed a student perk unthinkable today. In exchange for medical certificates declaring that her ladies were free of disease, the madam gave them discounted rates which they happily made use of, whether that certificate was true or not.

The madams also tracked the movement of soldiers and sailors to keep up to date on imminent arrivals so they could ensure adequate resources to maximise earning potential; this inventory included drink, drugs and of course women and girls. Their collaboration with their contacts on the docks and in the barracks worked both ways through the 'crimping' system found all over the ports of the empire. Crimpers were often madams or lodging-house managers who would take all of a sailor's wages and provide him with accommodation and access to red-light delights. However, he would shortly find himself out of money and in need of a new job, so off he would go back to the docks without overstaying his welcome. This system suited madams and dockmasters very much as it ensured a regular supply of money and labour, and both were happy to work in partnership with each other. The sailors themselves often didn't mind as they gained a more direct route to accommodation, alcohol and women, and then back to a job when they'd had their fill. Neither the employers nor the madams cared much about the long-term health of those they exploited as there was a constant supply of fresh bodies signing up – willingly or not.

The madams were transparent about their part in this circle of life for sailors, and the men accepted it as part of the price to pay for their fun, even incorporating this rapid withdrawal of services once their money ran out in their songs. With Jack being a common term for sailors, the Jacks of the brothels and lodging houses knew what they were signing up for:

But when the money's all gone and spent,
And there's none to be borrowed and none to be lent,
In comes old Grouse with a frown,
Saying, 'Get up, Jack, let John sit down'.

The madams also paid pennies to neighbourhood youths to operate as lookouts for police and to keep an eye on some of the women in case they dared to try to escape. Additionally, young boys like George Smith supplemented their incomes selling newspapers by passing on information on the expected arrival times of ships from the Dublin Ballast Office. He was told by one of the women, Belfast Bella, to use the cover story that his father worked on the ship and he was rewarded with a shilling for his efforts.

George's friends and fellow newsboys ran errands for the women and operated a strict code of discretion. If the women heard of this code being broken, the boys were out of a job. Living in Monto, they were poor enough to be easily manipulated by a few pennies, since those coins could mean the difference between going hungry or not. The boys may also have been able to make some money by favouring one of a madam's contacts with information on the newest women and girls available in the brothel. Groups of freshly arrived men were eager, too, to take up offers to be brought to the best brothel in town, if only for a small fee.

Despite the newsboys being young teenagers, there is some evidence that they were no strangers to violence. In the 1880s they attacked policemen and *Evening Herald* vans in a labour dispute and were described as quick-witted urchins who lured victims into narrow lanes to attack them and were happy to face

off with IRA men in the streets. While they may have been imma-
ture in age, they were proficient at using the combination of
violence and the architecture of the city to achieve their goals,
an ideal skill set for work in a red-light district.

The boys were not alone. Inhabitants of and visitors to Monto
developed the ability to turn their landscape into a tool for robbing
clients or escaping trouble, temporary shelter, a workplace and a
space for sexual violence. Dark and dingy alleyways, changing
street names and changing venues all served to make a client lose
his way and spend his money. Dimly lit laneway labyrinths also
provided a way to disappear from the prying eyes of the police
and to impede a woman's exit if she was being attacked.

The best example of using architecture to rob men in Monto
is found in the Man Trap. Situated next to Jack Meagher's pub
on the corner of Corporation Street and Purdon Street, the Man
Trap was a multidirectional maze which split off into several
laneways and cul-de-sacs such as Byrne's Square and White's
Court. Men were lured into its twisting warrens with the promise
of sex, but instead found themselves beaten up by bully boys or
robbed while their trousers were around their ankles. By the time
the man got himself together and figured out which door led back
to safety, it wasn't worth kicking off round two by challenging
the women or bully boys.

As well as the twisting streets, the indoor physical spaces were
used by Monto's madams to facilitate their goals. Monto resident
Tom Byrne, born in 1914, describes one method:

Donoghue [a publican] had a tenement house next to his
pub. Now, he had a big wardrobe along the wall in his living
accommodation above the pub – and another big wardrobe
along the wall in his tenement house. And they backed one
another! And clothes hanging in them. So, when there was
going to be a raid it was 'everybody upstairs!' So they ran

through the wardrobes [connected by an opening cut in the wall] and the door closed and he slides the clothes back on the rack! The police came in and raided the place – nobody there! Most ingenious!

Similar tricks could be used to take advantage of clients. In some brothels, if a client was in the front room, the bully boys reached in through the window to rob his belongings, relying on a greased lock to avoid noise. Across the pond in New York, some brothels had sliding panels through which an accomplice could slip to remove a client's things, and it is easy to see this occurring in Monto too. In 1868 Matthew Hale Smith described how this trick worked:

> The place selected is usually a basement in a quiet neighbour-hood, the more respectable the better . . . The room is papered and a panel cut in the paper, or one of the panels is fitted to slide softly . . . The bolts, and bars, and locks are peculiar, and so made as to seem to lock on the inside, though they . . . really fasten on the outside. And while the visitor imagines he has locked all covers out, he is really locked in himself, and cannot escape till he has been robbed.

Towards the end of Monto, when more of the buildings were slums than respectable brothels, madam Maggie Doyle changed her Georgian front door to a steel one to delay the police trying to raid her property. By the time the police were able to force their way in, any evidence of illegal activity was wiped clean, and clients were long gone through secret doors. Any illegal alcohol was hidden in gramophones and on the streets, which bought time and plausible deniability.

The women who had to resort to lower-class brothels, bare rooms or even the streets, did not have the same opportunities for advertising or the ability to escape through secret rooms.

Limited opportunities to access clients meant getting creative. They called to potential clients as they passed by, sometimes enticing them with a brief flash of their nude bodies under their raincoats. This was both a business tactic and a harsh reality of life for the women – there wasn't much under the raincoats because they would barely have any clothes left by the time they ended up touting for business on the streets.

In London, one client tells his story of being seduced by similar on-street tactics:

> Each woman had generally but one room, but two or three used to sit together in the front room in their chemises. There was the bed, wash-stand, chamberpot and all complete. Perhaps one lolled out of the window, showing her breasts, and if you gave such a one a shilling, she would stoop so that you could see right down past her belly to her knees, and have a glimpse of her cunt-fringe. Sometimes one would pull up her garter, or another sit down and piddle, or pretend to do so, or have recourse to other exciting devices when men peeped in.

Not every woman wanted to have sex with their clients, for a multitude of reasons. Monto women sometimes got their clients excessively drunk or drugged them, and in New York, William Sanger also saw this behaviour in the 2,000 red-light-working women that he interviewed in 1855:

> Sailors buy men and women drinks . . . [and] by such a course he very soon gets intoxicated, when a girl whom he has honoured with his special attention conveys him to bed, and leaves him there to sleep himself sober.

The women also used the same tricks found in European and American brothels, one of which was the 'badger game', where the bully boy would pretend to be an angry husband and burst in at a compromising moment and demand the client give him money or face a beating. This was successful because of the reputation of the bully boys and the clients' need to get out safely with their lives and reputations intact, even if their wallets were gone.

Martin Coffey tells the story of a trick his mother helped pull off as a child in Monto:

Sometimes when a prostitute was expecting a customer, she might send over to one of her neighbours who had young children and ask that one of the children be sent over to her for the day. The young child would be instructed by the prostitute to lie on the bed and pretend to be asleep when her customer arrived. He would become irate over the child being on the bed. The prostitute would then suggest that they take the child for a walk around the nearby shops. The customer would then be '*stung*' to buy something for the child, perhaps a new coat, a nice dress or perhaps a little doll. On their return to the room the child would once again climb onto the bed. This would very often result in the customer putting his hat and coat on and heading out the door but not before the prostitute would demand her money and of course she had the boyfriend standing outside the door with a lead pipe in his hand, just in case. Some people would be horrified to think my mother was involved with that. She didn't, she felt no shame, no shame at all. It was helping someone, somebody who was looked on as the worst type of individual in society.

Advice for men on how to avoid robbery was often included in another advertising tool brothel owners used: guidebooks. These books, also known as 'sporting guides' or 'blue books', advertising brothels and prostitutes were prolific in the Victorian era. Author Katherine Hijar describes these popular publications as being small enough for a gentleman's pockets, containing reviews of a woman's skills, costs and quality of the brothel.

They also contained tips on avoiding venereal disease, and towards the end of the 19th century, they began to feature ads for condoms. Like a shopping catalogue, the well-thumbed pages often included photos, although often they were not truly of the girl described. These pamphlets were made to be taken away on ships and journeys, folded in pockets or hidden from superiors, their pages destined to be soaked with beer and discarded. Only eight copies have been preserved in the US.

Blue books not only provided advice on the best providers, but also warned clients of the risk of blackmail. The *Gentleman's Companion* from 1870 advised that some brothels contained 'plunderers' who would take everything from a client, including his reputation.

While these guides proliferated across the British Empire, we must ask – was there a blue book for Monto?

We know that blue books existed in Scotland from at least the 1770s. *Ranger's Impartial List of the Ladies of Please in Edinburgh, with a Preface by a Celebrated Wit* was published in 1775 by James Tyler, a client of the upper-class brothels. Containing the names and descriptions of 66 women working in the brothels of Edinburgh, it was circulated in the pockets of clients. In London, *Harris's List of Covent Garden Ladies* sold thousands of copies a year and was the most popular blue book in the 18th century, but examples from the 1660s have also been discovered across Europe.

Wanting to have the best access to the wealthiest clients, a blue book must have seemed like an excellent idea to the madams, spotting the potential in an international distribution network for increasing their supply of fresh clients and prostitutes. They had access to cameras and they could afford to print photos; although not all blue books featured photos, so access to a camera was not mandatory for a book's success.

Blue books could be produced via a thriving pamphlet printing and distribution system in place across Britain and Ireland. Multiple print and stationery shops were a mere stone's throw from Monto on Sackville Street, Talbot Street and Sean McDermott Street, increasing the ease of access to making a blue book for their recruitment efforts. From 1800, printers lived on Mecklenburgh Street and knew who the madams were. If they could make some money on the side, it was surely an opportunity not to be ignored, and they may also have been the ones to print the business cards that the madams gave to sailors.

In 1865 over 30 new Irish newspapers came into existence, so it is not a stretch to think the madams saw the value of this form of communication. We also know that the printing industry was sometimes led by men who were no strangers to the brothels themselves. Seventy years before the heyday of Monto, queen of the red-light scene in Dublin Peg Plunkett threw a grand masquerade ball and invited Dublin-based printer Bartholomew Corcoran, whose speciality was chapbooks. Chapbooks were short, cheap printed publications intended to be sold on the street for a penny. They were used for a large variety of topics, from folklore to ballads, poetry and religious preaching, raising the possibility that blue books could be numbered amongst them. Bartholomew was clearly comfortable with the sex trade and happy to do favours for his favourite madam.

Some Dubliners protested the sale of 'spicy postcards' in Dublin newsagents, which depicted nude women. Vigilante groups such as the Ancient Order of Hibernians and the Dublin Vigilance Committee called for the Indecent Advertisement Act of 1885 to be enforced against shops such as Easons for selling 'pernicious' material, and organised pickets and protests to protect Irish social purity.

Another potential clue lies with Ned Nowlan, an editor of the *Freeman's Journal*. This newspaper ran for 166 years in Ireland until 1924. It was not only widely read, but Ned was also a guest at Peg Plunkett's masquerade ball and propositioned her on the night. Sadly for him, he was unsuccessful. But these party guests show a connection between people with power in the printing and distribution businesses and those in the sex trade, making a blue book of some kind a real possibility.

The madams in Monto may have known this history or been informed about blue books by their clients. Sailors were viewed as importers, bringing a mixture of foods, curios and clothes with them whenever they travelled. Contributing to a thriving black market with transitory sellers and buyers, clients also brought blue books into the brothels, and back to their barracks and cabins, and on to their next adventure. Perhaps one day a scrap of paper will be unearthed in an old dockyard halfway across the world with the names of Monto's inhabitants and their specialities splashed across it.

In the 1880s pornographic pamphlets thrived, such as *The Pearl* in England, which printed bawdy songs, pornographic images and poems. Because the printers knew these publications were destined for the underworld, they could forget about obeying the social rules of polite society and indulge the demand for folk erotica. This freedom resulted in these pamphlets becoming a record of the sex trade across the British Empire:

> . . . these texts, liberated from the imperative to maintain a veneer of propriety, rove across a startling range of territory: women's suffrage, physical disability and sexual impairment, secret sex societies, interspecies coition, India – rubber dildos, slave rape in the West Indies, duels, mock crucifixions,

Turkish harems, prophylactic devices, friendships ratified by the exchange of pubic hair – the list goes on . . .

However, this freedom may have swung in the opposite direction where the printers decided to just make up as much content as possible to sell quickly, knowing that the men probably weren't too bothered if the book was not completely truthful. Speculation and graphic descriptions of the taboo were alluring to many, and alluring meant money to the printers.

British soldiers also had a culture of showing off their treasures from red-light districts and talking openly about their experiences with the women. In his memoirs, Brigadier-General Crozier discussed what this post-brothel debriefing looked like:

They 'show kit' on a [train] carriage seat. The result is astounding! Two pairs of silk stockings and a chemise, one nightdress and a string of beads. A pot of vaseline, a candle, two boxes of matches, and an envelope full of astonishing picture postcards, completes the list. 'Souvenirs', says one rascal.

Blue books could have been passed around at events like this, pointing out the women they'd visited and showing off their souvenirs from them. Given that many soldiers and sailors interacted with each other during their travels through the British Empire, there was a shared knowledge of the best places to go onshore. It is conceivable that this knowledge included a blue book on Monto. Most likely, if such books did exist, they perished on their onward journeys or were deliberately destroyed by vigilantes or reformers. The popular press has been under-studied in Ireland, with so much more to discover in the print history of Dublin's underworld and working classes.

These examples show that the people of Monto, and indeed other red-light districts, were competent in finding ways to survive in extremely difficult circumstances with a lack of other options. They were also able to harness new inventions and make use of their networking skills to create a world where they had more power, control and money. New technology has always been instantly connected with sex and the sex trade – the first films and photos included naked women, and the porn industry has deftly used tapes, DVDs, the internet, smartphones and more to reach its audience. Those in the sex trade long ago learned to adopt new technology as a survival method against censorship and to skirt the rules, and the women of Monto need to be included in this history and understanding of sex, money and power.

CHAPTER 7

SEDUCERS AND
THE SEDUCED

While many historians have unfortunately shied away from including sexual content in their documentation of cultural history, we can learn a lot about the personal experiences of the women of red-light districts by looking at what kind of sexual activity was present.

While holding our breath for an authentic Monto blue book to miraculously emerge, we can see what kinds of sex acts were common in similar brothels with similar demographics by looking at nearby blue books. A Scottish version enjoys delving into descriptions of the sexual skill sets offered by their favoured women of the flash houses of Edinburgh:

Miss INGLIS, at Miss WALKER'S.
This Lady is short, black hair, bad teeth, and about 24 years old. She is foolishly good-natured, and many one takes advantage of her upon that account. Notwithstanding, she is no novice at the game of love, for she is remarkably fond of performing on the silent flute, and can manage the stops extraordinarily well. She twists round you like an eel, and would not loose a drop of the precious juice of nature, not for a kingdom.

Bella Cohen was rumoured to specialise in the wilder side of sexual services in Monto.

The songs sung by lower-class brothel clientele hint at sex acts featuring dildos and anal sex, showing there was awareness and potential availability of these practices on the brothel menu.

Writers such as St John Gogarthy and Joyce give us clues to experiences of sadomasochism, foot fetishes, groping of bums, and verbal degradation – specialties in Bella Cohen's brothel. Historian Aongus Collins suggests that even the most niche of fetishes were catered to in Monto:

One prostitute recalled an unusual errand. She was told to have a bath and await her customer. He arrived with two bunches of scallions. Her mission was to chase him around the table, beating him with the scallions while he was nude.

For this she got £20 [around €3800]- 40 times the normal rate.

The men expected a lustful time, and it did not go well if they did not get what they wanted. One client in Monto complained that the woman he had bought sex from was not enthusiastic enough for his liking. He whined to the bullies that 'there was more bounce on a bog' and demanded a refund. Predictably, this was not received well and his complaint was resolved less than amicably.

Clients could be encouraged by lust to spend more than they planned when their time was up, as this client in London details:

> One night I saw a woman with very fat breasts looking out of the window (I was then fond of stout women); and after talking a minute, asked her if she would let me feel her cunt for a shilling. 'Yes,' said she. In I went, down she shut the window, and in another minute I was groping her. She did not let me feel her long. I had not felt such a bum since Mary's [. . .] and it so wetted my appetite, that I struck a bargain for a fuck. She was soon stripped, and all I now recollect about her is, that her cunt was large and covered with hair of a brownish colour; that her eyes were dark; and that she seemed full twenty-five years of age. I fucked her on a sofa.

One source that explicitly tells us what went on in brothels is soldier memoirs. Their diaries often contained records of their exploits in the red-light districts, including occasions such as having sex for the first time. One such adventurer was 17-year-old Irish soldier Private Casey, who attempted to lose his virginity in a Parisian brothel in 1914. It didn't quite go to plan:

> . . . sitting on my knee, kissing my cheek, never my lips, and rubbing the nipples of her tits on my face, across my lips, all

in view of the crowds of men who were doing the same thing, putting her hands inside my fly, and murmuring, Oh Darling you are so hard and big, you will like a short time with me, I am very good, and I make you very pleasurable . . . I was amazed when she took hold of my business, and examined it very carefully, satisfied I was free from the Gonna [*sic*], laid on the bed her bit of cheese was off, opening wide her lovely white legs . . . I was told to lay on top of her, then my trouble started, I went limp. And though this French hussy, [*sic*] tried everything she knew, even putting my thing in her mouth, I could not get hard, then she got very angry, am I not very beautiful to you, that you do not want to love me, you English are very cold, and do not know how to make love, I leave you now, get dressed, I have work to do.

Casey did manage to have sex on another occasion and shared intimate details of his briefly momentous experience:

I felt a little proud of myself because my member was standing out as stif [*sic*] as a ramrod, pulling me on top of her, and guiding my stifun [*sic*] into her, she began to move her body, in a circular motion, and with making a move I ejaculated, I got the shock of my life, I was finished before I had start [*sic*].

One surprising reason for the gap in knowledge of brothel practices was that American brothel guides were extremely sparse about the sexual activities that went on behind closed doors. This was not due to embarrassment but was a deliberate attempt to appeal to the upper classes, who prioritised discretion.

Sex toys are a staple in many brothels and bedrooms now, but Monto mostly missed the era of these add-ons to the sexual offerings. Around the late 1890s vibrators became more popular – they were originally designed to help men with blood disorders, but women soon copped on to their potential. The early 20th century saw more women using these devices for their own pleasure, and manufacturers soon realised this and began marketing to women with the unspoken acknowledgement that women were not just using them to massage their necks. They were cumbersome, electric and cost $10–$30 at the time. By the time Monto was on its path of decline this may have been out of reach financially, but if they could have afforded it Monto would certainly have included the buzz of vibrators in its soundscape.

Perhaps James Joyces' love of farts were catered to in Monto, and we can glimpse just how he liked to indulge this kink in his love letter to Nora:

> You had an arse full of farts that night, darling, and I fucked them out of you, big fat fellows, long windy ones, quick little merry cracks and a lot of tiny little naughty farties ending in a long gush from your hole. It is wonderful to fuck a farting woman when every fuck drives one out of her.

We do know that many sexual interactions were brief, due to a clever brothel time-management system. Candles that resembled matchbooks were used to time clients: when the candle burned down to its wick, time was up for the gentleman. Of course, the women manipulated this system by trimming the candle so that the time would be subtly shorter. If they didn't want to have penetrative sex, the women could have adapted a trick known by international male prostitution circles in the 1840s. This involved using a prosthetic vagina to trick clients into thinking they were having vaginal sex, which may also have been used by women during menstruation.

Returning clients like sailors and soldiers made a beeline to see their favourite woman, and sometimes spent all their time and money with her, essentially living as husband and wife while in

Monto. A German woman in London outlined how this arrangement suited her down to the ground:

> I know very many sailors – six, eight, ten, oh – more than that. They are my husbands. I am not married, of course not, but they think me their wife while they are on shore. I do not care much for any of them; I have a lover of my own.

The Irish sailors working in transporting goods often made short visits to Britain, allowing them to make frequent trips back to Monto, and these relationships sometimes resulted in marriage. This arrangement offered the women a way to live the lifestyle they wanted to while their husbands were away. This could include enjoying a sense of independence that may have not been available in more 'traditional' marriages, or perhaps allowing them privacy to explore their sexuality with other women when the rest of society might judge them for being queer women.

The men knew that the women were not faithful when they were away, but neither were they. They enjoyed having their cake and eating it – a roster of women and a sense of home without having to provide support while they were gone. For the women, their continuation of selling sex was sometimes less about enjoying the work and more about surviving without the income of their 'husband' while he was away.

From being heard and seen on the streets of Monto for decades, sex fell silent not just in Monto but across Ireland as the state and the Catholic Church built a conservative society that confined women in the home as wives and mothers. It is a shame we have so little first-hand information about the sexual side of Monto in the women's own words, as it could tell us much about the sex trade through history and women's experiences in Ireland at that time. Academic Heather Miller-Lee asks some thought-provoking questions about what such gaps mean for our understanding of the historical sex trade:

> How could one describe the life of a prostitute or the sexual life of women (whether heterosexual or homosexual) without discussing the sexual activities in which they engaged, the desires they experienced, or the images around which they fantasised? Was the fact that prostitutes had sex for a living unimportant? Was it simply taken for granted? Or was the assumption that prostitutes were inevitably participating in sex that they could not have enjoyed and were simply the sexual and economic victims of men and capitalist society?

Some of the women who found themselves in Monto had been 'seduced'. This was a catch-all term that could mean the woman had either experienced sexual violence or fallen for a man who made empty promises to marry her but instead abandoned her after sex, leaving her with a shattered reputation and heart. Some 'seduced' women were pitied, some were blamed for the man's actions, and most felt excluded from society as they had now become damaged goods. This stigma limited their options and kept them in poverty, often leaving them with selling sex as their only option for survival. It was not unheard of for the madams of Monto to order their bullies to rape a woman if she got on the madam's bad side, and some cases of women holding down another woman's legs for men to rape her have been recorded in previous decades in Dublin. The status of women in the sex trade made them more vulnerable to extreme violence, as Eve Southworth suggests:

> As 'fallen' women, prostitutes lacked the protection of an ideology that prevented attacks upon domestic, good women. Often seen as sexual objects, some men asserted their dominance over prostitutes through sex and violence. This is not

to say that a husband or family could not assault the wife or daughter striving for ideal Victorian womanhood. Prostitutes, however, as public women, were at risk of being attacked and abused in ways that respectable women would not be.

Religious reformer William Logan recounts the experience of a 17-year-old girl that he felt was representative of a common experience. A naive rural girl came to Dublin with a friend and was immediately flagged by the bully boys as fresh meat:

> This monster saw she was a 'fresh girl;' the house was very throng, and, from his harsh treatment, he had few girls. He gave her three glasses of spirits, then she was taken up stairs, and after having had ten or twelve visitors, she did what she could to get over the window. He heard the noise, came up stairs, and threatened to take her life if she did not keep quiet, and she was actually compelled to receive other visitors that evening.

In conflicts and war zones, women and children are especially vulnerable to sexual violence. In the fight for independence, sexual violence from Irish revolutionaries, British soldiers and the British Black and Tans was another risk for the women of Monto. Forced hair cutting, known as 'bobbing', was done to women who were viewed to have betrayed the cause and to mark them as traitors. It involved holding women down and roughly chopping off their hair, visibly tainting them with stigma. Historian Gemma Clark outlines how bobbing was part of the spectrum of sexual violence:

> If a woman's hair is key to her femininity and attractiveness, then, its removal thus marks out physically women who have transgressed social and sexual norms (by collaboration with the enemy, for example) – and symbolically defeminises the target.

This act was often done with maximum cruelty intended, with women snatched off the street or their doors kicked in at night, and they were also at risk of 'other indignities and insults'. The use of hair to brand some women as 'wrong' women was also replicated in the laundries and refuges where their hair was also bobbed or shaved.

While the upper-class flash-house clients had the power of their reputations and wealth to protect them from allegations of sexual violence, lower-class clients may have enjoyed protection from army and naval superiors who needed them back and not in a police cell. Clients and/or perpetrators of sexual violence may have felt invincible because they were untraceable or untouchable, and so felt freer to commit sexual violence on the women.

Sexual violence was not just a terror-inducing reality for adult women in the red-light district. It was a common belief in Western Victorian societies that sex with a virgin would cure syphilis. Known as the 'virgin-cleansing myth', this belief has been around since at least the 16th century and has stubbornly persisted to the present day in some countries. The exact origins of this myth are unclear, but it may be connected to Christian ideals and the emphasis on virginity and sexual purity. Virgins proved to be a desirable commodity in the brothels, not just for those who were seeking a cure for an STI, but also for those who sought an opportunity to rape a child. These men felt relatively safe in doing so being, as mentioned above, untouchable or untraceable, and in the case of landlords, extremely powerful in Monto. Terry tells a heartbreaking story on his tour of how a 14-year-old girl was viewed as payment in lieu of rent, as a landlord indicated to her mother, Mrs O'Reilly:

> He was coming up for the rent, and the poor woman was saying 'Mr, I don't have the rent money. Could you see it in your heart to let me off for a week?' The landlord would say 'Not to worry Mrs O'Reilly, not to worry, how's young Mary doing? Tell her to drop down and see me.'

In this situation, Mrs O'Reilly had little choice but to hit the streets that night to try to get the money for rent to save her daughter from the landlord. The impossible choice between homelessness or the rape of her child led to a desperation that increased her vulnerability as she had less power to refuse a client or his terms.

Evidence of child sexual abuse was also seen in medical settings. Children with acquired syphilis, as well as those who were born with syphilis, were admitted to lock hospitals (hospitals which treated sexually transmitted diseases) in Scotland, London and Ireland. They could have been abused by brothel clients, family or the leaders of the institution they were in, such as the workhouse. F. W. Lowndes, a surgeon in the Liverpool Lock Hospital, discovered that the belief that raping virgins would cure venereal disease was sometimes facilitated by parents, often for money. No amount of sheen can hide the fact that children were present in the sex trade across the British Empire at the time of Monto and horrifyingly, are still found in the sex trade of today.

Taking advantage of those who were looking for virgins in the brothels, madams applied their creativity to meet this demand. In New Orleans, clients could add their names to a year-long waiting list for a virgin, showing that the demand for virgins was less about curing an STI and more about the desire to rape a child or take the virginity of a very young woman. In London, virgins could cost double the usual going rate: £5 compared to £2–£3.

If anywhere in Monto was going to offer this service, the brothel of one woman appears more likely than others: May Oblong's. May and her establishments prided themselves on offering children at least as young as 12 for her clients, enjoying a large personal fortune acquired through the rape of children behind her brothel walls. Marketing the children under her roof as virgins may have been a successful tactic for May, who was known as a cruel woman.

While in 2024 the age of consent in Ireland is 17, in 1875 the age of consent was 13. The children who survived the workhouses

Annie Meehan's opera glasses, now belonging to Pearl.

were also viewed as independent from age 13, making sex with 13-year-olds in Monto not an illegal act. Author John Finnegan reports that the girls and young women of Monto ranged from 12 to 20, and some young children were brought there via kidnapping. Annie Meehan herself was pregnant at 13 and married at 14 to a man more than twice her age, and went on to run multiple brothels. Her great-great-granddaughter Pearl has found herself reflecting on this reality over the years, since she still has many of Annie Meehan's possessions.

What's weird is that I have her stuff. And I wonder how many people out there can say I have items that belonged to one of the madams of Monto. I wake up every morning with her opera glasses sitting there on the chest of drawers that she had custom made. I think about the duality of the life that she lived. When you think of the word 'madam', she was glamorous with the opera glasses but then she was also the madam, the brothel keeper. It's bizarre to think that I'm looking at these glasses and those girls probably paid for them through selling sex. The picture that comes to my mind is one of poverty, just thinking about the sadness and filth that was in Monto, but she was rich and went to the opera and lived well.

There is no conclusive way to guarantee virginity, despite many cultures' efforts in the time of Monto and even now. Since blood-stained sheets were seen as 'proof' of tearing the hymen, women could fool their clients by inserting a sponge soaked in pig's blood into the vagina, which would hardly be felt by the client. In Monto, Pearl recalls her family explaining how the women used knotted pig's intestines placed in their vaginas to simulate the blood and for basic contraception. This method may have also been a way to protect themselves from violence from clients who would have felt they'd been tricked if there was no blood after intercourse. One wonders what the impact of pig's blood was on their vaginal health, or how clients reacted if they somehow discovered this subterfuge.

A common trick was getting a younger teenager to pretend to be a virgin. This was so frequently used in the red-light district of San Francisco in the 1890s that the madams had a well-oiled system in place:

> Each of the parlour houses in Commercial Street boasted a chamber called the 'Virgin Room', where a gullible customer could be accommodated at double or triple the usual price. Usually, the room was staffed with a girl young enough, and enough of an actress to simulate fright and bewilderment. She was usually paid slightly more than the other prostitutes.

Given that she was meant to look like a teenager or younger, there was a high chance of her actually being quite young. She had to pass as fresh-faced and beautiful, which became harder to do the longer she was in the red-light district. The fact that she knew how to act convincingly also shows a solid trade and plenty of opportunity to fine-tune her acting skills. Her expressions may also have been genuine, and they speak volumes about men who like to have sex with women – and children – that they know do not want to have sex with them. This also highlights that many men liked the impression that the young girl was a 'true' virgin, which goes beyond excusing this violence as attempts at STI treatment.

It wasn't long before such tricks were rumbled and some clients became more demanding about accessing a 'real' virgin. In London, in 1885, British journalist W. T. Stead asked a police officer about the realities of such women or children being genuine virgins, and he firmly believed that real virgins were readily available and cost around £20 in 1885, which is around £3,000 in 2024. This demand still exists today, although now the internet plays a multifaceted role in this trade.

CHAPTER 8

PINK LADIES

While we can't learn about the experiences of the women of Monto in their own words, their clothes, make-up and hairstyles offer us a way to understand the impacts of class, violence, trauma, poverty, homelessness and addiction. Clothing was more than just fabric – it was shelter, a way to attract clients, a marker of sin and a conduit for violence. In the theatre world, costumes are used to convey meaning, to tell the audience something about a character. The emotional response to the character's appearance is described as 'kinetic empathy', and clothing is part of evoking that response, which creates a deeper connection between viewer and actor, or prostitute and client. In the brothels, this tactic was also employed in the hopes of eliciting more sexually explicit responses.

Common clothes for many women around the time of Monto were floor- or shin-length dresses, crinolines, petticoats, shawls, ribbed stockings and skirts. When people could afford multiple outfits, they often layered them to adapt to the changeable Irish weather. Coats, hooded cloaks and capes were also common, often made from fur, cotton or tweed, although the shawl became the most popular form of outerwear in the 19th century. It grew in popularity due to its versatility as it could be used as a head-scarf, for carrying items and for warmth. Shawls came in a mixture of styles, from block colours for poorer women to paisley or check patterns if the wearer could afford it. Most clothes were dark in an attempt to hide dirt and made of hard-wearing material such as cotton or wool, made to be mended over and over and handed down.

Like their American and European counterparts, those that found themselves in the flash houses had access to fine garments like silk and lace dresses, furs, high heels, quality lingerie, jewellery, make-up and regular visits from a couturier outside of shopping trips to department stores such as Arnotts (Henry Street), Clerys (O'Connell Street), Switzers (now Brown Thomas, Grafton Street), McBirney's (Aston Quay) or Todd Burns (Mary Street). Clerys also had a ballroom where the women could show off their fashions at high-society events and pick up potential clients. The women were no strangers to showcasing their cleavages in low-cut dresses and tightly pulled corsets, which in turn influenced mainstream fashion. They kept their coins in secret pockets and purses known as a miser's purse, a world away from those who had to resort to using a stocking to hold any valuables.

Clothing was a way to attempt to cement their status as 'respectable' women. Style inspiration was found in the pages of *The Lady of the House* or *The Irish Tatler*, which printed illustrations of late 19th- and early 20th-century fashions for middle- and upperclass Irish women. The madams had the money to keep up with the latest fashions, a mere pipe dream for those with just the rags on their backs. As the madams' incomes grew, they purchased the finest fabrics and got their trusted dressmakers to tailor dresses for the women under their control. If they became more conservative about expenses – or meaner in personality – the quality of the fabrics declined. They also had access to a network of women who worked as milliners and dressmakers who engaged in prostitution on a casual basis. The fierce reputations of many of the madams meant it was not a wise idea to refuse their requests for fear of violence or losing income – or a home. In 1901 madam Annie Mack listed amongst her household a dressmaker, a milliner and a lacemaker, making a 'no' from these women impossible if they wanted to keep a roof over their heads.

The upper-class men who frequented the flash houses expected their high standards to be exceeded, and clothing was a part of the sensual utopia they sought. Humans are visual creatures, and seduction is often just as important as the physical act of sex itself. They expected a well-dressed woman, with stockings, heels and fine fabrics, who smelled enticing. This was not only for aesthetic reasons but also taken as a sign that the woman had a higher chance of being free from syphilis. Thus, they equated the sophisticated appearance of the women with health and less risk, which increased the necessity for the women to dress the part to keep their incomes flowing. This material culture is still part of the sex trade today, with appearance and clothing an important part of many commercial sex spaces.

Finely dressed women from the flash houses were sent to upper-class society events and encouraged clients to come back to Monto for some after-hours entertainment. In addition to being a form of advertising, clothes were also a way to access upper-class society and enjoy the perks of wealth. The women's intrusion into 'respectable' society was sometimes welcomed, sometimes merely tolerated, as one commentator remarked disdainfully:

Under the influence of whiskey or absinthe they ride about in their hired hacks and carriages and intrude their presence at all sorts of assemblies. [. . .] They seem to take delight in making their presence felt and making themselves obnoxious to everybody.

Madam Becky Cooper was also remembered by Monto resident Jem King for her well-groomed appearance: 'She was a very well dressed woman. She had long hair down to her shoulders and she kept herself looking well.' A madam Frank Duff nicknamed

Kitten Carr was remembered for the impression she left on those she interacted with:

> She was peculiar in appearance. In particular, her complexion was decidedly odd. The whole effect conveyed by her was far from pleasant. [. . .] She was self possessed, almost icy; that was her invariable manner.

One of the most successful Monto madams and costumiers, Annie Mack, resembled a real-life cartoon villain, at least if writer Oliver St John Gogarty's description is to be believed:

> Her face was brick red. Seen sideways, her straight forehead and nose were outraged by the line of her chin, which was undershot and out-thrust, with an extra projection on it, like the under-jaw of an old pike . . . Mrs Mack had a laugh like a guffaw in hell.

Other madams, like Meg Arnott, preferred to project an image of quiet elegance, and Martin relays a similar approach by his great-grandmother Margaret Carroll, one of the most infamous madams of Monto:

> She didn't go around in fancy clothes. She didn't go to Brown Thomas; all she would have gone to is Guiney's on Talbot Street; they wouldn't have been throwing money around. She was a very private woman, and that's why some of them never became famous, they were very private and kept their business to themselves.

Long hair was common for the women of Monto and was often tied up with hairpins and covered with hats, shawls, headscarves and bonnets. A photo of Becky Cooper shows her hair styled in a

Becky Cooper, one of the most successful madams of Monto and the last surviving madam by 1949.

glamorous updo to complement her sparkling earrings, necklace and tiara. Hair could be let down in the brothel, showing a departure from polite society into a world where behaviour that was frowned upon outside was welcomed. Loose hair became a symbol for rejection of the social control of sexuality and part of the aesthetic of the boudoir. The madams may also have been customers of the many wig shops and hairdressers found on nearby Sackville Street, following the fashions of their Parisian contemporaries.

Dripping in blood diamonds in more ways than one, sparkling jewellery was a highly visible way to showcase wealth and style. In New Orleans, infamous madam Lulu White was known as the Diamond Queen and was often spotted wearing a tiara, multiple diamond rings, bracelets and brooches. Her Monto counterpart

May Oblong displayed similar taste as she glided around with rings on every finger and a well-groomed appearance:

> She sometimes used to sit outside her shop with a group of women around her. She had her hair tied back in a bun and held together with hair clips. She wore this snow-white blouse and she had this beautiful gold cameo brooch pinned onto it. She also wore these beautiful big ear-rings.

Mary Foran recalls seeing May Oblong going about her business: 'She was a lovely-looking lady as well. She wore the most beautiful clothes I've ever seen.' Another resident hints at a mixture of awe and envy at seeing how May swished through the streets of Monto: May used to travel around 'all decked out like the Queen of England, with her fine clothes on her'.

May was a long-standing part of Monto, spending 45 years of her life there. She started off her Monto career selling sex then ascended to upper-class brothel-keeper, and during the last few years of her involvement in the trade, she became a costumier. Frank Duff describes May as a handsome, tall and clever woman, whose name was known all over the world. She was a fan of garish make-up, making no attempt to copy the soft, delicate make-up of the upper classes. May was six foot two inches tall, while Becky clocked in at six foot three, and together they were a sight to behold as they made their presence known across Dublin.

When Duff visited May in 1925 to try to secure her support for Monto's closure, she had maintained a formidable appearance despite her age:

> [She] was a most impressive-looking person. She was fully six feet tall. Though fairly advanced in years, she retained elements of her earlier beauty. She dressed quietly, but with discrimination.

She was nicknamed the Pink Leroy by Duff, who also dubbed her the 'flaunting extravagant queen' of Monto:

> Anywhere, anytime, you were liable to encounter the one and only Pink Leroy, an imposing figure, colourful in more than her name, draped with jewellery, going her rounds, one hand outstretched, so to speak, for the weekly dues on the clothing or money advanced by her; the other, amazing to relate, collecting for her favourite charities! Was there in all the land a stranger mind than hers?

Duff's choice of nickname is an interesting one. Delicate pink was a colour upper-class women used to signal their femininity, wealth and high status. Pink's social status exploded further when English chemist William Perkins attempted to make a medicinal drug and failed. In his misstep, he inadvertently changed the course of fashion forever by inventing a mauveine dye, a blend of pink and purple. Queen Victoria kicked off mauve mania, and the instant love for mauveine clothes led to an affordable fashion revolution where the working classes embraced mauveine with open arms, leaning into shades of pink and magenta. The frenzy led to the 1860s being dubbed the 'mauveine decade'.

Over the Atlantic and across the Wild West of America, legendary madam Pearl De Vere embraced the seductive power of pink in an $800 shell-pink dress, translating to an eye-watering $30,000 today. Not that the cost was her concern, as it was rumoured to be a gift from a millionaire client. Her dress earned its price tag as it was crafted from the finest chiffon, adorned with pearls and sparkle, and imported from France. Sadly, its sparkle dulled quickly as Pearl overdosed on morphine in the dress and was sent to her final slumber still wearing it.

Lingerie too began to be dominated by this pink wave, with madams and costumiers capitalising on the trend to keep their women at the cutting edge of sartorial style. None other than James Joyce had a fondness for pink underwear as the cherry on top of his arousal by how his love interest Nora dressed:

> Fuck me into you arseways, lying on your face on the bed, your hair flying loose naked but with a lovely scented pair of pink drawers opened shamelessly behind and half slipping down over your peeping bum.

The lock hospital noted the 'pink wrappers' of the women, and historian Maria Luddy also notes the women swanned about in the 'pink of fashion'.

Embraced by the brothels and the lower classes, the mauveine fever did not last long in wealthy circles. For the upper classes, the gaudy bright-pink and purple outfits of prostitutes and madams marked them out as frauds who didn't truly deserve a place in polite society. The clothes that prostitutes wore were often described as 'flash' or dismissed as immoral 'finery' to distinguish them from *truly* respectable ladies. This doomed attempt to elevate themselves from poverty and stigma is explained by academic Mariana Valverde as them wearing clothes that were 'too showy, clothes that looked elegant and striking but were in some unspecified way cheap, if only because the woman wearing them was herself a cheap imitation of upper-class womanhood'.

Dismissing notorious New Orleans madam Lulu White's appearance as fake and gaudy, one upper-class man described her crassly:

> She was a monstrosity . . . laden with diamonds worn not selectively but just put on any place there seemed to be an inch to accommodate them. [. . .] She, in her way, acted the grande dame to the hilt, although she gave the impression that she'd never seen a real grande dame. Her efforts to appear cultured were quite ludicrous. Her quick smile was as fake as the colour of her wig.

While Lulu and the wealthy madams of Monto used their appearance to gain social status, for the women that earned the money for them, clothing represented violence and precarity instead. For many women in the brothels, access to glamorous clothes was a gilded cage rather than a path to freedom. The shimmer soon dimmed for those who were unable to get out of the trade before things turned sour for them. The clothes and accessories the women were provided with were used to coercively control them, through the threat of violence and a crash landing into poverty or prison:

When they enter the infamous dens which traffic in their shame, they are supplied with dresses which they are never allowed to look upon as their own, and with trinkets which they are given to understand are stolen property; and by a hundred ugly phrases they are made to feel that escape with these clothes on their backs, and trinkets about their persons, would not only be theft from their taskmasters, but, in some hidden way, complicity in robberies which have been committed by others. Prisoners have escaped from Bastilles, but from bondage like this there seems to be almost no possibility of escape.

Madam Annie Mack found that it was an easier and more profitable life for her to become a costumier. Charging extortionate rates for clothing was a common tactic used across red-light districts, and it was impossible for the women to keep up, as Frank Duff found:

True, the dressing could be gay, sometimes elaborate. Once, in the course of an hour or two, we saw a girl appear in three quite different, expensive outfits. But all that finery represented a dead weight of debt, which pressed down on the wearer like a load of a slave. Often enough, the burden of debt outlived the garments themselves.

The reason for May's reluctance to support Duff in his efforts to close Monto was discovered by a chance sighting on a visit to her house as they caught a glimpse of an array of fine clothing:

> You may ask why should it jar us to see a few furs and silk things? Well, it meant only one thing to us. It told us that [she] was the costumier to [Monto]. The costumier was a notable limpet on the sorrowful sisterhood.

May is listed as a 'wardrobe dealer' living at 15 Corporation Street in 1915, and she had become the lead costumier and money-lender for Monto, enjoying an almost total monopoly on where the women could find clothes. She bought clothing wholesale and resold at double the retail rate. If the women needed clothing on credit, they paid dearly – up to three shillings a week. If a woman couldn't make the payment, she paid an even more expensive price. The madams had no hesitation in ordering their fancy men to strip the clothes off a woman's back and kick her out on to the streets.

Monto resident Billy Dunleavy explains how clothes were used as a tool of violence towards the women:

> If they picked up a man and, after doing the business, they tried to keep some of the money back on the madam, or the man ran off without paying, she'd have them beaten up in the kip houses. All their clothes would be torn off them by the madam's 'fancy men'. They were left in rags for not bringing the money back to the madam.

If a woman found herself in this situation, she was dehumanised and vulnerable. She was reduced to a commodity that the madam no longer had any use for. The woman was left desperate for survival and reduced in agency regarding how she sold sex and to whom. Women in the second-class brothels were more likely to be found advertising in the doorways of the brothels, still clinging on to any part of their former lifestyle. They sat on the steps in evening dresses, while some of their colleagues who fared a little worse were in their nightdresses.

Local woman Mary Corbally describes seeing the women standing on the street looking for business:

> Looking back on it you can never say whether they were young or old 'cause of the way they were dressed. The usual thing was a big white apron and a skirt underneath it and a shawl. The white apron was clean-looking and it drew the attention. Oh, they were always clean. There's one woman I remember, and I can picture her as if it was only yesterday standing at the lamp post at Jack Maher's and she didn't wear a black shawl, she wore one of the big coloured Galway shawls, grey and fawn and all the flowers on it and all the big long fringe.

Aprons were a sartorial staple in Monto.

*Cardigans kept the chills away as the women went
about their business; Monto resident Dennis Farrell's sister
Julia is in the middle.*

Many of those who took to the streets operated from dark lanes or basement steps, especially around Mabbot Street and Faithful Place. These women could be found barefoot and half naked under lamp posts, with only a flimsy raincoat to protect them from the elements. Clothes were often dirty and wet, with minimal opportunities to take care of them or change into spare clothes while they dried off. This was in stark contrast to the experiences of the women in the flash houses who had their clothes cleaned by the women in the nearby Magdalene Laundry – their former colleagues, in some cases.

Those down on their luck bought second-hand clothes at markets such as Iveagh Gardens and the Daisy Market. Annie Ryan, one of the Daisy Market dealers, said the girls would often come in and not have any money:

> I always remember me aunt one day here taking off her cardigan and giving it to this poor girl . . . a winter's day and

*Julia Farrell, standing on the same streets
she used to work on.*

she was nearly naked. Penny, they used to call her. Wrapped
her up 'cause she'd hardly nothing on her.

Duff described some of the women he met as having 'savage
moplike' tangles of hair and, shockingly, one woman was described
as having the 'look of having lain in a sewer for a week'. When he
attempted to rescue some of the women, a lack of clothing was a
barrier as some had mere rags covering them and clothing had to
be sourced before they could leave Monto. Descriptions of women
in London brothels observed on a rescue mission also help us visualise the state these women existed in:

Her face was grimy and unwashed, and her hands so black
and filthy that mustard-and-cress might have been sown

successfully upon them. As she was huddled up with her back against the wall she appeared an animated bundle of rags. She was apparently a powerfully made woman, and though her face was wrinkled and careworn, she did not look exactly decrepit, but more like one thoroughly broken down in spirit than in body.

Upon forcing entry into another room, they found an Irish woman in a dreadful condition, similar to the reality at the end of Monto:

There was not an atom of furniture in it, nor a bed, and yet it contained a woman. This woman was lying on the floor, with not even a bundle of straw beneath her, wrapped up in what appeared to be a shawl, but which might have been taken for the dress of a scarecrow feloniously abstracted from a corn-field, with any very great stretch of the imagination. [. . .] Her face was shrivelled and feminine-stricken, her eyes bloodshot and glaring, her features disfigured slightly with disease, and her hair dishevelled, tangled, and matted. More like a beast in his lair than a human being in her home was this woman.

While shocking, it is hard to fully discount the possibility that such descriptions were embellished for dramatic effect to secure access to funding and status. It wasn't only the women of Monto who wanted social mobility. The clothes the women wore may have been 'won by the wages and worn to tatters in the service of sin', but the words that many social reformers wrote were driven by self-satisfaction and to access wealth. They wanted to be welcomed in upper-class circles that wished to appear to help the working classes. It does not mean they had evil intentions – like the women, their work may have been a response to the horrors of the Famine and a desire to not fall prey to another precarious situation of life or death. Of course, some did have altruistic motives, and many accounts were factual, or at least mostly factual, but the end result was still social mobility, access to resources, and having their names remembered more than the 'poor unfortunates' they aimed to help.

The next step for many on the streets was to seek refuge in a laundry or lock hospital. In these institutions, ruthless haircuts were used to remind the women they were the wrong kind of women and were not deserving of respect as they repented their involvement in prostitution. They were forced to wear yellow clothes in the London Lock Hospital, which led to them being nicknamed 'canaries'. In Dublin, they wore brown smocks and were punished if they attempted to improve their uniforms with any personal touches. If the women escaped, they were easily spotted, as they stood out from 'decent' women. Brown marked the women out as different once they left the laundry too, according to Gemma:

There were six of them and they'd go to Talbot Street to the exact same shops. They all had long brown coats, and they all walked in a line linking arms. Everybody in the area had the greatest respect for them because they knew what life they had had.

Paula Meehan details how the shocking appearance of the women in the Sean McDermott Street Laundry has stayed with her to this day:

A lot of the old prostitutes ended up as Magdalene's, penitents, working in the laundries for the rest of their lives, for the religious. I remember those sad women the times I used to haul our family sheets down to the laundry up the street from us, with their brutal haircuts and their cowed spirits.

Women in flash clothes were viewed as unwanted visible symbols of bad, immoral character and a corrupting force to protect 'good' women from. Writing about a red-light district of Melbourne that employed many Irish women, a policeman blamed those in the trade for tempting respectable young women by preying on their 'love of dress':

> Even respectable girls notice them, though they do not like to be seen looking at them, still they are peeping side-long, and one will say to another – 'I am as good-looking a girl as that, and I may be a drudge in the kitchen, and that girl is flaunting about in silks and satins'. Flash girls are the ruin of many girls.

One could argue that it was primarily the violence of the clients, madams and bully boys, combined with societal stigma and poverty, that was actually the ruin of many girls. Reducing clothes to a mere symbol of indulgent vanity means ignoring how the women themselves used clothes as a tool of physical and social survival.

Similarly, social reformer William Logan framed the women as soulless, immoral, selfish deviants because of their clothes:

> Their innate love of dress will continue to be fanned into a passion; and, in the case of many, will reach its gratification at whatever cost – perhaps through dishonest dealings with the property of others, more probably through the nefarious, degrading barter of personal prostitution. Terrible paradox! They will have fine dress to bedeck the body; and they sacrifice the body – ay, and the soul too – to obtain that dress!

This 'lust' for glamorous dresses was presented by Rev. Dr. A. Macleod, as something silly and a foolish desire of a woman, who was at once a victim, a fool and a corruptor.

The want of clothing which she can call her own – so small a thing comparatively as that – is often the chain which binds her to a life of which she is long ago tired. There was nothing in all negro slavery more atrocious than the methods by which girls in her condition are terrified by their want of clothing into continuance into a life of shame.

Instead of clothing being an 'innate love' worse than the ravages inflicted upon Africans stolen from their homes and enslaved, perhaps it was in fact a trauma response to barely surviving the Famine and all-encompassing poverty. This statement also grossly minimises the savagery inflicted by the slave trade. There should be nothing shocking about a person deprived of almost every-thing, including their life, wanting that to change and to enjoy some luxury for perhaps the only time in their lives. The women's love of dress and property was seen as a moral failing, but the lure of decadent clothing, jewellery and carriage rides to the theatre in glamorous dresses must have been strong in the face of the reality of ragged clothes and bare feet. As well as being a taste of luxury, the clothes were a reminder that their survival was precarious and could be taken from them at any time. Keeping themselves in good clothes was a way to keep themselves from poverty; the real failing here is how these women were treated.

For the women of Monto, their dress may have been a repre-sentation of freedom, happiness, a feeling of agency, violence, trauma or simply survival. They maximised their appearance to escape poverty, avoid state violence and navigate class borders and social mobility. They also used their clothes to hide weapons for self-protection or deliberate infliction of violence. They concealed pokers in their skirts and shawls and hid messages about the movements of the British in their underclothes to give to the Irish revolutionaries. For them, clothes were a way to change their immediate present and future.

For those more interested in judging them than trying to understand them, the women's dress was a glaring symbol of being the wrong woman – one who failed to stay quiet and conform to the tightening social norms enforced by the Catholic Church and solidified by the Irish state from 1922. The gaudier the clothes, the more visible the woman was, and thus the more despised by polite society. Being marked out by clothing could also lead to violence from people who suspected she was a prostitute rather than a high-society woman who had access to support and police, as well as the safety of a 'good' reputation.

While the words of social reformers have survived for centuries to tell us their views on prostitution, we are left to hunt for clues for the women's thoughts on their own experiences. Clothes are more than just fabric: they are a way to attempt to understand the realities of life in Monto. The changing ensembles of Monto visually portrayed financial downfall, with some also calling this a moral downfall, but clothes tell us also about the trauma the women of Monto faced.

CHAPTER 9

WAGES OF SIN

In every red-light district, money is constantly moving. Monto's money flowed as fast as the Liffey, passing through the hands of clients, prostitutes, madams, bully boys, police and judges.

In London, a woman nicknamed Lushing Lucy had weeks where she could make ten pounds, and some where she made as little as three shillings. This insecurity of income was also seen in Monto, with the arrival and departure of ships and army units, one-off events such as horse fairs, and personal ability to attract clients. The price a woman could charge correlated with what stage of her journey through Monto she was at, and this undulating precariousness is still generally the international pricing system for selling sex.

Entry to Monto's flash houses cost a minimum of ten shillings. For £5, a client could buy alcohol and sex and have an experience in a well-furnished first-class brothel. If a person wanted to spend the night with the woman, it could cost them a minimum of £50. The price for sex dropped to £1 if it was one of the less fancy flash houses. Second-class brothels could charge five shillings, and the women on the street were lucky to get one shilling per sexual service provided.

We have some first-hand descriptions of the negotiation process from an anonymous memoir, *My Secret Life*, dating from 1888. The writer documents his experiences of buying sex from the women of the Whitechapel red-light district in London:

I used to look in and long. Sometimes had a shilling peep, and then bashfully asked for a feel of the cunt for it. I so often succeeded, that ever since then I wanted that amusement, have offered a shilling for a feel, and met with but few refusals in any part of London. Sometimes it ended in a fuck. Once or twice to my astonishment they took mere trifles, and as I think of it, there is wonderfully little difference between the woman you have for five shillings, and the one you pay five pounds, excepting in the silk, linen, and manners.

Rent was one of the biggest costs for the women of Monto. For basic rooms in Monto, rent could be three shillings or up to eight shillings for better dwellings. Cheap lodgings allow for a red-light district to flourish, since they draw in transient clients such as soldiers and sailors and the women themselves. Many women selling sex lived chaotic lives, and access to temporary lodging helped when they couldn't afford regular rent. With no stable roof over their heads, protecting any money from being robbed was a tall order, and skipping out on rent was common but came with consequences if they were caught. This was another reason for frequent name changes.

The women on the streets also had to stretch their earnings to try to cover fines for convictions for being a 'common night walker'. These fines increased from one or two shillings in the 1850s to 20 shillings in the heyday of Monto. Since those most likely to be arrested were the lower classes, they were also generally the poorest women. If they could only charge a shilling for their services, to pay the fine they would have to have saved the proceedings from seeing 20 clients, and that is before rent, bribes, food and alcohol. If the woman could not pay this exorbitant amount, she faced two weeks in prison. Nor was this fine or imprisonment a one-off possibility. Historian Maria Luddy notes that out of 41 women arrested for prostitution, only four had not been imprisoned previously. Trying to get oneself above the poverty threshold must have been impossible with fines so high in proportion to the realities of the women's incomes. Duff noted that one girl was arrested three times in a week and her fines immediately paid, leaving us to wonder at what interest rate she was charged by those who paid her fines for her. She may have been freed from the prison, but she was now trapped in the brothel.

Madams were usually fined for selling alcohol rather than brothel-keeping and were able to keep money safely aside for bribes for judges. Not all bribes were of a monetary nature; these bribes could also be in the form of free services as an ongoing preventative measure against arrest.

Because of the fear of being on the radar of the police, the women were vulnerable to coercion and blackmail from clients, the police and the madams. Women had to pay protection money to the bully boys as well as the police. If they couldn't pay with cash, they were expected to pay with sex or face violence. If they felt coerced by the payments demanded by the legal system into selling sex to multiple clients to gather enough spare cash to put aside in case of a fine, they were also at high risk of traumatisation. This increased the likelihood of their turning to alcohol to self-medicate, which further decreased their capacity and desirability for clients. It also increased their exposure to syphilis, which would end this miserable cycle with an excruciatingly painful death.

To see an example of the financial circuit of a brothel at this time, we can look at social reformer William Logan's account of life in brothels in Leeds. He identified 175 brothels and madams thriving in Leeds in 1840. A brothel with four women in it could service 80 men a week, according to his investigations. However, while over £4,200 was generated weekly in Leeds brothels through selling sex, the women themselves were only taking home 30 shillings a week. This obvious wealth discrepancy was a motivating factor for many women's decisions to become madams themselves or to supplement their wages by robbing clients.

If the women successfully robbed a client, they had to give the madams a share, as well as the bully boys. The same applied to any money made from selling sex. The bully boys would report back to the madam how many men a woman had seen, and if the totals came up short, she was subjected to violence. The fear this generated meant that the women were exploited by the bully boys who demanded money from the women to stop them lying to the madams and avoid the inevitable beating that the bully boys would gleefully dish out themselves.

Some madams were illiterate, which impacted their chances of making more money, but their street smarts made up for it and they found creative ways to bring the money in. Alcohol was sold at an unapologetically astronomical inflated price. Whiskey was two or three pennies a glass in the pub and three to five shillings in the brothel, with profits shared between madams, the women, the manageress and the bully boys. This was a hefty mark-up of 60 per cent. In Becky Cooper's brothel, a bottle of beer was a pound, when it was eight pence in the pubs and shebeens. While cheaper than the more expensive brothels, Becky still made a tidy profit at an extortionate mark-up of 37 per cent.

Many of the madams, such as May Oblong, Polly Butler, Annie Meehan and Becky Cooper, also ran shops which sold clothing and groceries to the locals and from where they could keep an eye on their fiefdoms. The Meehans would later buy May's shop on Corporation Street. The madams also operated as moneylenders in this black-market economic zone. They would lend sixpence with 33 per cent interest, which was charged per day in some cases. They were more than aware that official banking was an issue for those in Monto, being a community of urban poor. The madams were therefore assured of a built-in clientele desperate enough to agree to their interest rates and who wouldn't go to the police if things got ugly.

However, moneylending was not all nefarious. We don't know if the madams always charged interest or if they wrote off loans, or gave lower or non-existent interest rates to those they took pity on. They were an option for financial support in a time when there were no other choices for marginalised people, functioning as a form of mutual aid. This fringe banking still happens in communities around the world today, as many of those who sell sex today report being refused banking services.

As well as being a way to keep women trapped in prostitution, money could also be a route out of poverty and stigma. Social status could be accessed through the ability to afford dressmakers and valued customers or becoming an employer. Many women managed to sell sex on a temporary basis and leave with savings, viewing it as an option to see them through difficult times. At the start of the 1900s, when other jobs were as low paid as less than three shillings a week, even the women earning a shilling each time they sold sex were in a better financial position, at least initially. This possibility of accessing a better life must have been hard to resist for many who struggled, regardless of how they felt about the morality of selling sex.

Earning a lot of money in a brothel could be a way to free themselves from poverty, class and gendered restrictions on how they could live their lives. Prostitution could offer a route to home ownership and independence as they would not have to marry a man for survival. They could elevate their lives and increase their chances of meeting a well-to-do man as they mingled at the theatre or the horse shows. However, the pathway to riches for those selling sex was a narrow one, mainly open to those who were young and beautiful and who could leverage their skills to access wealthier clients and transition to being a madam or a courtesan. Many settled for marrying a sailor or soldier and lived a modest life away from Monto, with privacy more important than profit.

As they were also at risk of being robbed or spending their money on an alcohol addiction, many of the women were constantly chasing financial stability. Some found it in abundance; for others poverty would never end. Even if a woman had access to money, it was not guaranteed to last as the impact of her work, the legal system, the laundries and any addictions could mean a quick return to poverty.

For the madams and landlords, a property empire did not always mean intergenerational wealth, as Martin discovered when he tried to unravel the mystery of his family's former properties:

> I couldn't find any documentation to let me know what houses belonged to my family. Now, my uncle told me that there was never a house that the family lived in that was not theirs. They never rented a property, and I have found probably the best part of twenty houses they had in a five-year period in the early 1900s. They couldn't read or write. Cash was what bought and sold everything. So when Dublin Corporation moved in to knock down all the tenements there, you had to prove by paperwork that you owned that house. My mother told me because they couldn't produce the necessary paper-work, they got nothing. Imagine if they had kept all that property, I'd be living in Foxrock today as a millionaire.

The 200 properties that formed the Meehans' empire were also lost, albeit to gambling by Annie and Charles's descendants, with Pearl sharing the same sentiments as Martin. But the cost of life in Monto was not just monetary: the women paid a steep price with their health too.

Chapter 10

In Rude Health

Living in the extreme poverty that came to define Monto impacted the health of many residents. Those living in tenements were vulnerable to viral diseases such as tuberculosis, since whole families of up to 20 members shared one or two rooms in overcrowded tenements. Hunger was far from unknown to Monto bellies. Pots of sheep's head and cabbage stew – which Terry grew up eating in his Monto home and he assures us is quite delicious – were happily shared amongst neighbours.

In addition to health concerns from their diet, alcohol became a coping mechanism for women who struggled with the violence and poverty they were exposed to. They often turned to drinking ether, also known at the time as methylated spirits, and Frank Duff describes the hold it had on the women:

> You would want to see people who were addicted to it to realise the fantastic demoralisation it brought about. It made its victims look like and act like devils . . .

Ether was used in medical operations as it induced 'a state of perfect quietude' with no pain; no wonder then that it was also used on the streets to block out trauma. However, drinking ether often led to brain damage, which exacerbated the symptoms of syphilis and trauma, hastening the deaths of sufferers if they were unable to get help. Some so-called refuges only offered their help to young women who had 'freshly fallen' and were therefore considered 'reformable', while those longer in the trade were viewed as unsavable and thus refused. This rejection from redemption must have carried its own psychological impact as they were sent back to their pain.

Health issues also arose from the poitín that was commonly consumed alongside methylated spirits which was also known as 'Irish moonshine', illegal and extremely potent. Being made locally under the cover of darkness and away from the eyes of the police meant that its strength could vary, with bad batches causing untold damage.

The 'remedy of intoxication' was viewed as the 'only cure for low spirits' by the women of London, who had similar experiences as their Monto counterparts:

When I am sad I drink . . . I'm very often sad, although I appear to be what you call reckless. Well! We don't fret that we might have been ladies, because we never had a chance of that, but we have forfeited a position nevertheless, and when we think that we have fallen, never to regain that which we have descended from, and in some cases sacrificed everything for a man who has ceased to love and deserted us, we get mad. The intensity of this feeling does wear off a little after the first; but there's nothing like gin to deaden the feelings.

It would be more shocking if alcohol *wasn't* a coping mechanism, especially when the options for support were often more violent than the women's current situations. Many of these women had acquired their fallen sisterhood status due to sexual violence, which was then compounded by social stigma, violence from family, the state, precarious accommodation and poverty. The decline of conditions in Monto coincided with a rise in alcoholism, with over 50,000 ether addicts at this time, who often found themselves in

*Then, as now, alcohol was a common feature of
daily life for many.*

asylums or in the lock hospital as their syphilis took over. One in
ten admissions to an asylum were connected to alcohol misuse by
the turn of the 19th century. Being drunk could earn a woman
seven days behind bars, as Margaret Carmondy from Elliott Place
discovered in 1912.

In addition to alcohol, drugs were part of life in Monto. Opium
was openly sold in pharmacies across Dublin. Used to soothe
babies and as a medicine for a long list of ailments, it was also a
recreational drug for many people across all aspects of society,
from middle-class women who injected each other at afternoon
parties, to parties in the Hell Fire Club, to those who used it in

the brothels and on the streets. The sickly smell of opium was present in many parts of daily Dublin life, its consumers described as 'opium eaters' or 'drug fiends'. Opium was used for relaxation and was a key part of brothel life, since it was often used to drug clients and rob them. If the dosage was right, the client might think he'd just consumed too much alcohol and passed out, making life easier for the woman trying to get as much money as possible.

Laughing gas may have made headlines in the 21st century due to its rebrand as 'hippie crack' for use at music festivals, but it was enough of a part of Victorian Dublin to lead to the coining of the phrase 'gas man'. Laughing gas was used medically, but it was also used unofficially for recreational purposes, from the streets to the upper classes, a common option alongside the painkiller and sedative laudanum. Laudanum was easily accessible, but when unregulated it led to overdoses and addiction. It was also a known method of suicide for hundreds of years.

Pearl explains how it is no surprise that the women's experiences led to addiction:

People dismiss them as just addicts, but they had a lot of trauma to cover up. The doctor Annie Meehan employed would often prescribe sleeping tablets like laudanum, and it must have been for the trauma they went through. They would come in as they'd be so traumatised that they'd have to have help to sleep because of whatever they'd just gone through out on the streets. I remember telling my granny, when I was very young, that I was very interested in dreams and what they meant. And she would say, 'Ah, your great-granddad used to tell me that his mother would tell the girls that they just had a bad dream'. So, they didn't even believe half of what had happened to them. And that was something that I hold quite dear; I'm quite proud of the fact that she actually wanted to erase the trauma from them.

Sophie is a sex worker from Dublin who advocates for the inclusion of the voices of those selling sex in all conversations about the sex trade, especially the voices of those who may be vulnerable. She outlines her experiences of going through hard times while also selling sex:

> If you're on the street or in the harder end of the business, it does take a toll on you. It takes that physical toll, and you feel like you slip down further and further. It's harder and harder to make money. I used to see some of the women that would have been around working about 20 years, but they were heavily in active addiction and by the time they're in their late 30s or 40s it's taken a huge effect on them. None of us want to see that, and we try and look after them while we are out there, but it does become a very hard life when you're in that stage of it.

By the time they hit adulthood, the women of Monto were already dragging a sack of trauma behind them, which got bigger and bigger as they survived the Famine, the workhouse, sexual violence, family estrangement, poverty, homelessness, stigma and precariousness. They experienced all kinds of abusive interactions that society did not yet have the language to adequately describe. Emotionally stunted through traumatic upbringings and living with the resulting fear on a permanent basis, life was exhausting. Childhood trauma can mean a higher risk of adult trauma, and for many survivors in Monto, complex post-traumatic stress disorder would be something they could perhaps relate to if the diagnosis had been around in their day. The result of going through trauma after trauma after trauma can make a person feel like they are living in a constant state of terror, a state of being where there is no real peace as the person waits for their house of cards to tumble, their survival as fragile as a newborn bird's. The more traumatised they were, the less likely it was that they could dip into Monto's sex trade and escape major consequences. Multiple experiences of trauma makes a person extremely vulnerable, and being kept in the brothels for longer than they wanted compounded their trauma. They dealt with this terror in a few different ways.

Suicide was as underreported during Monto's era as it had been before and since, but records did show an increase towards the end of the 19th century. Kevin C. Kearns, for his book *Dublin Tenement Life: An Oral History*, spoke to Dubliners who remembered suicide being sadly far too common in the days of Monto. Growing up in the tenements of the Liberties, May Hanaphy empathised with those who found themselves in difficult circumstances:

Oh, you were never kept once you became pregnant. A woman often went on the streets if the fella didn't want you, that was a cause of many people going on the streets. Some of them went into prostitution. And some drowned themselves. Out of despair. And the Church had no sympathy in those days. [. . .] Oh, many a girl took her own life. Oh, the Church, she's a good mother, but she's a *hard* mother.

The situation was as grim in London, with many of the women who ended their lives by jumping into the Thames having had the same experiences as Monto women. Another Londoner in the sex trade, who went by the moniker China Emma, wearily explained to the social reformer interviewing her that she was struggling to keep going:

I have fits at times – melancholy fits – and I don't know what to do with myself. I wish I was dead, and I run to the water and throw myself in; but I've had no luck; I never had since I was a child – oh! Ever so little.

For the women, drowning was a common method of taking their own lives, an obvious option with the proximity of the Thames and the Liffey. When their bodies were pulled from the water, they would be judged as poor because of their clothes or their scars from having their faces slashed. Syphilis scars might also have marked them as fallen women. The subsequent lack of interest in identifying them by the police led to them being consigned for dissection by medical students, echoing the fate of many women who died in the workhouses. In Monto, if the woman was not successful in her suicide attempt, she faced the possibility of more hardship, as Cissy Carr found out in 1917. Carr lived in Faithful Place in Monto, and the result of her attempt to end her life was a six-month prison sentence.

Some women who ended up in the lock hospital on Westmoreland Street seized the chance to end their pain on their terms. One patient named Annie Evans used the opium given to her for a toothache as her method of suicide. Physician Dr Donnelly duly lamented that 'instead of applying it to that purpose the prisoner had drunk the contents'. Perhaps Anne knew what fate awaited her and she chose a more merciful route. Many of these young women and teenagers had no support networks, and the fact that suicide was chosen by some over going into a laundry or a mother and baby home tells us that these women of Monto made one final act of rebellion against surrendering to the violence of Church and state.

When it came to sexual health, the women of Monto had access to a choice of birth control methods. The rubber condom was invented in America in the 1850s and made its way slowly over to Ireland, replacing the earlier Victorian animal-skin condoms that were tied with ribbon around the base of the penis. A 1925 article in an Irish newspaper exposed the widespread availability of condoms, especially in Dublin:

What are known as 'rubber goods' can also be had without difficulty, the only difference between Dublin and English cities in this respect is that here they are not publicly exposed for sale in attractive shop windows; but, nevertheless, the 'business' is proceeding and developing.

These 'rubber preventatives' were often thick and designed to be cleaned and reused. They could be purchased in chemists such as Hamilton Long on O'Connell Street, and they were advertised in Irish newspapers, where readers could request a catalogue of goods to be sent discreetly. This discretion continued long into the 1990s and 2000s, where sex shops in Dublin such as Condom Power on Dame Street posted catalogues to customers, and women accessed information on birth control and abortion through pamphlets and peer networks.

If they couldn't afford condoms, they could try the withdrawal method, but this may not have always been an acceptable option for a client. Other popular methods in Monto and similar red-light districts were sponges soaked in natural spermicides such as vinegar, douches and condoms that just covered the tip of the penis. Half a lemon inserted into the vagina has been used as birth control for centuries, as lemon juice was believed to be a spermicide. Large amounts of pessaries have been found in Australian brothels, and many Vaseline and Listerine bottles have been unearthed from brothels around the world, used as disinfectants and spermicides. Women also washed their vulvas with vinegar, water and caustic soda to burn off any infection. These examples show us that women would try whatever they could to manage their fertility and sexual health, even at personal cost.

Interestingly, the modern copper IUD may have its roots in historical red-light districts. Archaeologists found copper coins in New York brothels that captured attention due to being much older than the average coins in circulation at the time, suggesting they were kept aside and not used as currency. Instead, it seems they were covered in Vaseline and placed in the vagina to cover the cervix. This was essentially an early attempt at a diaphragm, preventing sperm entering the cervix. This trick dates back to ancient Rome and suggests female knowledge about the contraceptive power of copper has been preserved through whisper networks and the sex trade for millennia.

When the impact of syphilis became clearer, soldiers in World War I began to be provided with some early preventative measures, such as creams purported to disinfect the penis after sex, but these concoctions were often damaging and painful as they contained mercury. As a result, many soldiers didn't bother with them.

Ads for contraception regularly ran in Irish newspapers such as the *Irish Times* and the *Freeman's Journal*, whose editors were familiar faces at upper-class brothels. Abortion pills such as Damoroid Tablets were advertised in the pages of *Ireland's Own*, with references to addressing 'earlier mistakes', alluding of course to sex. Sex education and contraception were also explained in pamphlets such as *The Marriage Problem* (1868). This was an Irish publication by pro-contraception feminist Quaker Thomas Haslam, although he wrote under the pen name 'Oedipus'.

A rant about these pamphlets in a medical journal makes the existence of Monto blue books even more of a safe assumption. The *Dublin Medical Press* condemned the circulation of pamphlets such as *Marriage and Reproduction* in December 1864 and dismissed any cures for venereal disease as quack remedies or snake oil. In 1868, a pamphlet entitled *The Complete Herbalist* circulated in Dublin and explained the 'regulation of the passions' and where to get contraception. The *Dublin Medical Press* didn't hold back in its disapproval, labelling these pamphlets 'a disgustingly indecent trap for the unwary and the prurient'. *The Complete*

Herbalist also ran adverts looking for 1,000 salespersons to sell it amongst their friends and contacts, with women given an extra bonus as an incentive. The salary of £30 a month plus a bonus of half a guinea was extremely attractive in 1868. The women of Monto were hustlers and survivors, so turning friends, family and clients into revenue streams was surely a no-brainer. If these pamphlets circulated freely in Dublin, the blue books of Monto could have done the same, via the same networks.

Historian Sandra McAvoy suggests that the pamphlets related to birth control were suppressed by those working to cement an Irish Catholic society, and blue books would certainly be included in these 'diabolical handbills' that threatened the control of sex, pleasure and women. In 1889 the Indecent Advertisements Act made it illegal to advertise condoms, further diminishing the chances of survival for these guides.

Irish folklore was a vital way to share information on abortion methods as well as contraception, passed from woman to woman and across whisper networks. Abortion was far from unknown, and Irish women sought to end their pregnancies in incredibly varied ways. Many used herbs to induce abortion, including goldenrod, motherwort, black bryony, savin and honeysuckle, some of which grew freely in the wild. Irish women preferred to take tablets or herbs over surgical abortions, both to avoid a high-risk procedure and to minimise recovery time. Some used quinine powder for home abortions, and Cara Delay suggests that in Dublin most surgical abortions were carried out by backstreet abortionists. Folklorist Anne O'Connor recorded testimonies with women in the 1990s who remembered their mothers' and other women's stories of ingesting disinfectant or Jeyes Fluid to end pregnancies. These were common cleaning products across Ireland and a staple of Monto tenements. They also used a Higginson syringe to douche, which was used for the treatment of syphilis as well as to induce abortion. Knitting and crochet needles, baths, gin, excessive exercise and 'accidentally' falling down the stairs were also known to be abortion methods, although they were not always successful. The *Sunday Independent* ran ads for pills discreetly advertised as 'prompt and reliable' for women, such as Thomasso's 'Magic' Female Pills, and imported British newspapers also contained ads for abortifacients that could be secured by post.

After the passage of the 1861 Offences against the Person Act, abortion was outlawed. Unsurprisingly, this did not stop abortion but instead led to the inevitable rise of backstreet abortionists. These were often women helping other women out, or a dedicated service from a community member, but were extremely dangerous and involved a high mortality and injury rate. The rooms and implements would often be dirty, and some had to resort to having abortions in alleyways, making complications even more likely. In Monto a local midwife called Mrs Dunleavy, sometimes referred

Mrs Dunleavy, the most well known and well respected midwife of Monto.

Mrs Dunleavy had no problem standing up to madams and the bullies in order to help the women with birth.

to as the Granny Dunleavy, helped out a lot of the local women with pregnancy and childbirth; now, thanks to Gemma Dunleavy, we also know she supported women with abortions too:

> My uncle said 'I always knew about the abortions but I wouldn't tell your mother that. Because I wouldn't want people interpreting that the wrong way. She did an awful lot for them. She used to help the women know if or when they'd get pregnant through telling them about their periods. She also taught them how to clean themselves, and protect themselves from STIs.' Me auntie said 'I think me mother Mrs Farrell used to carry out the abortions on the side. Becky Cooper used to make the women have abortions. Now, some of them wanted them because they couldn't make money, but not all of them wanted an abortion, but Becky still forced them. She was the cleaner and wrapped them up in newspapers to dispose of.'

If a woman could not access an abortion in Dublin, she might find herself making the journey to England that Irish women have had to make for decades. It was far from an easy journey, physically, financially or emotionally:

> Some contemplated slipping overboard during their passage to England, rather than face the ordeal at journey's end. A few allegedly did. Others remained abroad when it was all over. Not for a holiday, but to start a fresh life.

Pearl recalls stories of a Protestant doctor whose services Annie Meehan contracted for her establishments:

> She used to bring this Protestant doctor down to look after the girls. He lived in Parnell Street or thereabouts, which was owned by the Meehans. In exchange for his services, he lived rent free. I think it was abortions and venereal diseases and he would delouse them too. Seemingly he took on one of the young girls as a nurse, because it was a way to help remove her from that lifestyle. He saw the spark they had, and the intelligence and humanity in them.

This continued decades of Irish madams having doctors on their payroll to deal with sexual health and abortions. The women were highly incentivised to get an abortion for fear of being kicked out of the brothel, losing both their income and accommodation. Some madams were kinder than others, and Annie did not always throw the women out, as Pearl shares:

> One girl was so badly deformed from doing a backstreet abortion herself, or one of the girls doing it on her. She was just sewed up and she was no use to anyone for sex. So, Annie would give her a job housekeeping or nannying.

Without a doubt, syphilis and gonorrhoea were the dominant health concerns for many of the women of Monto. In the Victorian era, they were referred to as 'venereal disease' or VD, as these two sexually transmitted infections were often found together or not yet understood to be two separate infections. It was also called the 'pox' in the streets of Dublin. Known since at least the 15th century, syphilis is still the most common STI in Ireland. Scores of countries blamed other countries for the disease over the years – the Italians blamed the French, the Russians blamed the Polish, and Ireland, to absolutely no one's surprise, blamed the British. Monto regular James Joyce was alleged to have syphilis, did he catch it or spread it in Monto?

The first stage of syphilis involves painless ulcers appearing on the genitals or mouth a few weeks after infection. These would often go away on their own, lulling the sufferer into a false sense of security, thinking it was gone for good. This hope was dashed a few months later by the second stage of rashes on the hands and feet, occasionally accompanied by hair loss. Again, these symptoms resolved themselves and the infection settled into a latent stage, ranging anywhere between three and fifteen years.

This symptom-free stage was why quack treatments survived for so long, since they appeared to work, but in reality they facilitated the spread of syphilis as the sufferer assumed they were cured and went back to their indulgences. That was, until the disease returned with a vengeance and destroyed the person's body from skin to bone and everything in between. The weakened immune system of someone experiencing trauma, addiction, homelessness and lack of access to services hastened the arrival of this stage for its victim.

As with most aspects of life in Monto, class had a huge impact on health. Richer women could afford private doctors, as many in the middle classes were able to do. Their money also bought discretion and protection from stigma. Status also meant a different experience within the hospital walls as they were kept separate to avoid being infected physically or emotionally by the fallen sister-hood of women who came from the brothel or the streets.

As well as being a sexually transmitted infection, syphilis can be passed from mother to baby during pregnancy or birth. This method of transmission was suspected but solidly confirmed with the spike in cases after World War I, when British soldiers spread the syphilis that they caught in European brothels to their wives and future children. In the London Lock Hospital, most of these babies died before their third birthday. Babies born infected with syphilis are often smaller and can start displaying symptoms as early as a few days old, resulting in physical and intellectual disabilities, and infected mothers face a higher risk of miscarriage or stillbirth.

Due to the taboo of acknowledging that children were being sexually abused by family, true numbers of infections by this pathway are impossible to uncover as they were not recorded. The idea of child abuse by family members across the class spectrum was so unutterable that the founder of psychoanalysis, Sigmund Freud, had to recant his belief that many of the patients he saw were telling the truth about being abused by fathers, brothers and others. The backlash led him to revise his theories to state that the true source of women's suffering was hysteria, not the fact that they were being violated in a multitude of ways across all strata of society. This reframing helped solidify the stigma that abused children faced as they were labelled damaged goods, which influenced the kind of life they could hope to lead.

While the men in charge pointed their fingers at women, the men in the brothels continued to spread syphilis on their travels. By the start of Monto, one in three army patients were infected with syphilis, rising to almost half in 1867. Female admissions for syphilis to Dublin hospitals in 1850 were reported to number 3,000 infections from soldiers.

Official statistics for infection rates are, however, hard to trust. Women who had thrush or discharge as part of their normal menstrual cycle were often accused of having venereal disease, since doctors thought all vaginal discharge was the result of infection. However, it is safe to say that the hundreds of reported cases a year could have added a zero or two to their tally.

Men who wanted to avoid the battlefield or the open seas resorted to drastic measures despite the consequences. Some deliberately infected themselves with syphilis or gonorrhoea: in the face of certain death, syphilis became a survival mechanism for the men. Soldier Robert Graves documents the lengths men went to in order to avoid battle:

> Such respite from the sphere of battle was so desired by some soldiers that Men bruised their penises. They deliberately sought out prostitutes infected with venereal disease or, if these exertions came to naught, they faked venereal discharge by injecting condensed milk into the urethra.

Infected men would be quarantined to a base hospital for months, and despite how stigmatised they would be, still chose this option rather than face war. Some never sought treatment, knowing they were infected but not caring about infecting others. In saving themselves from the battlefield, they gave a death sentence to the women they paid for sex, their wives and girlfriends back home, and the children of the next generation.

Many hospitals refused to admit patients with venereal disease for fear of spreading it to other patients. That is, of course, apart from one of the most notorious institutions in Ireland – the lock hospital.

CHAPTER 11

(NOT QUITE) LOCKED IN
THE LOCK

An institution that became just as infamous as the local brothel, the lock hospital was a staple accompaniment to many prominent red-light districts across much of Britain's colonial empire of the Victorian age. It was a dedicated hospital to treat venereal disease, specifically syphilis and gonorrhoea, which at the time had no cure and could mean an agonising death. The term 'lock' hospital is assumed to come from the names for the bandages used to treat its previous leprosy patients, although some patients may have preferred to use this term because many women were forcibly locked up behind their doors.

The lock hospital had long played a role in the history of prostitution in Ireland. In 1755, surgeon George Doyle opened a dedicated hospital to treat venereal disease in Dublin which moved a few times around the city, as far out as Donnybrook in South Dublin, before finally settling on Townsend Street from 1792 to the 1950s. The site is now occupied by the building hosting the *Irish Times* newspaper offices. When it was in its temporary home of Donnybrook, one of its surgeons, Charles Bolger, offered the use of the hospital as a venue for one of madam Peg Plunkett's hedonistic parties. The hospital switched to exclusively female patients in 1820 and was known as Westmoreland Lock Hospital for the

Incurables, or for those in Monto, simply 'the Lock'. Named after the earl of Westmoreland John Fane, who offered support to establish the hospital on Townsend Street, it was kept busy as Monto provided a steady supply of thousands of patients over the years.

While the Donnybrook site was considered good enough for a wild orgy, would Bolger have made the same offer for the Townsend Street site if it was as bad as historian Susannah Riordan describes it? She paints a bleak picture of a damp, dark, rotting, run-down building in dire need of repair, where residents were often restricted to their small, dark wards:

> The laundry, in which patients continued to labour, was a 'very poor type of hand laundry'. The hospital's yards, shaded by high buildings, could not be used on the three days when laundry was dried each week. Then, and in bad weather, patients were still 'strictly confined to their wards'.

Perhaps Bolger would decline to offer in this case. However, that is not to say sex did not happen – one of the reasons the Lock started accepting only women was due to illicit encounters between the patients. Sex with hospital staff was also not unheard of, but while some encounters were consensual, many women may not have been in a position to refuse or resist.

In 1881, the Lock was clearly struggling to keep the wheels turning:

> The walls and ceilings ... could not be white-washed, cocoa-nut mattresses could not be supplied in place of straw for bedding, and the dilapidated roof could not be repaired owing to the want of means.

Its financial situation continued to be rocky until it was finally demolished, having been a health and safety risk for decades, and the women and children still present were accommodated elsewhere, more than eager to escape its decaying walls.

Meals were basic and uniform across the network of lock hospitals throughout the British Empire.

Breakfast: – 8 oz. Bread; ½ pint Cocoa.
Dinner: – Five days – ½ lb. Meat; ½ lb. Potatoes. Two days: –
1 pint Soup; Soup Meat. 1½ oz. Rice.
Tea: – 6 oz. Bread, ½ pint Tea.
Supper: – 1 pint Gruel.

Meat Diet
Breakfast: – As above.
Dinner: – ½ lb. Meat, ½ lb. Potatoes, every day.
Tea: – 6 oz. Bread, ½ pint Tea.
Supper: – 1 pint Gruel.

Beef Tea and Pudding Diet
Breakfast: – As above, and 1 pint of Milk.
Dinner: – 1 pint Beef Tea, 2 oz. Rice in a pudding.
Tea: – As above.
Supper: – 1 pint Gruel.
Mutton Chop or Fish, when ordered, instead of Meat Diet or ordinary. Rice occasionally instead of Potatoes. Extras Porter, Wine, Spirits and Milk.

The system, rules and physical layouts were familiar to those who had been in the workhouses or laundries, where freedom was a malleable concept. The women of Monto were also segregated from the women who had been infected by their husbands for fear of their deviance contaminating those good women. As the women moved from district to district, they may have found themselves in more than one hospital, becoming well acquainted with the rules:

1. At 6 a.m. Patients to rise, strip beds, turn mattresses, and open windows at the discretion of the Nurse, and leave beds to air. Wash and dress in lavatories.
2. Make beds and tidy wards before breakfast. Patients confined to bed will be attended by the Nurse.
3. 7 to 7.45, Morning Prayers and Breakfast.
4. 10 a.m., Ward, Lavatories, and bathroom to be in perfect order.
5. Morning hours to be occupied in needlework, writing letters, reading, or attending in Surgery if required.
6. 12:00 p.m., noon, Dinner.
7. 2 p.m., The Afternoon and Evening to be spent in [staying inside].
8. 4 p.m., Tea.
9. 6:30 p.m., Supper, followed by prayers.
10. 8:00 p.m., All patients to be in bed and lights lowered; no talking allowed afterwards.
11. Bad language and disorderly conducts or talking over past wrong-doing are all strictly forbidden.
12. All letters for patients will be opened by the Matron, and such as are objectionable will not be given.
13. The Nurses are authorized to report to the Matron any breaking of the rules, or disobedience to those in authority.

The lock hospital system became ground zero for the merging of the police, judicial and medical professions to create a system of invasive monitoring of the wrong women. This nightmare became reality in the form of the dreaded Contagious Diseases Acts (CDA), designed to tackle the blight of syphilis.

The CDA gave the police the power to arrest any woman they suspected of being in the sex trade. This decision was subjective and could be based on appearance, location, tip-offs or the personal inclinations of the arresting officer. The woman was brought before a magistrate who would order the woman to submit to a vaginal examination to be checked for disease. If she was found to be suffering with venereal disease, she was admitted to the lock hospital and detained there for months at a time until her symptoms cleared. Her name was added to a register and she was now on the radar for further police attention, thus beginning a cycle of institutionalisation and exposure to state violence.

The CDA did *not* apply to the Westmoreland Lock Hospital but did cover the majority of lock hospitals across the rest of the British Empire, including Cork City, Cobh and the Curragh in Kildare where the wrens were based. There is often some confusion about the status of the women in the Westmoreland Lock, and this confusion existed even back in 1882, with one disgruntled doctor complaining that he was tired of hearing that the women of the Dublin Lock Hospital were imprisoned. He claimed that they did have the choice to leave when they wished, preferably made after some 'gentle admonishment' that she would 'no doubt gratefully listen' to. For some Dublin-based doctors, it didn't make sense to exclude the Westmoreland Lock from the CDA since it had the most cases in Ireland, with 830 women admitted in 1861–2, and 772 women in 1881. They actively campaigned for this gap to be addressed by joining the Association for Promoting the Extension of the Contagious Diseases Act of 1866 to the Civil Population of the United Kingdom. However, they were ultimately not successful, and the Westmoreland Lock maintained a voluntary admission system. As some of the women came to Monto from the countryside, they may have been escaping to the relative freedom of Monto and the ability to leave the Lock whenever they wanted, unlike their visits to Kildare or Cork.

The CDA was, in theory, meant to halt the spread of VD amongst sailors and soldiers; in reality, it was women who were targeted, particularly visible, poor working-class women accused of being in the sex trade. Syphilis was 'feminised', says author Mary Spongberd, as women, especially those working as prostitutes, were blamed for being transmitters, not the men they had sex with or were raped by. This belief also led to medical information targeted to men only, placing all shame and blame squarely on the woman's shoulders. Or rather, her genitals. The women stopped being innocent victims and were framed as 'paid murderesses, committing crime with impunity'. Their bodies, souls and morals were seen as both polluted and polluting and therefore they were in dire need of control and containment.

The middle-class hatred of women who sold sex was made quite public when *Sherlock Holmes* author Arthur Conan Doyle spewed his misogyny in letters to *The Times* newspaper:

These women are the enemies of the country. They should be treated as such. A . . . Bill should be passed empowering the police to intern all notorious prostitutes in the whole country, together with the brothel keepers, until six months after the end of the war. All women found to be dangerous should be sent to join them.

In 1882, a surgeon at the Liverpool Lock Hospital was also happy to lay the blame squarely on the women in the sex trade, viewing his role as both moral and physical rescuer:

And I may here repeat, that in every one taken from off the streets while in a state of disease, and prevented from following her trade, a humane act is done to her, since she is prevented from making herself worse. At the same time she is prevented from spreading her disease to innocent as well as guilty people.

The wrong women were seen as inherently diseased and able to carry and transmit infection in a way that good women simply did not. While there was empathy towards those infected as children, their status meant they would grow up as outcasts and inevitably find their way into the sex trade for survival. Women who caught syphilis through sex were viewed as degenerates, far from the ideal asexual woman who turned a blind eye to her husband having his needs met in Monto. Syphilis, and thus by extension women having sex outside of marriage or those selling sex, came to be seen as 'a menace to the maintenance and advancement of the physical and intellectual standard of the race'. This divide between categories of women meant there was an attitude that women selling sex were not 'normal', and indeed 'scarcely human', and therefore less deserving of inclusion in society. Indeed, the acts' supporters boasted that 'The Acts are not directed against *women*, but against prostitutes'.

This framing completely dehumanises the women in the sex trade – seen not as people, but as objects. When people are objectified, it becomes easier to commit acts of violence against them because they aren't seen as victims. This objectification was clear in the lock hospitals – despite the test for venereal disease in men being painless and more accurate, they chose to test women instead since they viewed them as 'a certain class of deplorable objects'. Historian Paul McHugh notes that those who supported the CDA believed that 'men would be degraded if subjected to physical examination, [but] the women who satisfied male sexual urges were already so degraded that further indignities scarcely mattered'. It was the women who were portrayed as biomedical threats, not the men. One British regimental officer was outraged at the thought of subjecting his men (and perhaps himself) to tests for syphilis as it was 'both demoralising and unnecessary'. He outright denied that any of his men had any form of venereal disease. Statistically speaking, this was of course highly unlikely; an inspection of just one other regiment found 40 cases.

The text of the law related to the Kildare lock shows us how the system was to be operated in the Curragh from 1869:

1. All women subject to the provision of the above Acts to be called upon to sign the Voluntary Submission Paper (2nd Schedule Form H).

2. Should any woman object to sign, she is to be informed of the penal consequences attending such refusal, and the advantages of voluntary submission are to be pointed out to her.

3. Any such woman still refusing to submit herself is to be proceeded against under section 4, of the Act of 1869 her name being first reported to the Sub-Inspector of Constabulary at Kildare and his sanction obtained.

4. A complete register is to be kept by the police of all women subject to the provision of the Act.

5. Periodical examinations are to be made of such women at the time and place hereafter mentioned.

6. Such examination being made by visiting Surgeon in the presence of a female attendant, and no other person, until further ordered.

Place of examination: Lock Hospital, Kildare.

Time of such examination at 2.00pm.

One-third of the women weekly and absentees from examination at the next examination to that which they ought to have attended.

All newcomers into the District to be brought immediately under the operation of the Act.

If a woman refused to be examined, she could be locked up for five days before being forcibly examined. Despite knowing the women were mostly illiterate, they were still asked to sign forms that gave their rights away. Officers were encouraged to be 'excessively stringent' in apprehending 'suspected' women, safe in the knowledge they were essentially immune to consequences.

Dr Samuel Chaplin was the main surgeon in the Kildare Lock Hospital and was supported by special CDA enforcers Constable Robert Kennedy, Sub-Constable John Dempsey and Sub-Constable James Plant. The women would come before the Right Honourable Major Forbes in the Curragh court. Together, these men operated a system of containment for the women of the Curragh who sold sex, 'looked' like they sold sex, or were brought in for any subjective reason the men wanted. To avoid corruption, the CDA police enforcers had to be married men who were long-standing employees with a good reputation. As we have learned over millennia, public reputation or marital status is no guarantee of an absence of poor behaviour behind closed doors or in dark alleys. In fact, according to one victim of this Act, hypocrisy was well and truly flowing: 'I did find it rather hard that the gentleman on the bench who gave me the casting vote for my imprisonment had paid me five shillings the day before to go with him!'

Domestic servants were particularly vulnerable to this law being used to inflict multiple forms of sexual violence on them:

If poor innocent women are in danger from soldiers when they are drunk, they are in greater danger from lecherous gentlemen and profligate rakes in high life, even when these are in their sober sense. If such a gentleman has a good-looking servant, and she refuses to comply with his desires, he *may* drop an anonymous note to a spy requesting him to take up that girl for instrumental examination.

An 1878 letter from Fredrick Walter Lowndes, who acted as a chaplain in the Cork hospital but also as a surgeon in the Liver-pool Lock Hospital, shines a light on how the CDA created a system of containment that worked across institutions:

Dear Sir,

I have been acting chaplain in the Lock Hospital in Cork since it was opened under the Contagious Diseases Act. I have also been chaplain of the Cork Workhouse for nearly twenty years. I have over three thousand Church Protestants in my parish, of which I have been rector for nearly twenty-one years. You may judge that my experience as a parish clergyman must be considerable. I look upon the Contagious Diseases Act as one of the greatest blessings, socially and morally (and, so far at all events as poor little children are concerned, physically), that has ever been conferred upon this country. You may make any use you please of this letter.

Yours faithfully,
F. W. Lowndes

To compound the harm caused by being targeted by police and detained, the women were then accused of enjoying the examination so much that they had become addicted to the speculum, reduced to being labelled as 'uterine hypochondriacs' who craved the exam, and this belief was spread in the pages of influential medical journals.

So what was the procedure that these women were so feverish to go through that they might willingly submit themselves to several times a week as a sexually satisfying experience?

Historian Hugh Crawford describes the start of the process in Kildare:

Hospital dress was worn in place of their own clothes (which were kept by the matron), and there was a towel at each bed. Off the wards water was laid on and basins were provided for the women to wash their faces. Baths and a bidet were also provided and every effort was made to prevent any possible contagion. The patient before presenting herself to the surgeon for examination was required to use these facilities. The examination was carried out on the special chair and this involved the woman having her ankles secured.

Listening to the women who were subjected to this ordeal destroys the credibility of statements suggesting they enjoyed it. The process was violent from arrest to examination. One woman in England described what the doctors did to her:

> It is such awful work; the attitude they push us into first is so disgusting and so painful, and then these monstrous instruments – often they use several. They seem to tear the passage open first with their hands, and examine us, and then they thrust in instruments, and they pull them out and push them in, and they turn and twist them about; and if you cry out they stifle you with a towel over your face.

This gynaecological violence blended with police violence to terrorise the most marginalised of women. The speculum was reviled by the women and by feminist campaigner Josephine Butler, who called it an 'instrument of rape' or 'steel rape', while women in France called it the 'government's penis'. Butler was told by victims that 'the pain is dreadful – I have never been free from pain since', and she described the impact on one woman who was subjected to this process *repeatedly* while pregnant:

> [Her] lips were white and her hands blue, and whose fainting was certainly not feigned. Am I to suppose she dyed her poor garments (which were drenched with blood) to make me believe she had those floodings after every violation with instruments!

Some doctors were in favour of twice-weekly inspections, others wanted them conducted every second day, and one advocated for daily inspections that would continue for up to two years. One woman who had to endure these inspections shares the horrors committed on the women and girls:

> When I was in the hospital they examined me by instruments every day, and some other girls three times a week. There were three doctors – one of them a young student – present. Some of the girls scream dreadfully when examined, and I have seen the blood dropping from them as they walked away.

Blood doesn't sound surprising, sadly, given the violence described and the use of a 'widener', which was sometimes used to open the vagina even more.

If a patient didn't have venereal disease before she found herself in one of these torture centres, she was likely to have it after her time in the doctor's office. In Paris, women reported being subjected to doctors using equipment that had just been used on 30 other women before them. In London, social reformer William Acton alleged in parliament that he personally saw 150 women examined in two hours. However, this claim was disputed – these numbers meant the doctor would process more than one woman a minute for a straight two hours. But even if the numbers were somewhat fewer, there could hardly have been enough time to properly sanitise the equipment between patients.

In Kildare, the speculum was dipped in a solution of permanganate of potash after use, an antiseptic that is not recommended for internal use as it can burn the skin upon contact. Infection sites included the speculums, wideners, spatulas, syringes, catheters and more. This lack of hygiene all but guaranteed infecting the woman and changing the course of her life irrevocably, and violently.

While they were only in effect for less than 19 years, the acts brutalised hundreds of thousands of women. Over a mere six-year period at least 50,000 women were subjected to these examinations across Britain. In another study of a four-month period in 1870, 13,139 were subjected to this examination, with fewer than 1,000 showing symptoms of venereal disease. In Britain, girls as young as 11 were subjected to this examination, which could last up to 45 minutes.

Social reformer Robert Wilson blisteringly condemns the men involved in this system:

> If these men did not love violence they could not practise it. What man of moral principle could constantly enforce a shameless exposure? What man of tender sensibility could constantly stretch on the rack? What man who cared for his soul's salvation would become a vile panderer – would degrade science – would torture woman – in the insane attempt to make prostitution harmless, while many of the suffering ones hurled curses at this head with grinding teeth?

Many women turned up drunk to the examinations as they were so traumatic, or tried to die by suicide as an escape. One woman fainted every time she had to undergo this violation – and this apparently was not enough to stop subjecting her to this procedure on a regular basis.

But why *would* it be when the system was terror *by design*. This purpose was unashamedly admitted by the surgeon of the Plymouth Lock Hospital in England, H. S. Sloggett, who made it crystal clear that he wanted the woman to be in fear, because he proclaimed that 'without terror the woman will not submit'. For supporters of the acts, the women were nothing more than collateral damage in their fight to keep their armies and navies stocked with fresh recruits to satisfy their colonial bloodlust and capitalist greed. F. W. Lowndes, the surgeon in Liverpool Lock Hospital, admitted that the function of this process was not just to treat the clients physically, but to judge them morally and socially too. Many of these hospitals used stigma as a treatment. The system was designed as a punitive measure, not a holistic one, although their reports do detail some cases of women who went on to get married and leave the sex trade behind them.

In the lock system, the women were used as cheap labour to repay their moral debt, following the same path as the laundries. The board appeared to be quite happy with this arrangement, remarking in 1878 that:

> One feature of the Westmoreland Lock Hospital which we particularly admire is the utilisation of the labour of the patients, combining as it does the advantages of a reformatory system with those of a well-regulated strictly managed hospital.

There was 'little evidence of charity or compassion' and the meagre amount available was reserved for those who were 'innocent victims'. Even then, so-called 'innocent' women were not safe from violation, as historian Susanna Riordan found in the case of a woman called Mrs Holland, who was not, in fact, working as a prostitute but forced to undergo this treatment:

> . . . she suffered for a long time from nervous prostration, and . . . had never been the same since her unpleasant experience.

After the brutal examination, those discovered to be suffering with venereal disease had to have wondered if the treatment was worse than the disease. Since there was no cure yet for syphilis, treatment methods were experimental but often contained mercury.

Patients were prescribed mercury ointments, pills, catheters or vapour baths. Injections in the urethra and enemas were also used. The women were often knocked out with chloroform, which brought its own dangers of injury or death. Ulcers were burned off with nitrate of copper and patients could drink specially prepared tonics. Vomiting, diarrhoea and excessive salivating were just a handful of the side effects of mercury treatment. Unfortunately, the *British Medical Journal* acknowledged, death was another, which a 27-year-old woman found out as a result of the mercury tablet placed inside her vagina. This resulted in pain, diarrhoea, vomiting and death six days later.

Dr Thomas Byrne was a surgeon at the Westmoreland Lock Hospital for three decades. He used a variety of methods to treat the women of the Lock, from mercury pills to creams and occasionally a bichlorite tablet, which was a mixture of mercury and chloride and often resulted in side effects spanning rapid tissue loss, vomiting, diarrhoea, weakness, anxiety or an inability to pass urine for over 24 hours. He also administered mercurial vapour baths and Dover powder, which was an opium blend commonly used at the time for pain relief.

The treatments must surely make us relieved that syphilis is now treated with a course of antibiotics. Historian Hugh Crawford explains how the Kildare Lock Hospital operated by forcing patients to inject themselves into their vaginas up to four times a day with a solution made from lead, zinc or tannin. Treatments escalated if there were any visible symptoms:

In cases of inflammation and tenderness, the house surgeon, when the speculum was used, which was at least twice a week in all these cases, inserted a strip of lint dipped in the lead-lotion, and this was allowed to remain for three or four hours. If the inflammation was acute, the application of the strip of lint was repeated daily through a small speculum.

As treatments developed, Salvarsan tablets became the standard medication for syphilis, although they contained arsenic and could lead to convulsions and jaundice. Despite these effects, it meant many people avoided the wards and could be treated in their local hospital, easing a sense of stigma as well as physical symptoms. If they couldn't afford Salvarsan, they often had to resort to the old mercury-based treatments.

While the CDA system was often violent, there was at least some kindness reported in the Westmoreland Lock which remained free of the rule of this law. In the Westmoreland Lock, according to historian Susanna Riordan, the staff worked under very difficult conditions for decades, trying to provide a space for patients who were vulnerable and rejected from other hospitals. Miss Whyte, the matron of the Westmoreland Lock, would refer clients to external services such as the hostel for 'rescued' prostitutes set up by religious campaigner Frank Duff. She would also accommodate last-minute requests to host a woman until a space became available, and weekly visits from Duff were also facilitated.

Some refuges and asylums would not take back repeat offenders, preferring to concentrate their efforts on women that had freshly 'fallen', but there were exceptions to these rules and evidence of the women using these institutions to suit their needs and leaving on their own terms. However, the Westmoreland Lock was keen to admit all patients, regardless of how many times they had presented before:

> None are so helpless and so hopeless as those whose own errors and vicious life bring them to our doors; to them all access to private benevolence is closed, and their very approach is contamination to the virtuous and pure of their own sex. Shut out, therefore, from all means of relief from the hand of private benevolence, and excluded from the partici-

pation in those public charities which scrutinize the moral character of their recipients, these unhappy ones must be left to perish under the eye of charity itself, were it not for the refuge afforded by this Institution.

A report from 1885 states that 'some of the patients had been in the hospital no less than 12 times'. Many 'frequently left while they were very bad' because of the restrictions under which they were placed. However, the women were welcomed back time and time again, which hints at an environment they had some sort of positive relationship with, as they returned repeatedly despite challenging some of its aspects. The patients built a positive relationship with the staff, according to the chief medical officer, who claimed that 'girls of the unfortunate class preferred going to the lock hospital in preference to any other, no matter what ailed them'.

In Dublin, surgeon Edgar Becket Truman came out against applying the CDA to the Westmoreland Lock Hospital, stating:

My experience has taught me that the lowest harlot is quite as anxious to be cured of venereal disease as any peer of the realms; I should say more so. And I am sure that voluntary institutions, well conducted, will accomplish infinitely more good than any vain and aggravating efforts at police control.

This support suggests that Truman listened to the women and saw the first-hand effects of the failure of the CDA in the other hospitals and the impact of state confinement on the women's quality of life.

The post-hospital journey was not particularly optimistic either. This report from the Westmoreland Lock Hospital tells us how it was for the women there in 1909, when their already fragile selves became even more institutionalised:

Of the 473 treated during the year, 25 were sent to Magdalene Asylums; four to other hospitals; 11 to workhouses; five were taken on in the hospital as ward maids; five as laundry maids; 81 left contrary to medical advice; 18 were discharged for insubordination; 14 were restored to friends; 31 were sent to extern department.

Many of the women also ended up in the Lock Penitentiary on Dorset Street in the northside of Dublin, close to their former homes in Monto.

When a woman entered the front door of the Lock, she entered a stage of life where she was contained – perhaps for the first time, perhaps as yet another type of institutionalisation. She became a woman to be kept from public view, confined to the borders of Monto, rescue homes, laundries, the lock hospital, Mountjoy Prison and so on until she managed to leave. If she did leave, her Monto experiences were kept separate from her new life, never to be shared for fear of further institutionalisation or social stigma. The women of Monto who were unable to leave often ended up in a mass paupers' grave in Glasnevin Cemetery. Zoned off from others even in death; a life and death measured by restriction and rebellion.

One of the victims of the CDA laid the stark reality of this system bare:

> Men-police lay hands on us. By men we are examined, handled, doctored, and messed with. In the hospital it is a man, again, who makes prayers and reads the Bible for us. We are had up before Magistrates who are men, and we never get out of the hands of men till we die.

Speaking of their deaths at the hands of men, we need to explore another rumour about the fate of the women in the Westmoreland Lock Hospital.

CHAPTER 12

SMOTHERATION

According to a chilling centuries-old rumour, some women in the Westmoreland Lock Hospital were smothered instead of receiving medical treatment.

Author Maurice Curtis describes how this process apparently worked in his book *To Hell or Monto*:

> Another example of one who ended up in the Lock Hospital was Rose, a 16-year-old prostitute living in one of the Monto brothels. The harrowing way in which Rose met her death in 'The Lock' was typical of the fate of many of the young Monto prostitutes. Having contracted venereal disease she ended up in the hospital. There she was 'euphemised' (another local expression, meaning 'euthanised') by the nursing staff who were in the habit of smothering young women too far gone with venereal disease, after moving them to the end of the ward from which they could be silently evacuated at night without alerting the other diseased 'brassers'.

Maurice credits Terry as his source, and Terry confirms that he was told this by those living in the Monto at the time:

> I was told by two or three locals that there was a place for the women, and some said it was the lock hospital and a lot of women died there. One man told me it was an awful place

for women. He said he remembered the stories being told that these women were screaming in pain, and the orderlies used to go in and smother them. It's murder, and that was all brushed under the carpet for the want of a better word. That's what they did to these women. Some of the women told me that the lock hospital was a terrible place for women to go. They didn't know if they were going to come out.

One of Terry's main sources of information for this claim is Monto resident Billy Dunleavy, whose words can be found in Kevin C. Kearns's collection of oral folklore from Dublin tenement dwellers, including those who grew up in Monto. Billy's description paints a disturbing picture:

But we had a hospital here then called the Lock, over here on Townsend Street, and you know what they used to do with the girls (with sexual diseases)? Smother them. When they had syphilis and all . . . *incurable*! They used to be smothered. See, there was no such thing as pills at that time. They couldn't cure them. Smother them to take them out of their pain, or give them some kind of a needle. They were so far gone and at that time there was no cure. The hospital was built for that purpose. That's right. They wouldn't do them all, just an odd one. They'd be nearly dead before they'd do it.

This rumour is even one of the selling points for a Dublin ghost tour promoted by talking about the women whose 'misery was ended in The Westmoreland Lock Hospital with many apparently being suffocated to death'. Billy Dunleavy's account is mainly the original source for this information.

But is Billy adding some local flavour to a salacious story or letting us know about real injustices done to the women in the Westmoreland Lock Hospital?

In London, the story of a young French woman named Anille leaves us in no doubt of the realities of end-stage syphilis and why pleas for mercy might be made or granted. She had been trafficked to London at the age of 14 under the false promise of a domestic servant job. Anille was described by her surgeon in a London lock hospital thusly: 'She bore her illness with childish impatience, continually wishing for the end, and often imploring me with tearful eyes by the intervention of science to put an end to her misery.'

According to the following account of Anille's death by the surgeon, it's no wonder anyone would wish to avoid such a horrendous death:

Her mind wandered, and she spoke wildly and excitedly in her own language. After a while she exclaimed, 'J'ignore où je suis. C'en est fait' [*I don't know where I am. It's done*]. An expression of intense suffering contracted her emaciated features. 'Je n'en puis puis' [*I can't take it any more*], she cried, and adding, after a slight pause, in a plaintive voice, 'Je me meurs' [*I'm dying*], her soul glided impalpably away, and she was a corpse.

Kevin C. Kearns, whose book Billy's claim is published in, is cautious about believing Billy as he wrote in an email when contacted:

Billy Dunleavy is the only person of perhaps 500–800 oral history subjects I interviewed on the tenements over about ten years who ever mentioned such a thing. I would not place too much credence in his words since he had other 'unusual' beliefs that he swore to but without much evidence. Though I cannot now, perhaps 60 years later, recall what they were. He was a nice man, very poor, but generous with his words.

Terry disagrees with this assessment of Billy's credibility:

I found that Billy is credible enough because Billy was able to come and tell me exactly where the pub was where they shot and killed his brother. He was credible enough on the madams. I found with the stuff he told me that he was telling the truth. I know it can get hyped up, but you have to allow for that when you are talking to people. But I found him okay.

Gemma describes her great uncle:

Billy had a real funny way of talking. If he came in and my ma was cleaning the place and the place was spotless, the place is gleaming but he would say "ah the place is horrible clean. She has the place horrible clean", meaning that actually it was spotless, clean and it was lovely. He just had a really, really strange way of wording things. Terry sent me a transcript of the interviews one day and I got goosebumps because I heard the tone of his voice, because the way he spoke was so unique to him. He died when I was five or six. he was the loveliest in my memory, the loveliest man. Every single day for me lunch, he'd go up to my playschool on Mountjoy Square and he'd put his hand through the bars, and he'd say 'shake me hand kid'. And I had a tiny little hand at time, and he put a pound in me hand and I always remember the pinching, you know, at that time a pound was huge'.

Billy *is* right in a few aspects of his story. Syphilis wasn't curable then, and if by pills Billy means antibiotics available in later years, he is also correct. Mercury tablets were available at the time, but they did more damage than saving. The hospital was built specifically for 'incurables' and modified to suit the needs of the venereal doctors. The statement 'They'd nearly be dead before they'd do it' tallies with the testimony above where the woman begged for mercy at the very end of her life. None of the stories about smotheration suggest that it was done in a malicious way – it was rather an act of kindness to someone suffering and about to die in agony.

The claim can be traced to other locations too. It was repeated in the pages of the *Irish Times* in 2009 by Hugh Oram, who claimed that in the lock hospitals 'Often, the women were put out of their misery; the favourite form of euthanasia was "smotheration"'. Oram repeats the claim that the Westmoreland Lock had the power to detain women, but it did not as it was not subject to the CDA.

Dr Susanna Riordan, historian in UCD, wrote a letter of response challenging Oram's claims. She referred to Oram's claims as 'outrageous myths' and protested that:

> The staff, and more particularly the patients, of the Westmoreland Lock Hospital were treated sufficiently shabbily without Hugh Oram's allegation that the former routinely murdered the latter.

Other lock hospital accounts can be examined for potential evidence, one way or the other. In Scotland in 1843, social reformer William Logan confirms one case of smothering, but by a peer:

> She soon became so diseased and miserable, that no person could remain in the house, and at last she entreated a few old associates to smother her, – 'O! Women, smother me; I cannot bear this – do smother me!' And they did smother her.

Logan scoffed at the mere suggestion that staff smothered the patients even if it was called for:

> I have visited several of these unhappy creatures, in Glasgow and elsewhere, in such a putrid condition, that they have, in the height of suffering, begged to be deprived of life. It, however, need hardly be remarked, that there is no such thing as *smothering* in our hospitals.

However, in an 1871 version of the sorry tale, he has dropped the strong disclaimer of his last sentence. His earlier viewpoint seemed to ridicule the idea that women were smothered in the lock hospitals, and he held the highest regard for the doctors. The use of italics on the word 'smothering' signals his incredulity and scorn for such a preposterous idea. But why then the omission in his later retelling? Perhaps he simply forgot to include it; maybe he thought it didn't *need* to be said because it was so ludicrous; maybe an editor insisted on its exclusion for various reasons; or maybe he came to see mercy in smothering. He also wrote of seeing many women dying in pain: 'In death their mental anguish is inexpressible. – When I recollect many of their death-beds, [I] reflect upon their dying yells, – "I am lost! I am lost! No mercy for me!"' Did this traumatising first-hand experience, in hospital after hospital, year after year, country after country, influence him in any way? Whatever Logan's reasoning, it is a curious omission given his beliefs and his earlier mocking rebuttal.

Another potential clue to the truth or otherwise of 'smotheration' is contained in a lock hospital inspection report from 1938. Prepared by medical inspector C. E. Lysaght, the report laments the decline in admissions amid the public belief in this rumour that 'all bad cases . . . are destroyed by being smothered between mattresses'.

This particular method of smotheration was a possibility if we are to believe Martin Coffey's take on the matter:

A friend of mine told me that some years ago, he was talking to this fella he met in a pub that he knew from the north inner city. He was an older man and said he had worked in the Lock Hospital on Townsend Street. Now he was a big man, a strong guy in his day. He told my friend that he often had to smother patients in the hospital. He said, 'I put the mattress over them and I had to lie on top of the mattress until they stopped moving, and I had to make sure they were dead.' I asked my friend if that was really true and he said, 'No, no, no, he told me honestly and I believe him.' But I guess it's a story where we've no evidence, because the evidence has been destroyed.

Lying on top of a squirming body is hard enough; the addition of a mattress would seem to make it harder and less discreet than a pillow or needle. However, hospital mattresses were also quite thin at the time, so perhaps it does hold some grains of truth.

Bodies were not problematic to dispose of, since many of the women ended up in a mass paupers' grave in Glasnevin Cemetery or the Royal College of Surgeons to be dissected. The Lock had a high turnover of patients and a high death rate; a few extra would not have raised any eyebrows. Nor would any family come looking for them and ask awkward questions.

When asked for their thoughts on the possibility of a system of mercy killings in the Lock, Sophie, Terry and Paula all had immediate empathic responses that acknowledged the hardship of this point in the woman's life:

Sophie: Oh, I hope somebody would do the same for me, if you've no way out and there's no cure and you're just in fuckin' agony, yeah, I would choose that.

Terry: The way it was told to me was, they are in hospital, the women are screaming and screaming, it's not beyond anyone's imagination that some staff would say 'fuck this'. But I'd nearly say it's true because she was the woman of a lesser god.

Paula: I don't know if you have read much about what death by syphilis is like, but I think I'd be looking for the pillow myself. Sometimes with information that's presented very negatively, if you dig a bit you find that there can be mercy in it.

Billy mentions the use of a needle, but if there was something nefarious afoot at the Lock, chloroform was also at the staff's disposal. It was used across Britain and Ireland for childbirth and surgery such as amputations as it minimised struggling and noise from the patient. Death by chloroform was quiet, with death occurring between five and ten minutes after administration, and this quietness is reminiscent of Curtis's story about needing to remove bodies quickly and discreetly from the wards. This process was seen in the case of one woman in a London hospital who accidentally died a mere five minutes after been given chloroform for treatment of venereal disease:

> The patient had gone through the usual stages of excitement, etc., and the last dose was scarcely used, as she sank off, almost immediately after its application, into a state of complete insensibility, unattended by any alarming symptoms.

Despite the risk of death, Lowndes, a vocal advocator of the CDA, admits to the use of chloroform in the lock hospital in Liverpool in the 1880s, albeit only a handful of times a year, and rationalises this choice with this statement:

> If I can save the funds of an [sic] hospital by shortening the residence of the patients, I consider that I am justified in so doing, and as for our results, see the Lancet for 6th January, 1882.

The phrase 'shortening the residence' is an interesting one that could be read in different ways. The same curious choice of words is seen again in the writing of Dr James Morgan in discussing the use of mercury alternatives in the Lock. He says some of them 'cannot "go wrong", as mercury, though most carefully administered, occasionally appears to do'. In what ways did it 'go wrong', and did this lead to accidental deaths or deliberate ones, and how often? Did they record these cases or investigate the doctors who administered the treatment?

One potential clue may lie in how the women were seen as collateral damage in the quest for finding the cure for syphilis and the glory that would bring. A woman's social class dictated how her treatment would go. If she was middle or upper class, she could avail of private and *respectful* treatment. Poor women and those from Monto had a completely different experience as their class position made them fair game for medical experimentation. The CDA and the lock hospital system were also racist and colonialist state weapons that were more violently enacted in Britain's colonies to regulate the sexuality of undesirable populations. The idea that these women may have been subjected to violence in many forms does hold water.

Feminist campaigner Josephine Butler doesn't appear to have mentioned reports of smothering or mercy killing Lock patients, and given her passion and time spent talking to the women in the system and communicating their realities, this would be an odd omission if she was aware of it. If anyone was well placed to hear this rumour, it was Josephine. She was willing to challenge the system and despite pushback, kept advocating on behalf of the women subjected to these examinations. If the women were being murdered and Josephine knew, this would surely have helped her campaign to repeal the CDA.

Women in many industries have kept themselves safe through whisper networks – was Monto any different? As the women were transitory in both the brothels and the hospitals, did they hear these stories of smotheration or witness them on their travels? Did their clients hear them in another red-light district across the seas and pass them on? Perhaps they were just *too* taboo to talk about too loudly, too close to home.

When discussing the sex trade, those at the heart of the discussion are often spoken over. Classism, racism, transphobia, homophobia and ableism add extra barriers for people to have their voices heard. Personal knowledge and lived experience are challenged, and some knowledge is suppressed or dismissed as fairy tales or propaganda. When activist Catherine Corless shared her work locating almost 800 children in a septic tank in Tuam, County Galway, she was accused of lying and dismissed as clearly wrong. That is, until ground penetrating radar proved her right.

Annie Meehan's great-granddaughter Paula challenges the outright dismissal of something as true because of the absence of historical records:

> You are going to find that working in the folk idiom – some people will find it unreliable. They say the same about me; some people say the same about Terry. Because it's about story, and story is about refining narrative for entertainment value in many cases. But in the wildest and outlandish stories you often find at least the signpost to more reliable information. So, I dismiss nothing. You only had to say the term 'Lock Hospital' when I was a kid, and you could feel the ripple of shivers in the room. Because to end up there you were *ending up there* and you may very well be screaming for a pillow.

Many historical records have predominantly been written by men wanting to represent their morals, their social norms, their truth, at the expense of women's truths, their humanity, and in some cases their lives. The hospital governors used records and reports to gain funding, which they did not have to account for. How many case notes were accurately reported and inclusive of the woman's voice? Did they note how she felt, how she accepted or refused treatment? Did they pass on any last words to family or friends? Were her symptoms exaggerated to get more money or minimised to reduce shame?

Unfortunately, a lot of the accountability for and knowledge of practices behind the walls of the Lock has been lost. Not to time but through deliberate action, according to historian Gary Boyd. He suggests that upon the closure of the hospital in the 1950s the staff deliberately burnt the records of its patients, from the most recent first, lamenting that:

Of all Dublin's major hospitals, the lock hospital remains the only one without a dedicated history. And, throughout its two centuries of existence, the 'lock' had often been a site of controversy and approbation.

Starting with the most recent records meant destroying the possibility of living relatives finding out what had happened to their loved ones and causing a scandal – an attack on history and women's dignity, yet again. Sadly, Dublin is in line with many other lock hospitals of this time, with few surviving records or artefacts; even the buildings themselves are mostly gone. What little remains of the Westmoreland Lock Hospital's records is now held in the Royal College of Physicians library in Kildare Street. The physical remains of the Lock consist of two pillars relocated to a garden in a private home in Howth, North Dublin.

As these institutions were not subject to checks, they appear to have enjoyed a sense of being untouchable, a reality due to their status and that of their patients. This was a period where the medical profession was becoming solidified as a professional organisation, one that was enjoying a ride to the middle and upper classes and a steady income. Did that power lead to corruption and exploitation of vulnerable women, as it has done in many different formats, contexts, eras and locations?

Was record destruction an unwritten policy, or is it a coincidence that most of the lock hospitals have had their notes erased from history? Or was the truth rooted in compassion, as the hospital very much understood the impact of social stigma and perhaps wanted to protect their patients' confidentiality? Historian Anne Hanley suggests this destruction was a collaborative effort: 'The acute stigma and shame surrounding VD has resulted in a dearth of historical records. Individuals and their families, often aided by doctors, actively suppressed knowledge of their affliction.'

Frustrating as this destruction is, this effort is understandable especially as the moral teachings of the Catholic Church became intertwined with the fight for independence and the establishment of the state. Being seen publicly as a 'fallen woman' meant serious consequences of containment. The staff knew life was bleak for their clients outside their wards, and by destroying their records, they were eliminating the opportunity for them to be identified by the state and brought to the laundries. Maybe they wanted to give them the dignity of dying with their families instead of alone on a hospital bed or in a laundry.

While the staff may have succeeded in setting the records ablaze, the embers from the ashes have floated through history, keeping the women's voices alive. Through the words of songs, folklore and local and academic historians, these smouldering remains can be compared to the records of other lock hospitals that shared similar conditions and demographics.

These symbolic cinders also remind us of the attempt to silence women by accusing them of being witches and burning them at the stake – a fate that befell infamous madam Darkey Kelly in the 1760s in Dublin. The types of women burned were 'troublesome' women who didn't conform, but in reality any woman was vulnerable to a man deciding to accuse her of being a witch. If she turned down his advances. If she thought she was better than him. If she lived independently. If she represented a threat to the social order. If she was the wrong kind of woman.

In attempting to piece together what could have been so horrific that the records had to be burned in a hurry, it's crucial to also ask: what *didn't* they record?

What did they do while the women were passed out and tied down, knowing they were essentially consequence free?

What did they subject the women to in order to climb the career ladder?

Did the women know what was being done to them?

One particular answer to these questions is one that changed the course of history. Reformer Robert Wilson alleged that the doctors in lock hospitals deliberately infected their patients with syphilis, disregarding their consent or comfort. This practice of syphilisation appeared to be common enough in France and England that Wilson remarked that

Since Paris, the holy city of civilisation! gives law to earth,
English surgeons are largely following in the same track.

These practices *did* happen, both to those who were confirmed to already have syphilis, and those who were suspected of it. In the London Lock, a 16-year-old patient being treated for syphilis given the initials A.B. was injected seven times under her breast with syphilis from another woman, resulting in fever and a multitude of painful sores. Another 16-year-old, given the initials A.C., admitted on 9 May 1851, was injected over 550 times on 89 occasions during her four-month stay. In 1867, surgeons James Lane and George Gascoyen shared the results of their experiments, where 27 patients were injected between 102 and 468 times with syphilis from other people. The resulting sores were then treated with mercury, taking at least three weeks to heal, scarring the patients and impacting their future health and life expectancy.

These sores were not always small. One woman suffered with a sore the size of one buttock and the upper part of her thigh as a result of the process, and her painful decaying tissues were not a rarity. Despite this, it was viewed that the process must go on, for 'to attempt her cure without it is to waste the time of both parties', according to the surgeons. In the London Lock, Case 11 was a woman who spent over four months subjected to this treatment but returned with sores around her anus. Her treatment involved rubbing nitrate of silver on the sores. The doctors lamented the fact that she wasn't seen again, but as nitrate of silver causes staining and skin irritation and her treatment took months, we can hardly blame her.

Patients in London who died while undergoing syphilisation were all recorded as dying from liver failure or from their facial tissues rotting away to the point of exposing their brains. None were recorded as dying because of the treatment, which does not necessarily mean that the treatment was not the cause or played a key role in their death.

Medical consent was not a consideration at this time. The experiments were often viewed by the doctors conducting them as a way for the women to repay the institution for their support, following in the footsteps of the workhouse making its inmates earn their keep – an unspoken social contract struck between desperate patients and doctors eager for test subjects. While we now know that this treatment did not work, it did contribute to the eventual discovery of the cure for syphilis, saving untold millions from a torturous life and death. It was claimed by the doctors in the London Lock that the women 'cheerfully submitted' to syphilisation. Similar was said about the response of the patients subjected to experimentation in America by J. Marion Sims, who is credited with inventing the speculum. What is often missing from his accolades is an acknowledgement that he also pioneered gynaecological racism by experimenting on enslaved African women and children without anaesthesia in order to enhance his career. The surgeons of the lock hospital system used gynaecological classism to do the same. The end results saved millions of lives, but that came at the cost of the women of Monto and their colleagues in other hospitals. The cure for syphilis was found in part because of the experimentation on the bodies of lower-class women who worked as prostitutes, and this acknowledgement is part of ethically remembering what these women went through. The women were viewed as guinea pigs to carve up and infect, and their consent mattered less than the doctors' efforts to develop science and medicine.

Did this happen in the Westmoreland Lock Hospital? Sadly, yes. This experimental treatment was tested and refined using the women in the lock hospitals under the CDA including Westmoreland Lock, despite it being outside this law. At the same time as animals were being used as test subjects for potential syphilis cures, the women of Monto who were in the Lock already for venereal disease treatment were also subjected to the artificial infection of syphilis by doctors.

J. Arthur Morgan, a surgeon at the Westmoreland Lock, was a strong advocate for extending the CDA as he believed it worked and confined the 'truly infecting character' of the prostitute who infected soldiers. While he did not get his wish, he did get to make his name by experimenting on the patients to find a cure for syphilis. In an article written by Morgan in 1870, he details how he subjected 1,582 women to this procedure over the course of two years. What Morgan called a close examination by experiment was the deliberate mass infection of women with syphilis, women who were predominantly from Monto.

Morgan took the vaginal discharge from one woman and injected it into another woman or rubbed it into open wounds on her skin. This would produce a sore, which in turn was rubbed on another woman, and on and on, one woman becoming patient zero for this chain of infection. He also rubbed the vaginal discharge of an 'intensely syphilised' patient on another part of her own body to check if it would produce sores; it did. He referred to this woman as 'a thoroughly infected subject' and claimed to have never experimented on those not already infected, or in his words, 'already undoubtedly tainted'.

He was further infecting those at an early stage of infection, not those at death's door. He noticed that the stronger the strain became, the more difficult it became to heal, leaving the woman experiencing more symptoms than she may have had and perhaps playing a role in hastening her death. Morgan also infected them with gonorrhoea by injecting samples from men into their arms, and he admitted on 'several occasions' to have tried to transmit the virus using the implements used in smear tests of the cervix. This did not appear to work all the time, but he was still aware that the potential for infection from the instruments used was high enough that even if the implements had a half-hour break between uses they remained infectious.

Morgan performed these experiments on eight-year-old children, and he also used mucus from the anus of a two-year-old who had been born with syphilis. It was common enough practice that engravings of the results of these deliberate infections were published in the *Medical Press and Circular* of 22 March 1871, with Wilson calling this 'iniquitous conduct' that should not be glorified.

That experience was not the end of the invasion of their bodies for the women. As a result of the 1832 Anatomy Act, the bodies of the poor were used for dissection, advancing knowledge of the medical field. Patients were viewed as 'recipients of charity' rather than autonomous humans, and therefore the hospital had more control over them, including their remains.

Historian Gary Boyd claims that because of 'unfettered' freedom to experiment, the Lock enjoyed being a space for 'innovation for environment medicine such as ventilation, fumigation, hygiene, [. . .] particularly suitable for clinical trials of new forms of medication and especially those relating to venereal disease'.

The bodies of the poor were much more acceptable to experiment on than the upper classes, and so medical classism was solidified using the bodies of poor women, most often those who worked as prostitutes. From the testimonies of the women who survived the laundries and the mother and baby homes, we now know that this institutionalisation and containment of the wrong woman behind closed doors, away from the ability to corrupt good men and women, was traumatising and certainly lasted a lot longer than their time selling sex. The desire to avoid such a horrific fate meant that the women were extremely vulnerable to violence from multiple sources around them, including harm from medical institutions.

CHAPTER 13

CRUEL INTENTIONS

Clients venturing into Monto were at risk of more than just STIs or a hangover. Monto had a fierce reputation for being a violent space, with religious reformer Frank Duff describing its notoriety in the 1920s:

> The corruption within its borders was apparently so extensive, so unhandleable, the stories in circulation so fear-inspiring, that even the holiest and bravest were convinced that nothing but harm could come of an attempt to grapple with the evil.

Sailors, soldiers and clients of the lower-class brothels were all but guaranteed to be robbed during their evening's adventures. They were aware that they were easy prey, since everyone knew they wouldn't involve the police and would often be leaving the country shortly afterwards. Blue books carried warnings about brothels with known pickpockets, explaining why certain madams may have been keen to destroy particular copies. Robbery in red-light districts was usual enough that at the same time as Monto, a third of those convicted for robbery in Edinburgh were also alleged to be prostitutes.

Women employed several methods of violence for either self-defence or to maximise their take, using their hat pins to stab clients or hitting them with pokers concealed under their skirts.

One rather salacious rumour suggests that Prince Albert, grandson of Queen Victoria, was not just a visitor to Monto but that his time there also started a very niche trend of penis piercings. If this rumour is to be taken at face value, the second in line to the English throne asked a woman of Monto to do something she didn't want to do, so she stabbed him in the penis with her hat pin. Not wanting to deal with Irish doctors, the Prince waited until he returned to England to seek treatment. By then it was too late for the hole to heal up, so he made the most of a bad situation and attached some jewellery. This particular style of piercing has become known as the Prince Albert. Sadly, this rumour cannot be proved, despite an unusual amount of literature on the penis of a royal family member. Some commentators believe he did have a piercing, but its purpose was to make his rather large appendage stay in place while horse riding or wearing tight uniforms. Still, we can at least entertain the image of a woman of Monto defending herself against an overstepping royal.

Some clients were less interested in the delights of singing and companionship and more interested in the opportunity to enact violence against women, targeting vulnerable women who were unlikely to go to the police or find the person's true identity. Previously stabbed in the arm with a bayonet, one woman in London's red-light area tells us how common violence was and how she fought back:

> The sodgers is such – cowards they think nothing of sticking a woman when they'se riled and drunk, or they'll wop us with their belts. I was hurt awful onst by a blow from a belt; it hit me on the back part of the head, and I was laid up weeks in St. George's Hospital with a bad fever.

Monto's visitors were known to carry knives and other weapons, and fuelled by drink, they became more likely to turn violent if

180

their weapons were not filched first. For survival, the women had to learn how to protect themselves as best they could.

The spoils of robbery were shared out amongst the madam, the bully boys and the women, and if one of the women attempted to keep any just for herself, she would find herself on the madam's wrong side very quickly. Tricking the madams was risky business, as they had sold sex themselves in their young days so were well acquainted with the ducking and diving of brothel life. Frank Duff highlighted how the madams were no stranger to personally keeping her girls in check through violence:

Such punishment was physical; it was drastic; it was terrific. Once I saw the aftermath of one [. . .] The girl had been terribly beaten up; as well her clothes were torn off and ripped into small pieces.

Independent women selling sex were also part of Monto. They solicited men from O'Connell Street and took them to the dark streets of Monto or scouted for business in the shebeens, but this was also risky as neither the madams nor their women appreciated the encroachment on their turf, as Terry explains:

You see, it's like the drug trade. Each of the madams had the areas carved up between them. They didn't want people taking away their business. She could get killed, get stabbed, anything could happen to her.

The women who worked in lower-class brothels and on the street may have been targeted by the bully boys to reduce the other brothels' competition or just for sport, since they appeared to enjoy inflicting violence. Monto resident Mary Murphy, who grew up seeing what these men did to the women, calls them 'dirty rotten lousers', and Terry describes their role in brothel management:

The pimps were under the control of a madam. You are not going to damage their goods without them knowing. To be a bully, they had to be able to handle themselves, and they certainly did.

The bully boys reported back to the madams, who sent their women out to the street. They would take up positions at either end of an alleyway to make sure that the clients didn't escape without paying, and also so they could keep an accurate tally of clients. For the women, keeping these men on their side was a survival tactic since the bully boys had a lot of power, as Terry shares:

If a woman said she had three clients, but the pimp said she had six, May had the girl stripped naked [. . .]. If money was found on her body May had a habit of slashing her face so she would be of no use in future. The girl would then be thrown out onto the street – it was a way of warning the others what would befall them if they messed with May.

Black eyes were also dealt out by madams like May, who had no issue inflicting the violence herself. This violence came in many forms, and escaping it was not easy. Terry outlines some reasons why it was hard to leave Monto, even if a woman had willingly entered and enjoyed her time there up to this point:

They had to pay the madam, and the bully boys and then the cops, then the clothes and lodging. It's hard to get out of that cycle. Once you are in it, you can't get out of it. The women also knew that the madams had contacts all over the city, and if the women fled, they could get them.

Monto resident Jem King remembers the fearsome reputation of May and her weapon of choice: 'Madam Oblong was a hard woman and you could not argue with her, begod. She would lift up a bacon knife and slash at you with it if you tried to cross her.'

A slashed face was not just an injury: it was a symbol that the woman was a troublemaker and made her occupation ever more visible while simultaneously reducing her earning potential. This visibility led to an increased risk of violence, and Martin recalls his family explaining this system:

That was to keep the girls in place. Because if your face was cut nobody would want you, nobody would want you at the price you were looking for. The price was lowered if you had a big scar on your face. Some of them, and I've come across this with my own family and in prison records, they would have cuts on their arms. Originally, I thought that was self-harm. But my family said no, they were warnings to the women – *next time it could be your face.*

Martin's Monto family also included a very violent man that he describes as one of Monto's 'thugs':

He was just a thug. He got into more fights with men, and he would pull out his cut-throat razor; he thought nothing of using it. When he died and they had the autopsy they discovered scars on the back of his neck where he had been fighting other men with knives. There were two sailors he took on one night, but he didn't realise that they had cut-throat razors as well and they beat the living daylights out of him. He ended up in hospital.

Violence went hand in hand with Victorian red-light life and could occur at any moment from a variety of sources. However, the women themselves were no strangers to committing acts of violence, often fighting with their competitors or maximising the take from their clients. The madams sometimes faced violence from local mothers; one woman from Foley Street courageously stood up to May Oblong, ripping her hair out and leaving her with two black eyes when she had had enough of May's behaviour. We can only speculate what repercussions she faced for her stance, and from whom.

The madams' reputations and income were something they were willing to protect at all costs, and if someone challenged the status quo, they were swiftly dealt with, as Pearl remembers: 'Annie Mack hated Annie Meehan because she was paying her girls too much, so she taught her a lesson. She threw something at her fur coat and tried to set her on fire. Not her house, but *her*.'

This was not the only time fire was used to target women in Monto. Folklorist Terry Fagan tells the story told to him by Monto resident Mrs Byrne, who knew a woman nicknamed the White Lady of Monto. Mrs Byrne chatted with her on the steps of the tenements of Railway Street when she was 12 years old, and described her as a pale, small old woman who wore heavy white make-up and paid the local kids pennies to go to the shop for her. This woman had worked in the brothels of Monto after leaving the countryside due to heartbreak over a man she was forbidden to marry. Her father paid her lover to leave, and despite her last-minute efforts to reach him in Dublin before his ship set sail, she was too late. Feeling like she could not return home after what her father had done, she had few options for survival and thus ended up in a brothel on Faithful Place in Monto. Mrs Byrne believed that the White Lady wore so much heavy make-up because she'd been set on fire by a bully boy. This man, Mrs Byrne said, was believed to have thrown paraffin oil over this vulnerable woman inside her room before setting her on fire and locking her inside. She was rescued, but badly burned, with her haunting screams added to Monto's soundscape. Since then, she had used make-up to cover her scars. The sheer premeditated wickedness of doing this to this young woman shows how ultra-violent the bully boys were prepared to be.

The women at the lower end of the rungs of Monto were more public than those kept in luxurious surroundings, who had the ability to mask their identities as 'wrong women' through their glamorous appearance and social climbing. Those on the streets stood in their coats and dirty rags and had to announce their presence verbally and visually if they wanted any clients. They had to make men come to them, unlike in those more private institutions that operated waiting lists and screening from a line of willing and wealthy clients. Their lack of choice and visibility made these women vulnerable to violence not only from clients or police, but also from society, which stopped seeing them as women and started seeing them only as 'poor unfortunates' or 'fallen women'. They lost their identity through stigma, and the option of reclaiming their identity lessened the more Catholic and independent Ireland became. Their Monto experiences became memories best not talked about in order not to risk their safety in this new age of morality.

The minute a woman wasn't the shiny, sparkly new addition to the brothel, her risk of violence swiftly increased. Her highly sought-after youthful peachy skin became less of a commodity when it was mottled with bruises, accompanied by black eyes and broken bones. Her smile became less frequent because of broken teeth and trauma, and if she was extremely unlucky, the ravages of syphilis had also begun to take hold. At this point, her options for help were limited and came with their own risks of violence. Instead of being supported, she was now in danger of being institutionalised for decades in desperate conditions that left their mark on too many women.

Violence against women selling sex in Ireland did not originate with Monto. In 18th-century Ireland, prostitution was culturally viewed as an exclusively female profession. While this does not rule out other genders engaging in selling sex, violence against prostitutes was almost always male violence towards female victims. The Pinking Dandies were a street gang who assaulted people with swords and caused terror amongst vulnerable women. They assaulted Peg Plunkett in 1779, leading to the death of her unborn child and her two-year-old daughter. They followed in the footsteps of the strawboys, groups of men who meted out punishments to women they decided had broken the moral code by marrying someone they did not approve of.

Religious vigilante group the White Cross Association was also present in Monto to try to shut it down. The impact of the men being deterred was a reduction in available clients for the women, therefore leading them to take riskier clients or face a drop in income. Most of the women in Monto were selling sex to survive and very few got rich, so actions such as these could mean the difference between making enough money for the night or facing the wrath of the madams and bully boys.

Many of these young girls had to live with the ever-present potential of sudden violence from madams who enjoyed slashing faces, ordering their bully boys to assault them, and turning a blind eye to sexual violence. If the girls didn't manage to escape, they made their way down the brothel system until they hit the streets, which was where the most vulnerable women selling sex were. They were often anonymous, lacking support, addicted, homeless, in poor health and historically targets of violence – including murder – from clients, police, madams, serial killers and institutions. Ruining the looks of the women under their roof might seem counter-intuitive but the madams could afford to be cruel because another girl would soon come along, not leaving the madam out of pocket for very long.

Monto's approach to regulation was a self-contained system, as Duff explains:

The place had its own 'bosses', its own law, its own financial system. This was not a written code, but it operated efficiently. Its driving power was crude violence operating swiftly. It did not argue. It simply ordered and struck.

Arriving in Monto was often a result of personal violence, but more violence kept many women there longer than they wanted to stay. This violence came from people who should have looked after them but did not – including the police.

CHAPTER 14

POLICING THE BODY

Shortly before Monto solidified itself as a centre for prostitution, the police of 1844 were found to have high rates of venereal disease. It wasn't viewed as too big of a problem; if the men were caught in brothels, even in their uniforms, they were fined or demoted rather than fired. It was viewed as just a part of life for them, and the fines were not excessive. The Dublin Metropolitan Police's medical officers explained that it was not the policemen's fault that they caught venereal disease, since they were innocent rural young men who were not used to the vices of a big city, and 'finding themselves surrounded on their beats with vice and infamy, under many attractive forms, they were probably unable to restrain themselves from the influences brought to bear upon them'. They were an all-male police force at a time when it was women who were blamed for immorality, not men, thus enjoying an added power dynamic over the women of Monto.

The women were sometimes charged with offences related to being drunk and disorderly or selling alcohol illegally, rather than offences related to prostitution. In 1882, madam Annie Mack was charged several times with selling liquor without a licence, at one point being fined £6. Meg Arnott, who used several different names including Maggie Arnott, was arrested in 1885 for selling bottles of porter without a licence when a policeman raided her brothel. He found numerous clients and young women, all drunk, and plenty of empty bottles that Meg couldn't hide from his policeman's eye. Fleeing to Scotland, she got away with it, but others weren't so lucky. Some women, such as Kate Caulfield from Elliott Place and Annie Taylor from Faithful Place, were charged with larceny in a brothel and faced prison.

Religious reformer Frank Duff complained that Monto was de facto 'free from police interference', while Paula Meehan suggests the police left Monto alone as they knew exactly what went on there but, more importantly, *who* was there:

> The police didn't want to go in there, they didn't want to find some lord in bed with some young one, or indeed young fellow. They didn't want to find the soldiers in the same place as the revolutionaries, drinking in the shebeens. It was a no-go area where the laws pertaining to the rest of the country just didn't hold, so the police didn't go in. It was sort of a territory unto itself.

However, while this may have seemed true on the surface, in the sense that brothels were essentially free to operate how they wished, in reality the police were very much a part of the Monto experience. It was a natural progression from the previous century, where police and judges worked in unison to rent premises to the madams around Christchurch in Dublin city centre and sell them their alcohol for a tidy profit. This might have been a comfortable situation for all parties involved, but it equally may have been one where the women were not in a position to say no to the police or judges for fear of being shut down or evicted.

The police knew the clients ranged from the everyday person to the upper classes – and themselves. Timmy 'Duckegg' Kirwan confirms the visible presence of the police in Monto:

You had policemen in these places drinking all night as well! They were from Store Street. I knew most of them. All Mayo men, all big men. And they were 'on the take' – or them places wouldn't have been *open at all*. They *should* have been closed up. But they closed their eyes and they got that (money) every night. See, they'd come on duty and they'd slip into one of these places all night. And there was fights outside the houses at nine in the morning when they'd all be coming out stupid drunk. Ah, the police drunk as well! Never sober.

Despite the Criminal Law Amendment Act of 1885, which should have shut down 'disorderly houses', it was in reality mostly ignored. Instead, the police demanded free services, protection money or bribes from the women in order not to be arrested. The most visible women were the ones on the streets, and these were most at risk of intimidation from the police. Monto resident Sara Fagan recalls a particular individual she refers to as a 'bastard' taking advantage of the women:

There was this policeman; he was a cow in his heart. When he was on the beat in the street he would not go near the girls on the weekdays, but on the weekend, he knew that the girls would make lots of money and he'd collect his share of their takings.

Accusing women of selling sex proved lucrative for some police officers, who were already used to supplementing their relatively decent wages through side jobs. Their demands for bribes from the women were in keeping with the behaviour of the police in red-light zones across the world and across centuries. In Scotland, proof of police interactions with women selling sex was seen in the very system that was meant to 'protect' the public from venereal disease. Out of 120 special constables brought in to monitor women they suspected of selling sex, 64 of them were found to have caught venereal disease and had to go on sick leave.

Historian John Finnegan makes the shocking claim that 'I knew one sergeant in the Dublin Metropolitan Police who, instead of bringing prostitutes to court to be charged with soliciting, brought them instead to bed'. Of course, as our understanding of the spectrum of sexual violence has grown, we can see that he did not 'bring them to bed' – he used his position to coerce them into sex that in reality was rape, as saying no would have meant facing prison.

The police were also well aware of what went on behind the doors of the Lock, since they had a history of being taken there to gawp at the women, who were used as a cautionary tale to scare the men away from sex workers. They therefore enjoyed a position where saying no to their demands for bribes or sexual favours was all but guaranteed not to happen. If the woman wanted to stay out of the system's revolving door of arrests and detention, she was at the mercy of the policeman's inclinations. She knew it, and he knew it.

Police also coerced women to report on where other runaways or criminals were, and pressured them to tell them where a woman they wanted sexual favours from was. They were also happy 'to frighten them into subjection by threatening imprisonment with hard labour' and had truncheons to enforce their official and unofficial powers.

Police violence towards those selling sex took another turn due to the Dublin Police Act of 1842 and the Police Clauses Act of 1847. These laws allowed the police to stop any woman they suspected of selling sex as 'a common prostitute or night walker loitering or importuning passengers for the purpose of prostitution', and fine her not more than £2. This essentially meant the police had free rein to decide who 'looked' like a woman of ill repute, and their subjective judgement could mean arrests, fines, an opportunity to make a little money on the side or freely commit sexual violence on women they knew wouldn't report it. The cost of an arrest was not just financial, however – she would be labelled a 'common prostitute' and shamed.

According to Tommy 'Duckegg' Kirwan, a particularly sadistic police officer enjoyed targeting some of the most vulnerable women of Monto – those sleeping in tenement hallways overnight. He compares the kindness of the tenement families towards the women sleeping there to the cruelty of this man known as 9c in reference to his badge number:

> He had a black tar stick and he used to go around looking for poor souls laying in the tenement houses all night. A big Mayo man. He'd go around at twelve at night and he knew every lobby where the poor devils would be asleep and he'd have his flash lamp and he'd hit them across the back with that, the poor old souls.

Police maltreatment of women selling sex was widespread enough that in 1891 the chairman of the General Prison Board, C. F. Bourke, complained that the women were not being treated fairly by police:

> I am of opinion they should be protected by law as far as possible and should not be driven by persecution into the class of heinous criminals or be deprived, on account of being prostitutes, of the protection and liberty accorded to other of her majesty's subjects.

The guidance that the police had in 1889 was that 'prostitutes cannot legally be taken into custody for being prostitutes; to justify their apprehension they must commit some specific act that is an offence against law'. On paper at least, once the women were not breaking any laws, they were to be left alone. By 1910, this approach continued with the Royal Irish Constabulary, since prostitution itself was not illegal.

It was in both the madams' and the women's best interests to keep the police on their side. This was not just a survival mechanism: it was good for business too. In New Orleans's red-light district, Storyville, one madam enjoyed a mutually beneficial relationship with the police. Madam Norma Wallace kept the cops on her side by tipping them off if someone they were after was going to be a guest at her establishment. They were more than happy with this as it made them look efficient, so they made her brothel a police-free zone, with strict orders not to raid it. Who knows what other activities she got away with, safe in the knowledge she was untouchable? Many of the Monto madams also enjoyed a cooperative relationship with the police – the officers would not interfere in how they treated the women, the clients or even their tenants or neighbours, as they were paid off by the madams.

One strong contender for the title of BFF with the police was May Oblong, according to resident Mary Murphy. She remembers her parents discussing May's hustling ways: 'She was a holy terror she was, always with the police and the army. They were never away from her house. They were her friends.'

Becky Cooper also enjoyed a close relationship with the police. Whenever she had a few too many drinks in her local Monto pub, she would get kicked out. The publican knew her next move would be to break the windows of the pub, so her policeman friend would be summoned to get her under control. This man was known as the 'Hump', and resident James Burke describes his relationship with Becky:

He would say to her, 'Come on, Becky, let's go home.' 'The Hump' would not arrest her; he would just bring her over to her house. You see, he used to get his free drink off her when she ran the speakeasies in Monto.

We can only speculate how much the police were paid and how much extra they received from bribes and protection money from the women. The blind eye the police turned also had the advantage of allowing the revolutionaries who frequented Monto to plan their activities in relative safety. This freedom was bolstered by the women of Monto passing their pillow talk from British clients along to the revolutionaries, providing information that was beneficial to planning the 1916 Rising and in the fight for independence.

It was common in British brothels that if a madam discovered one of her prostitutes had caught a disease, she would pass her details to the police, who could extort money from her or use her as a quota for their arrests. Considering some madams of Monto treated the women as little more than commercial products, they may have had no qualms following this example.

The police were also known to tolerate the madams' tactics for getting out of prison. The names of the madams were sometimes passed down to their successors or manageresses, which was a way to not only continue a notorious reputation, but also evade arrest. Pearl recalls from her family history a domestic helper who worked for her great-great-grandmother in their brothel:

Little Annie took the name, and I think she went to prison a few times as well for Annie Meehan because obviously she didn't want to go. So, she took the rap, but the deal was that if she did that, her family would be looked after or she would get some money. If anyone came looking, she was Annie, while the real Annie stayed out of trouble.

This story hints at the realities of a good relationship with the police – there was no doubt they knew exactly which madam was which, but they were happy to go along with the charade and reap the personal benefits.

Annie Meehan had other tricks up her sleeve for managing rowdy punters, according to Pearl:

> She also had a relative that pretended to be a policeman and he used to go around in a policeman's uniform, because if the police came and saw him on the door, they thought there was a policeman already there. He used to wear this policeman's uniform, but he'd just stand around the door walking up and down, like a bouncer. But he wasn't a policeman at all. It made the clients behave, as they thought he was real.

In 1911, the new commissioner of the Dublin Metropolitan Police, Colonel Sir John Ross, decided to tackle the open sore that Monto had become. The first Catholic to hold this role, Ross shut down the brothels of Elliott Place, one of the poorest streets in Monto. However, this led to the women moving their trade to O'Connell Street, since they still had to eat. Middle-class sensibilities were offended by the visibility of the trade, and so Monto was left alone again until Frank Duff facilitated the final blow in 1925.

Shortly after Monto's demise, a garda by the name of Lugs Branigan would go on to earn the title of 'Ireland's most famed garda' because of his reputation for protecting the women on the streets and his willingness to use his fists in his fight against crime. While he referred to the women as 'pavement hostesses', he operated a zero-tolerance approach to violence against the women and often arrested husbands or clients who were beating the women up or stealing from them. Branigan's stories of his work with the women contain reasons similar to those given for selling sex today: forced by partners, trying to survive, trying to afford occasions such as Christmas, or trying to pay for communion dresses. Pressure from police also continues today in many countries. Research from around the world has shown a correlation between police violence and higher rates of STI transmission and less power and choice in who the women saw as clients. Women also experienced being robbed and sexually assaulted by police and felt they were not taken seriously when they tried to report incidents of violence.

The organisation Ugly Mugs advocates for the safety of sex workers in Ireland, consisting of a peer-to-peer network where those selling sex can share details of dangerous clients to try to stay safe as a community. Organisations like these also draw attention to gaps in policies that mean vulnerable people selling sex are not protected from violence, including police violence. Ugly Mugs CEO Lucy Smyth outlines this gap in Ireland's domestic sexual and gender-based violence (DSGBV) policies:

> Ireland really needs [to] up its game in terms of dealing with Garda violence against women. The lives of people in sex work and victims of trafficking matter. The Government and NGOs heavily funded by the government cannot continue to not take Garda violence against women seriously because it doesn't fit comfortably within their agendas. We know Garda violence against women in sex work is a problem. We have brought to public attention cases showing this. If the new DSGBV does not address the problem of Garda violence against women, more women will surely suffer.

In 2015, a male garda arrested a woman selling sex, then later returned to her apartment to have sex with her. He argued that this act was consensual; the woman stated that it was rape and that she was afraid to say no since he had earlier arrested her. A fine was issued and the garda remained in his position, damaging the trust that many had in the gardaí.

This distrust appears to be widespread. In 2022 a report from University of Limerick and GOSHH – Gender Orientation Sexual Health HIV – found that one in five street sex workers interviewed had experiences of being sexually exploited by the gardaí. They also reported that gardaí were their clients, made jokes and threats at their expense, and took advantage of their lack of knowledge of the law, making them feel unsafe. The report coordinator, Billie Stoica, noted that for those selling sex on the street who had to navigate many challenges such as addiction, poverty or precarious housing:

> How sex work is policed only added to the pressure they were under and left them with little or no access to justice.

Linda Kavanagh, spokesperson for Sex Workers Alliance Ireland, says that less than 1 per cent of the sex workers they work with had enough trust in the gardaí to report crimes, a very stark contrast to the 81 per cent of the general population who do trust the gardaí. One can imagine the women of Monto could report similar statistics.

CHAPTER 15

BLOODSHED

Statistics seem to indicate that some of those in the sex trade, particularly those working on the street, and who are also in addiction, homelessness or crisis, are much more vulnerable than women not in the trade. Violent predators take advantage of this vulnerability, knowing that these women are less likely to be missed and more likely to be desperate for money so may go to a quiet location with them. In many areas, serving policemen have been convicted of murdering vulnerable women in the sex trade. The Sex Workers Outreach Project USA notes that they deal with reports of violence from law enforcement officers on a frequent basis. Even if concerns are raised about potential predators, police failures to take them seriously because of the status of the victims have allowed serial killers to claim more victims before being caught. The number of murders of people selling sex are impossible to quantify because they are not all reported, but many red-light-district workers have stories of women they know who disappeared one day without a trace.

Stories also abound about the murder of clients who were too innocent or stupid to play by the rules of Monto. If a punter complained about being robbed, it could be one of the last complaints he would ever make, according to Frank Duff:

Anyone who has been down there can visualise the scene: the cries proceeding from a struggling knot; a figure that does not rise, but lies still; awed whisperings, and in a little while the body is carried away for disposal in a backyard grave; then a universal conspiracy of silence!

Red-light districts in the same era as Monto saw their share of murderers and serial killers targeting women selling sex. In 1890, San Francisco's red-light district was terrorised by a man who by day was a respected member of society, as a medical student, and church volunteer, but by night was a serial killer. Theodore Durrant prowled the brothels and was in the grisly habit of acquiring birds to slit their throats and smear their blood over his body while he murdered the brothel workers. At the same time in England, Jack the Ripper was one of the most well-known serial killers of women alleged to sell sex. While his identity remains unknown, there were enough men of questionable character to produce over 20 suspects, from Irishmen to Monto regular Prince Albert.

Guns were very present in Monto, from the standard issues of the British Army to republican arms and the guns issued to the Dublin police, albeit for short periods at a time. Murder by gun was also a part of Monto life, especially during the fight for independence and the establishment of the Irish Free State. A military policeman, John Ryan, was shot in broad daylight as he read his paper in Hynes pub in Gloucester Place in February 1921. Becky Coopers' brother was also shot in Monto by the IRA for being an informer. The number of guns in combination with a transient population that was reluctant to engage with the police created a perfect storm for violence. A group suspected of being behind a series of armed robberies were believed to hide out in Monto, next to civil-war survivors who carried on the fight with their fists.

Monto's hostile architecture merged with a hostile atmosphere for women on the streets. As well as counting on social stigma against their victims, those with nefarious intentions made use of the landscape to cover their crimes. Jack the Ripper showcased how this was done in London as he navigated a similar landscape with similar victims. He was able to disembowel his victims and escape through the lanes and a maze of Victorian tenements – not once but several times. In Monto, a murderer could slip out of its boundaries and on to a ship off to a foreign land before anyone realised what had happened.

Monto was a ten-minute walk from the river Liffey and a much shorter journey by cart or carriage. As drowning was a common method of suicide, especially for women, recovered bodies may have simply been dismissed as unfortunate souls that took their own lives rather than having met a brutal end at the hands of others. Marks on their bodies that identified them as prostitutes would have automatically lowered the priority to investigate.

In London, accounts of those working in the trade alleged that women were murdered by the bully boys and disposed of in the river: 'There is an aqueduct of large dimensions, into which murdered bodies are precipitated by bullies and discharged at a considerable distance into the Thames, without the slightest chance of recovery.' Bodies in the Thames were a common enough sight that the river was known locally as 'the Great Stink' in 1858. In Cork, one woman working as a prostitute was almost murdered by three men when they threw her into the river from Pope's Quay in 1839.

Dublin local Maggie Murphy grew up in a family of dockers in 1920s Dublin and recalls disobeying her mother's orders to avoid the area due to the women using the docks to tout for business:

> The boats would come in and they had their own men. And many of the (women) were even thrown into the river. Like if you and me (two prostitutes) was down there and I have me man and you took my man I'd kill you, and maybe you'd be thrown into the river. Oh, many a body I heard going in.

Martin was told family stories about how unwanted guests were dealt with in Monto, and once again the Liffey makes an appearance:

My mother told me there were times, now she said it was very rare, but men would come into Monto looking for children. One night, some man came into the area looking for young children to buy for sex, young girls. It was brought to notice of the women in the area and they went to the men and told them to sort this out. But there was nothing happening. So the women came rushing in through the door of the pub where my mother was, and shouted, 'Are you fucking men or what, do we have to take care of this fella ourselves?' The men put their pints down, because they were afraid of the women, and they went and found this guy, beat him up, and threw him into the Liffey. I asked my mother if he drowned in the Liffey, and she said, 'I don't know, no one knows, and no one cared.' But he never came back.

If someone wanted a speedy exit from the scene of a crime, they could allegedly make use of the tunnels of Monto for a subterranean escape. But did these tunnels really exist, or is this another part of Monto lore?

Rumoured to lead to the Custom House, the tunnels were said to provide cover for important visitors to Monto, such as Prince Albert and other nobles. Other rumours say that while the tunnels *did* exist, they were less of a rabbit hole to a wonderland of sex and more of a political necessity. In this case, the tunnels were a built-in feature of the fine Georgian houses to help their wealthy upper-class residents escape in case of an uprising due to the push for independence, brewing since the 1798 Rising and political efforts to achieve Home Rule. Another possibility is that the tunnels were a reality but intended as air vents to keep produce cool, a trend in Georgian buildings where the pantries were located in the basement.

The possibility of tunnels being used for illicit brothel visits was revisited on the other side of the city when a hole opened up on Dame Street in 2015. Historian Gerry Cooley suggested it could lead to a tunnel that was used for politicians to discreetly visit brothels in the 19th century.

One item can serve two purposes, and where there's a tunnel there's often someone who has modified it for their own purpose, with plenty of reasons to keep quiet about it. The 1916 fighters were quite happy to discourage belief in tunnels so they could use them to move guns or plan their escape routes through them. Tunnels utilised in the Rising have been found under the Ambassador building at the top of O'Connell Street, a few minutes away from Monto, showing that such tunnels in the north inner city do exist and played a crucial role in Irish history.

In England, soldiers were no strangers to using architecture to get what they wanted. They would crawl through sewers to sneak out of the barracks and go to the local red-light districts. Were soldiers in Dublin aware of tunnels criss-crossing Monto, and did they adapt them to connect the neighbouring Aldborough Barracks with Monto?

Social reformer William Logan suggested that tunnels and secret passages were normal parts of red-light districts in Britain and describes how sneakily they had to be entered:

> I got on my hands and knees and moved along very slowly and cautiously till I reached the other end of the plank, when I felt something like a stair, and finding myself right in my conjectures started to ascend [. . .] Arrived at the top of the stairs I knocked at what turned out to be the door, which was opened, and I observed at a glance that the house was a third-class brothel, in which I found several young men and young women.

Secret passages in Monto were seen by resident Bill-Boy Preston, who was shown one in his Aunt Kitty's house as a child. He saw an IRA man run through the house and disappear, followed by a policeman. His aunt assured the policeman that he was mistaken. When he left, Bill-Boy was shown the secret in the walls:

> She walked over to a wall with a lot of holy pictures on it and she put her hand behind one of them. Next of all, a door opened. It led into the back of a grocery shop named Butlers that went out into Corporation St. I was amazed at it . . .

Frank Duff came dazzlingly close to proving the tunnels existed in the 1920s and 1930s. The nuns who had taken over the houses on Lower Mecklenburgh Street employed a contractor to incorporate the sites into the laundries, and under Mrs Curly's house quite the surprise was awaiting him:

> The understructure of the house was extraordinarily formidable, completely out of keeping with the house itself. He wanted to know if there was originally an extensive range of wine or other cellar!! [. . .] It does look as if the contractor turned up the shattered remains of such a [tunnel] system.

Duff lamented that he never managed to photograph the tunnels, but Terry fulfilled this goal a few decades later.

Terry, preserver of so much of Monto's history, says he has personally been in the tunnels in Mabbot Lane, off Railway Street. This tunnel backed on to Gardiner Street and was connected to the offices of a wine merchant. He knew of another that extended under Corporation Street, today's James Joyce Street, but it was too dark and dangerous to go deep into them and see what secrets their walls held. In the Mabbot Lane tunnel, he found coins, ink bottles, brass beds, money and dockers' buttons and said, 'Some of the tunnels were really massive [. . .] You could actually drive a carriage through them.' These spaces could have facilitated many violent incidents during Monto's existence. Terry once found

Terry made his way into the tunnels at long last.

a cache of guns which was taken by the police, and the council filled in all the tunnels that were uncovered. Tantalislingly, Terry claims there are yet more tunnels still to be explored, what could these add to our understanding of Monto?

Regardless of what method was used to commit acts of violence and murder against women who sold sex, far too many women of Monto met a gruesome end at the hands of clients, madams, opportunists or vicious killers.

In 1886, Elizabeth Doyle was brutalised so much by a soldier that when she arrived at the lock hospital, she died of her injuries. Despite being just 18, Elizabeth was well known to the staff of the lock, having worked in the trade for years. She wanted to be treated only at the lock, requesting while she was still conscious to be brought there.

A resident of 55 Purdon Street, Harriet Butler was only 28 years old when she was shot dead by Detective John McClowery on 1 November 1920. McClowery was a Monto regular who had wanted Harriet to leave Monto and start a respectable life with him, but she had refused. He was identified by two of Harriet's peers, but as the police moved to arrest him, he turned his gun on himself and evaded justice forever.

Pearl recalls the family story of a woman who disappeared in Monto and was never found:

There was one of the workers, she had very, very long curly blonde hair and it was very, very pale. I remember my great-grandfather talking about her and it used to stick in my head because I have a doll and every time I look at it, it always reminds me of her. She had long blonde curly hair down to her waist, and my granny used to say he talked about her like she had a curtain of gold falling from her head. One of the other madams wanted her to come and work for them, because she looked like a little doll, but she ended up going missing.

Towards the end of Monto, another woman who sold sex lost her life to male violence. Elizabeth Carberry, who also went by Bessie, was found dead in a Dublin laneway on 27 October 1920. She had extensive injuries, indicating sexual and physical violence, and her cause of death was suffocation, most likely via a hand clamped across her mouth. As a military badge was found at the scene, attention turned to Lance Corporal Albert Hadley. He was missing his badge and his clothing was in disarray, but he escaped prosecution because another soldier from the same regiment had also lost his badge that night. No other follow-up occurred as Dublin was being drawn further into the fight for independence at the time, and no justice was sought for Bessie after the case was dismissed. Her previous convictions for soliciting and her drunken behaviour had stigmatised her into becoming someone whose death was not worth pursuing.

We can see another sorry example of how vulnerable women were at the hands of British soldiers. In Tipperary in 1921, 45-year-old Kate Maher was left for dead after a brutal physical and sexual assault, but no one was convicted of her murder because of the War of Independence and focus elsewhere. How many other women were not given justice due to the lack of interest in pursuing cases where the victim had spent time with the enemy? Many of the clients of Monto were British soldiers, and some people resented the women for interacting with them.

In the 20th century, the police raids on the houses in Elliott Place pushed the women out of their usual surroundings and down to the docks to try to find clients. Kate 'Christy' Kenny, who lived at 1 Elliott Place, and Fanny Langford, who was homeless but worked in brothels in Elliott Place, were both old-timers in the trade. On the night of 7 November 1908, they joined their friend Mary Carroll for a drink in James McDonnell's pub on North Wall Quay before they went looking for clients. Both Kate and Fanny had been arrested many times for selling sex, but it is unknown if Mary did or was stigmatised as a prostitute because of the company she kept, being a widow, or daring to visit a pub.

The women split up, but upon Kate's return to their meeting point, she discovered Mary's body on the street. She had been stabbed in the chest, a six-inch puncture wound ending her life at the age of 36. The chief suspects were Scottish sailors who had been drinking in the same pub, but their ship left that same night, almost immediately after the murder.

Thankfully, Mary's case was taken seriously, and Scottish police managed to track down the six men who had been in the vicinity at the time and they were brought to Dublin for a trial. One defendant, Thomas Grant, was the prime suspect as a bag with a dagger sheath and bloodstained clothes had been found in his lodgings. He had also bragged about a knife and showed it off, its unusual design remembered by many witnesses and a perfect fit for the wound inflicted on Mary. A solid body of evidence meant he was convicted and sentenced to be hanged. In a foreshadowing of the 1926 trial of another murdered woman who was assumed to sell sex, Mary was demonised by the press who called her 'a miserable outcast' and part of 'that unfortunate class' of women, meaning those in prostitution. Her killer had respectable people lobbying on his behalf for clemency, and their influence worked. Grant's sentence was commuted to prison, but in the end, he enjoyed an early release and went back to his native Scotland. Despite the body of evidence against him, he resumed work as a sailor and no doubt stopped by other red-light areas on his travels.

Martin Coffey can not only make the claim of being related to a madam of Monto: he is also the descendant of a convicted murderer of Monto. His great-grandmother Margaret Carroll and her sister Nannie McLoughlin earned the moniker the Poker Sisters because of how they dealt with a customer in their brothel. On the night of 4 July 1896, railway worker John McKenna made the fatal decision to make a trip into Monto. He met Carrie Thompson, who was working as a prostitute, on Gloucester Street, and she brought him back to Margaret and Nannie's brothel on 3 Gloucester Lane. John was a repeat customer and had a bottle of whiskey with him, intending to make the most of his time away from work and his family. Nannie became furious when she wanted some whiskey and the last drop was gone, grabbing the bottle and hitting Carrie on the head with it. When John attempted to defend her, imploring them, 'Don't beat the girl like that,' Nannie, Margaret and others turned on him. Those would be his final words.

As related by Martin in his book *What's Your Name Again?*, their neighbour in 2 Gloucester Lane, Catherine Dillon, witnessed the brutal last moments of John McKenna:

As she looked out her window she saw Carrie Thompson covered in blood. She said there was a great row next door in number 3 and she knew the voices of the prisoners and heard

Johnnie Byrne call out, *'Leave him alone'*. She heard Nannie McLoughlin call out for a poker and saying *'I'm not done with him yet . . .'* and that *'. . . she'll do for him'*. Then she saw John Byrne and John McLoughlin drag a man out of the hall and lay him down outside their own door. Both of them began kicking the deceased. Nannie McLoughlin said *'Don't leave him there, throw him over by the wall'*. Witness said that Maggie Carroll robbed the pockets of the man while Mrs Higgins held the light for her. She heard Maggie Carroll saying *'It's gold'*. Then the two men and the two younger women carried the man to the Gloucester Street end of the lane. The witness identified a blood stained hammer/hatchet as the property of the prisoners.

Prison mugshot of Margaret Carroll, great-grandmother of Martin Coffey.

*Prison mugshot of Nannie McLoughlin, great-grandaunt of
Martin Coffey.*

Margaret was sentenced to five years in prison while Nannie got
seven, both with hard labour included. Carrie found herself at
huge risk after the trial as she was labelled an informer and had
her teeth knocked out by a woman called Anne Jane Doran. She
had to seek shelter in a police station from a crowd who were
threatening her, and Carrie knew well enough that threats in
Monto were not empty threats.

Those vulnerable to having their lives snuffed out early in
Monto also included children. If the women found themselves
pregnant, they were aware of the horrors that awaited them in

mother and baby homes, England, the streets or the workhouse. They also had to fear violence from their families, who might commit honour killings or punishments. Of course, not all women faced this fate – those who were wealthier had access to private abortion services or luxury trips to England, and while they could still face stigma, they were much less vulnerable than poorer women to familial, societal and state violence. Infanticide therefore became an option for some women's own survival.

Until the 1830s, the Foundling Hospital in Dublin provided a safety valve for those who could not raise their children and did not want to resort to infanticide. Women could leave their infant at the Foundling Hospital on a revolving wheel for anonymous drop-offs. These tiny children did not live long in the overcrowded hospital – many died within hours or days of arrival, their bodies dumped in a nearby mass grave that was prone to flooding. The closure of the Foundling Hospital in the 1830s led to an increase in infanticide, to the point that in 1860 it was the single biggest cause of violent death in Ireland.

For an impoverished young woman with no family support, being pregnant left few choices for survival. Historian Maria Luddy notes that infanticide appeared to be common enough that newspapers wrote hundreds of stories about infant corpses being discovered, alongside cases of women who were prosecuted for infanticide. Author James Kelly notes that it was single mothers and women who sold sex who were more likely to commit infant-icide, both demographics that are at higher risk of experiencing poverty. In 1913, Margaret Reilly admitted to throwing her child in the Liffey after she left the Westmoreland Lock as she was homeless, struggling to survive with no support from her husband, and could not raise it.

Children's bodies were found in rivers, dumps and manure pits, with suffocation, strangulation and drowning being the most common methods used. Some women did not know how to care for a child as they had never experienced a family with caring parents, or indeed a family at all. Some children died through neglect, through ignorance or with malicious intent. Babies born out of wedlock were more at risk of infanticide as they were labelled 'illegitimate' and could bring shame on the woman, limiting her options for survival. Sadly, their discarded bodies were often discovered by the children of Monto as they sifted through rubbish for anything to sell, according to Terry. If the woman was lucky, she had sympathetic family and friends who helped to conceal the pregnancy, birth and deceased body, and the less lucky might come up against those who would commit them to institutions or kick them out on to the streets.

Through her grandmother, Paula heard some of these tales growing up, a whispered glimpse into an underworld of butchery and survival that left its mark on her:

My grandmother would go in and visit old pals and they would go for hours, sifting through story and lineage. They could get three hours out of placing an individual exactly in their relationship to everyone else. I was under the table listening to stories I wasn't supposed to hear – there'd be people having babies, people disappearing, bodies and blood. Often in the way of childhood, you overheard things, rather than heard things. Some of the best things I ever heard were from under the table on the edge of the adult world.

The most publicised murder of a woman selling sex came just three months after Monto was forcibly shut down. Honour Bright would never know it, but her murder played a key role in the creation of the post-colonial Irish identity, not just of women, but of the nation as a whole.

As with many women in Monto, Honour Bright used several aliases as she made her income and dodged police. Known as

Lil since childhood, she was also known as Lizzie O'Neill, Lily O'Neill and Elizabeth O'Neill. Thanks to the work of her granddaughter decades later, Honour Bright was given her real name back: Mary Kate O'Neill. She was described by those who knew her as 'an attractive, fresh-complexioned, warm-hearted girl, with brown hair and deep brown eyes' who came to Dublin from her native Carlow as a teenager. Like many women of Monto, she worked in a clothes shop until she became pregnant and was forced to leave both her job and home. Turning to selling sex was a way to support her and her baby boy. It was at this time that she adopted the pseudonym Honour Bright.

Honour used the streets around Stephen's Green to try to pick up clients. She lived with her friend Bridie, also known as Madge Hopkins, who joined her for work on occasion as both women were trying to survive by selling sex. She paid another woman £1 a week to mind her son while she visited him as often as she could. Her life changed for the worse when Catholic campaigner Frank Duff came into it. He closed down the lodging house where she lived, at 25 Chancery Lane, with 25 other women who worked the streets and who had formed a community of their own. While many of the other women went to his hostel and retreat, Honour did not because it would have meant being separated from her son. She found new lodgings at 48 Newmarket Street with other women who had refused to go with Duff.

On the night of 8 June 1925, a mere three months after the closure of Monto, Honour met 30-year-old physician Patrick K. Purcell and 25-year-old Leopold J. Dillon, a garda superintendent. Lest anyone think 25 is a typo, that was Dillon's correct age – historian John Finnegan explains that because of the eagerness of the Free State to establish a successful and large police force, young men were promoted rapidly if they had higher education. Dillon was a previous University College Cork medical student.

The three were observed having a row on the street outside the Shelbourne Hotel at St Stephen's Green, before all three then got into Purcell's car. They appear to have suspected Honour of robbing them earlier in the evening. It was to be the last time anyone would see 25-year-old Honour alive. She was shot through the heart in the Dublin mountains and her body discovered the following morning. Honour's shoe was found nearby, leading the prosecution to suggest that she had tried in vain to protect herself with anything she could. Her desperate attempt was no match for a gun nor the hatred within the person pulling the trigger.

On the night she was murdered, Honour wore a black beehive hat that sported a red rosette, a 'dark pink blouse, silk flesh-coloured stockings, a slightly worn grey tweed skirt and jacket, and black patent court shoes with T-straps'. She had no identification on her, but when the newsboys ran through Chancery Lane the next day, her friends recognised her from the description of the deceased and, knowing she had not returned the previous evening, alerted the police. Her friends walked for almost three hours to identify her body. Other people apparently had the same idea as crowds turned up to gawp at Honour, who had been moved to a shed. Her body went unclaimed by family and she was buried in an unmarked grave in nearby Kilgobbin, near Stepaside.

Dillon voluntarily handed in a statement to the gardaí and was sacked from his superintendent job a day before he was arrested. He later pleaded not guilty when charged, as did Purcell. Both lived in Wicklow at the time of the murder, and Purcell was married while Dillon was single. A year later, the two men stood trial at Green Street courthouse near Smithfield, which is still in use today. The judicial personnel consisted of a male judge and an all-male legal team and jury. Honour was described in court by the prosecution as 'an unhappy girl of the unfortunate class', reminiscent of Mary Carroll's treatment two decades earlier.

The two men were identified by witnesses and the prosecution's case was supported by physical evidence. Their car was identified as being close to where Honour was last seen, and Dillon admitted having sex with Honour earlier that night. In some court cases, this evidence would be more than enough to convict; in Honour's case, the jurors took a grand total of three minutes to decide that the men were not guilty. Bonfires were lit in Wicklow to celebrate the verdict, while Honour was consigned to history, dismissed and blamed for her own death by those cheering the verdict.

Historian John Finnegan reveals a shocking piece of information that shines a light on Honour's murder. A woman named Esther Kennedy came forward in the 1970s to tell Finnegan that she had known Honour and had viewed her body. She stated that she knew another woman called Margaret Walshe, but did not know her real name, who said she was speaking to Honour on the night of the murder and told her not to get in the car with Purcell and Dillon. Esther believes that Margaret had earlier robbed Purcell and then swapped clothes with Honour. Purcell and Dillon must have thought it was Honour who had robbed them or who had their stolen possessions. Esther suggested that because Margaret had some famous clients, this information was not admitted to trial, and immediately after the trial she left for Canada, taking with her one possibility of solving Honour's case.

The following week an anonymous letter was published in the *Sunday Independent* boldly proclaiming that 'we must not waste words over this unfortunate girl' because what happened to Honour 'makes us realise what must inevitably happen when humdrum, ordinary, everyday life is debased by orgies of vice, loose-living and licentiousness'. Historian Cara Delay points out how Honour's independence and profession made her an acceptable victim for society, one to be held up as a warning to other

Irish women not to stray off the path prescribed to them by the Church and state:

> Drink, dancing, immodest fashions, sex, and murder: the sad path of Honour Bright was one that any Irish woman who was not careful and vigilant could fall victim to. *All* Irish women had the potential to be, or to become, Honour Bright.

Rather than blaming the victim for her murder, we should reframe this statement and ask instead: *could not all Irish men have the potential to be, or to become, Purcell and Dillon?* Rape culture enables the blaming of those who are subjected to sexual violence and the excusing, minimising or outright ignoring of the actions of those who decide to commit sexual violence on others. The lack of justice shown to Honour has been replicated in multiple court cases since, where women's underwear and their personal history of consensual sex has been used to smear their characters and excuse the violence perpetrated on them. In addition to newspaper letters and op-eds, we now also face victim blaming on social media, TV and across society within minutes of cases being publicised.

As with Kate Maher's murder previously, there was no further search for Honour's killers. Irish journalist Sarah McInerney has spent much of her career telling the stories of women who have died violently at the hands of men, including in her book *Where No One Can Hear You Scream*. Many of them, including Honour, have not received justice of any kind and faced speculation in the press about their jobs, clothes or sex lives. Sarah feels that Honour never stood a chance in the court of public opinion due to how she was perceived:

> The idea that two respectable and upright men would be associating with a lady of the night was not what the new

Irish State wanted to be connected with. The thing that really struck me from the court case was the extent to which she didn't matter, because this case was so notorious because it wasn't what society, particularly this new Irish society, wanted to project itself as. The really basic questions that weren't asked about why she was upset when she got into the taxi. In any trial, you would expect that would be a question that would be asked. But I was left with a sense that it wasn't asked *because she didn't matter.* You know, it didn't matter because either way, if she got killed it was seen as her own fault anyway, because she was on the streets, so her being upset just didn't matter to people. The whole thing is just tragic from beginning to end for her, and the media coverage of it was hugely influential.

It was a sloppy investigation. This woman was killed; she was shot through the heart, found on the side of the road with no blood around the place. Where's the blood? It makes me think that if it had been the doctor who was killed, all of those questions would have been asked and answered and pursued right until the end. One of the accused had made a remark that he 'could clear the Green of them in one go', and I remember just thinking, it's as if he's talking about rodents. The language is so revealing. My sense towards the end of my investigation is that there was sort of a collective national sigh of relief when the two men were found not guilty, and everyone could go back to accepting the world as we wanted.

How can the media address this today, bearing in mind the influence it has on the cases it chooses to cover or ignore? Sarah suggests the path forward for ethical reporting lies in under-standing how the stereotype of the wrong woman has survived since Monto and is still played out today across the pages and views of modern media:

You have those good victims and bad victims, and some cases just capture a nation's attention and people's imagination. We do have to ask the question as to whether or not the media plays a role in cases that *don't* capture the nation's attention because of the good victim/bad victim division. Some victims are painted as people that we can feel good about feeling really, really sad and sorry for without any complications. Grey areas start when moral dubiousness begins. The media does list occupations of the people they report on, but sometimes the media does make an editorial judgement by understanding that by including a particular bit of information you're potentially biasing the story in a way. That's where there's a lot of questions when it comes to media ethics, because then the journalist has to be the person to make that decision. We see this in cases of race or religion, too, in cases of mass violence. But in saying that, newspapers are very concerned about circulation, obviously, so sex sells and dead sex sells as well. A hint of scandal and the people can be lost in it completely. I don't think much has changed since Honour's experience. I think everyone would enjoy the scandal the way everybody enjoys scandals, especially sex scandals. And a few people's lives would be destroyed, and Honour would still be the prostitute.

This sensationalism was present even as Monto's roots began to take hold. While various editors over the lifespan of the *Freeman's Journal* attended high-class courtesans' parties and enjoyed the offerings there in many ways, their printed pages told a different story. They referred to the women as a problem to be solved urgently:

> . . . the swarm of these shameless and abandoned women that nightly prowl through the streets of this metropolis is really become a most intolerable nuisance.

The hypocrisy of this moralising has not disappeared and continues to harm people today.

Belinda Pereira's story reflects the same stigma that impacted Honour. Belinda was a Sri Lankan national visiting Ireland as a sex worker and was murdered in an apartment at Mellor Court on Liffey Street, Dublin, on 29 December 1996. She was murdered six days after Sophie Toscan du Plantier in Cork, and the coverage in the newspapers couldn't have been more different. Belinda lost her identity and became a nameless 'Sri Lankan prostitute' or 'slain hooker'. Her diary, which kept records of clients, was sensationally headlined as 'Slain Hooker's Diary Names Celeb Clients', these celebrity clients being seemingly of more interest than the man who murdered her.

Belinda's brother Hirantha remembers the shock of finding out Belinda was a sex worker through headlines like these:

She was obviously leading a double life which we didn't know about. The following day we took a flight out to Dublin and we stayed with some friends. They told my dad about the news coverage in the newspapers, which was quite shocking really, because we always thought of Belinda as a family person, and now we saw a totally different side in what they were portraying in the newspapers. So it came as a real shock to us. It really affected my mother more than anyone else because she was very close to my mother. It wasn't long after that my mother got cancer and she passed away. My mum always kept like a scrapbook of photographs of Belinda. And cut-outs from the newspapers. She made little effigies of her and kept them in her room. I think when Belinda died, a part of my mother also died as well. It was very tough for all of us.

I can probably understand the stigma that people have for that type of profession. It's not the sort of thing that people would like to have in their community, but at the same time, they don't see the other side of her, that she was just part of our family. I think it's important that people understand that she was a real person, and that she wasn't someone who wasn't loved because she was loved. People only see her from their point of view, you know, and they don't see her as a family member, as someone who was loved as a sister or a daughter. They just see her as a prostitute.

Hirantha is resigned to the fact that, despite renewed police appeals, his sister's murderer will never be caught. However, this does not mean he thinks they will escape justice of some kind:

Nothing is going to bring her back. And whoever's done it, they have to live with that guilt. And whether they pay for it in this life or the next life, it's immaterial to me; they will have to pay for doing this. It's a loss in our life, but even if they catch the person, I'm not going to feel any satisfaction for that, because it's not going to bring her back.

This vulnerability and stigma have continued to the present day, as Izzy Tiernan, former Student Union officer at the University of Galway from 2023 to 2024, explains. Izzy is also a self-identified sex worker and spoke to me about their experiences of stigma that led to people unable to reconcile how they could do their job as a welfare officer because of their past:

The stigma around being a sex worker hurt, and I didn't actively openly talk about doing sex work even though I was actually doing it. My friends, my family, I didn't tell them about it. I only started speaking about doing sex work this year, and it's been incredibly freeing, but even though I'm not still doing sex work the stigma around even having done it for a time is so very prevalent. I think if you are outside any of the boundaries of acceptable behaviour, specifically the Catholic ethos in Ireland, you were isolated and you were ostracised. But you can't just look at me as a former sex worker or a recovering drug addict. That's parts and pieces of the whole of me and sometimes when I do talk about my past vocation or my past substance abuse issues and then follow it up by saying that now I'm the Vice President of Equality in the Students Union at University of Galway, they get a bit of a shock and say 'wow that's amazing, you have come so far'. But really, I haven't come far from those situations – they were struggles that have put me in a position that I'm better at my job. I'm better at working with students and I'm better at working in welfare because of my lived experience as a sex worker. It's not that I have overcome the struggle of being a sex worker, it's that it has enriched my experience to be able to better help others.

In some cases, vulnerability can be fatal, especially when combined with stigma. In Limerick, Geila Ibram, a 27-year-old Romanian sex worker and mother of four young children, was stabbed to death on 4 April 2023. Her body was discovered by her fiancé, and her suspected killer was eventually caught in Northern Ireland; at the time of writing he is awaiting trial. Ugly Mugs released a statement at the time of her killing, sharing their distress at the lack of information from the gardaí, which was a barrier to trying to keep other sex workers safe and warning them of this man before he was arrested.

Limerick Social Democrats councillor Elisa Donovan organised a vigil for Geila when she heard of her murder. She felt she could not stand back and do nothing, and kindly agreed to share her speech here:

This time last week we heard the awful news that a woman had died here in our community. At the time, we didn't know anything beyond that a woman in her twenties had been killed in Limerick city.

Over the weekend, we came to know that this woman was named Geila Ibram, and she was murdered just a few short metres from where we are standing here today.

Geila was a 27-year-old woman from Romania, who had only been in Limerick a few short weeks and now she will never return home. We learned that Geila had children and had a family in Romania.

Even though she was only in our city a few weeks and so many of us in the community did not know her, she was a woman who would come to Limerick, and she deserved to be safe and protected in our city.

I called this vigil today so that we as a community could come together and show our respect for a young woman whose life was stolen from her at such a young age.

I want for Geila's family and friends and her children to know that we are deeply sorry for your loss. That we as a community are distressed and deeply saddened that your loved one Geila has lost her life in such horrific circumstances. We as a community find this senseless violence abhorrent. And I want to make a commitment to you that we will do everything we can to ensure that another family will not have to go through this ever again . . . Margaret Atwood called it the murders of our sisters and Geila Ibram is our sister.

On the anniversary of Geila's murder in 2024, Sex Workers Alliance Ireland (SWAI) released a statement to mark the moment. Linda Kavanagh, spokesperson for SWAI, said in a press release:

We recently learned through the media that another predator is preying on sex workers in Ireland. We have had no contact with the Gardaí about this, despite our attempts to open lines of communication recently. We can confirm that Ugly Mugs, a safety app used by sex workers, was also not warned. Outdoor workers, such as street workers, are sitting ducks while the Gardaí refuse to use what little safety networks sex workers have to keep them safe. Gardaí pose as clients and lie to sex workers to get access to them, under the guise of so-called welfare checks, but refuse to warn them of dangerous attackers operating in the area.

Sophie, a present-day sex worker, feels that because people associate the sex trade with death, a murder like Geila's doesn't attract much sympathy:

For a lot of people across society, we are expected to die in that way. Women who aren't sex workers are not expected to suffer in that way. People relate to them differently; they don't relate to us; they never see themselves in us. And they don't *want* to see themselves in us because it would probably be a scary thought for them. So, we're marked as separate in a lot of ways. I recently was over in London with people I don't know that well, sound people, who didn't know that I'm a sex worker. They were showing me around the area, and they were pointing out 'oh that house, there was a murder in there'. And one of them said in such an offhand way, with no deliberate offence meant by it, that 'yeah there was a murder here, a prostitute was killed'. That, to me, just captures exactly how separate we are to them in their minds. So, they're not really supporting us in the way that they would mark other victims of violence because they don't see us as that.

The tens of thousands of women and men passing through Monto did not all have a smooth passage. How many women stood up to state intimidation and paid the ultimate price? How many became victims of violence from clients of all persuasions, from royalty to local labourers?

The jury gave Honour a pitiful 180 seconds, but they continued a too-long legacy of those involved in the sex trade being failed by the court system.

CHAPTER 16

LIGHTS OUT

Frank Duff is the man credited with closing Monto down for good on 12 March 1925, although Monto's closure was not just a matter of turning up one day and politely asking everyone to leave.

Duff set up the religious group Association of Our Lady of Mercy in 1921, aiming to provide support for women in the sex trade and in poverty, with a team of female volunteers such as Rose Scratton and Josephine Plunkett, who became involved in 1922. He describes Plunkett as a brave woman who was determined to save the women of Monto:

> Nothing could have frightened her, or perhaps it is safer to say that fear could not deter her. She was a person with a single-track mind. If there was a soul in danger, she simply went after it. . . . [She] had a wonderfully charming manner.

Renamed the Legion of Mary in 1925, the group set up a hostel called Sancta Maria at 76 Harcourt Street in Dublin and arranged religious retreats for women who wanted to leave their previous lives behind. They operated on a policy of being non-judgemental, even providing their residents with five cigarettes a day, wisely picking their battles. Duff felt that things had changed since the last attempt to close Monto in 1911, and with fewer than a hundred women suspected to still be working there, he felt the time was right in 1925 to strike again.

Duff and his female volunteers were warned not to go into Monto given its fierce reputation, with rumours of knuckledusters and broken bottles just some of the many weapons awaiting them. The idea was dismissed as an inevitable failure:

> Most scaring of all – because it ended in a gruesome query mark – a vivid picture would be thrown upon the mental screen: two Legionnaires being called into a hallway; behind them the door shuts stealthily and firmly; then nothing more is ever heard of that rash pair! Why, it almost serves them right for being such fools!

However, they were not to be deterred from their mission. They found a way in by learning of a young woman called Mary who was at death's door. They arrived to see her, found her in a bad way and arranged to send her to the lock hospital, where her life was prolonged for almost two months before she succumbed to syphilis. Her willingness to accept their help inspired them to keep going. They made twice-weekly visits to Monto and built up relationships with the women there, who surprised them by giving them a friendly welcome, with many being more than happy to accept their help. Their first foray resulted in 15 women agreeing to come to the hostel and go on one of their retreats to Baldoyle in North Dublin.

They sought out the madams, current and former, to gauge how they felt about closing Monto, and May Oblong, whom he nicknamed the Pink Leroy, did not respond well, to put it mildly:

> 'That would be madness!' she said haltingly, as if after getting her breath: 'I implore you to do nothing of the kind. For forty-five years I have lived in and around [Monto], and I know

everything about it. I could not answer for your lives for a minute if you went into it on that business. Besides, you would be wasting your time in trying to take any girl away. They would only laugh you to scorn.'

Duff realised she was still working as a costumier for Monto so May's vested interest naturally meant opposition, since she enjoyed a large income from selling or renting clothes to the women for a hefty mark-up. Most of the women said they would like to leave, but they were trapped in debt and could not go without paying off the madams and bully boys for fear of being found by them and beaten. However, some seized any chance they could get. One evening, Duff's group found themselves in a gathering of the women who were drinking methylated spirits, and in the midst of a dancing session, one woman named Marcella Dean chose her moment:

> Still grasping my arm, she whispers to me with an earnestness which was startling by contrast with her wild gyrations of a minute before. She said: 'I want to get out of this life, but I will never be able to get over to the Hostel tomorrow. Would you not take me over there with you now? It is my only chance.'

They had no space in the hostel but anxious not to let this opportunity go, Duff asked the lock hospital to take her in for the night and they happily complied. Marcella came on the retreat and was happy to leave her old life behind. She later got married to an Artie Morrie, whom Frank Duff vetted, and by all accounts lived a happy life with him.

The group's early success buoyed them up, and they were further heartened to see women turning up at the door of the hostel asking to be admitted. They were not expecting this, but quickly adapted and made space for them. They took advantage of the momentum created by the annual Catholic Lenten Mission, to be held in 1925 at a church near Monto on Marlborough Street, to step up their efforts. At this time, they reckoned there were around 40 women left, so they felt sure that it was now or never. They also had the chief commissioner of the Metropolitan Police, General William Murphy, on their side. Murphy was well connected to politicians and had helped Duff to secure the hostel and was only too happy to see Monto closed for good.

A plan was set in place to buy the madams out and turn their properties into accommodation for new tenants not connected to the area. This was key as they didn't want new madams taking over the properties. The transition was to be swift – new furniture was found, transportation organised and the tenants would be ready to move in instantly.

A madam that Duff nicknamed Mrs Curley, who had been left her empire of vice by her deceased husband, Dicker Curley, was one of the madams they approached. She had eight houses with a manageress in each one. Meeting her in the nearby Belvedere Hotel, which still stands today, she surprised them by being only too keen to leave Monto behind, crying out:

> If you could close down this place, I'd be the happiest woman in the whole world. I've been going around attending retreats to try to get back to the Church but when I come to the point about my trade, I can't get absolution at all.

She agreed to forgive the debts of the women and close her doors if the legion would pay her debt of £40, which they agreed to in exchange for her selling them the properties. She also agreed to clothe the women, as this was a barrier to them leaving because they only had bare rags covering them. She rejoiced: 'Thank God this thing is ended . . . Now, I'll be able to get back to the Sacraments.'

It was less smooth sailing when it came to other madams, however. Ned Curran was described by Duff as a sergeant major of the bully boys, enjoying enormous power and status because he lived with a madam. Unsmiling, clean-shaven and of medium build, Ned was used to intimidating people. He informed Duff that the deal was off unless he agreed to pay two holdout madams £1,500, instead of the £76 previously agreed upon. These rebellious madams were nicknamed Kitten Carr and Betty Grey, real name Polly Butler, by Frank Duff. Duff baulked at this, knowing that it was not an option, financially or morally.

A solution was quickly found in partnership with Chief Commissioner William Murphy, who agreed to a police raid of Monto. This was scheduled for midnight on Thursday 12 March. Duff and his team got to work getting the new tenants ready and envisioned them moving in the second the rooms were evicted, viewing the new tenants as 'our garrison troops, occupying and holding the territory as we filched it, room by room, from evil'. With only around five houses left as brothels at this stage, they felt confident it would be a smooth and speedy operation.

All was going to plan until 7 p.m. on Thursday, when they heard that some police officers weren't going to bother and were 'hostile', planning to merely kick some doors in and leave it at that. Duff was not lying down, however, and called in Murphy to get the police in line.

Murphy rang the superintendent in Store Street station to reaffirm the course of action:

I have just heard a firm rumour that there may be a mistake. Now in case there may be something in it, just to get a grip on this and pass it on for those concerned to digest. If anything goes wrong tonight, there is going to be a little bit of hell knocking around. Degradations, I mean – and worse. Have you got that? Spread it about and keep your eye on things. That is all.

With that warning ringing clear in their ears, the stage was set for the raid. The police were made aware of the addresses of the brothels by Duff, who describes the heart-stopping tension and speed of proceedings:

> At 12, precisely, the raid began. It was expertly organised and carried through. There was no hitch and no misfire. An immense fleet of lorries suddenly arrived on the scene and a close cordon was thrown round the entire bad area. At a signal, many parties set to work to ransack the place. By the way, some shots went off – by whom discharged I cannot say; but there was no record of anyone being hurt by gunfire. Every room was entered; and every person was made to account for himself or herself. It will be appreciated that time could not be thrown away. If a door was not opened in a reasonable interval after demand, it was just pushed off its hinges, and the forces of the law poured in, so to speak, over its dead body.

Those who fought back were subdued and brought to Store Street police station and then transferred to Bridewell station. Fifty clients were bundled into police transport, along with 45 young women and the holdouts Betty Grey, Kitten Carr and the notorious Ned Curran. This trio were tracked down by female volunteers who knew the importance of securing them.

The jovial atmosphere of Monto was replaced with panic and confusion, screaming and smashing, its wildness extinguished in a brutal, swift end.

Once the glass stopped shattering and the reality of Monto was over, the court process loomed large. The 50 or so clients and the 12 bully boys were mostly released without charge, and Duff and his volunteers advocated for the 45 women arrested to be released without charge too. Duff was aware of the rumours that some clients of note were amongst those arrested, but claimed there were no famous names on the charge sheets. Rumours suggest otherwise. Historian John Finnegan alleges a Donegal politician was present but claimed to be just there for the shebeens.

Many of the women went to the hostel and were happy to do so. Miss Carr was unrepentant in her cell, with Duff describing her as being her 'queer, sardonic self', quite unruffled by her ordeal. In stark contrast, Betty Grey, aka Polly Butler, appeared to have spent the night in tears and was full of remorse. In time, Grey was sentenced to a few months in prison and renounced her previous life. Carr got off on a technicality and disappeared, never to be seen again; rumour has it she escaped to Scotland.

Duff wasn't quite finished. Despite the fear of vengeance, the next day Duff and his female volunteers decided to go back to Monto for their usual Friday visit. They were warned of dire consequences if they set foot in Monto again, but to their welcome surprise, they survived the process and even found more women who were keen to go with them. They feared one moment of violence when Polly's daughter stormed up to them in the street. She had grown up in her mother's brothel but wasn't involved in the trade. She confronted them in quite an animated fashion before being kindly supported away by the locals:

At first we thought she was going to throw herself upon us to rend us. But for the moment she contented herself by inhuman screaming and shaking her fists at us. She was like a possessed person. Suddenly she hurled herself upon her knees, and, raising her hands to Heaven, she invoked from her children.

The incident broke the ice and the woman calmed down. Duff faced no more obstacles. The new tenants settled in and there was no room left for the madams to set up again. The rest of the plan for Monto's closure was carried out on Sunday 15 March 1925. The Church's Lenten Mission marched through Monto's streets, and every house was blessed with a picture of the Sacred Heart affixed on each former brothel door. Accompanied by missionaries carrying candles and holy water, a cross-bearer led the procession to the high wall in Monto. A crucifix was nailed into the wall by Duff after a speech from Father Mackey, symbolising the final nail in Monto's coffin and the permanent reclaiming of the area. The crucifix stayed on the wall for years and is now kept in the offices of the Legion of Mary in Dublin.

Duff reported that most of the women were happy to leave their previous lives behind, with many going on to be married. Duff acted as best man for several of these marriages. The hostel operated for decades, changing its name to the Regina Coeli, and provided support for homeless women well into the present day. Some women did continue to sell sex, since they had no other option, but it was on a more ad hoc basis than Monto's previous system of madams.

Despite his efforts, Frank Duff cannot have sole credit for closing Monto. The tide was turning against it due to the dual process of the fight for independence and the rapidly spreading influence of the Catholic Church. Duff's crusade simply rode this wave at the right time.

The strength and pace of the establishment of the Catholic Church as an instrumental and powerful force in Ireland was nicknamed the 'devotional revolution' by historian Emmet Larkin. Irish women were framed by Church and state as chaste housewives and mothers, with Catholic writer Nora O'Mahony writing in 1913: 'The true mother has no thought of self: all her life, all her love, are given to her husband and children, and after them, and because of them, to all and everything that have next most need of her.'

Attitudes towards sex were changing too. In 1875, the age of consent in Britain and Ireland was 13, which was raised to

16 in 1885, increasing to 17 in 1935. Information on birth control was banned in 1929, with birth control itself becoming illegal in 1937. Decent Catholic Irish women had to be protected from vice at all costs – even fashion magazines were blamed for corrupting them, leading them to want to dress like the English and becoming associated with the enemy. Cara Delay's research into how the Church and state joined forces has found this rebuke to the influence of the English on Irish women printed in a Catholic magazine in 1926:

> England is doing far more harm to Ireland today than ever she did in her 700 years of occupancy. What she failed to do by persecution, tyranny, and oppression, she is now accomplishing only too successfully with her *Press*, her *Spirit*, and, let me add, her *Fashions*.

The decline of the British Empire meant a lack of soldiers in Dublin. There just wasn't the same money to be made in the trade, so those who would have used Monto to survive now had to find other options.

As well as these factors, one role has been less acknowledged in the resolution of the 'problem' of Monto: the unique role of women.

CHAPTER 17

DISRUPTERS

Frank Duff may have scooped the accolades for being the one to end Monto, but he did so by standing on the shoulders of women.

Women played a multitude of roles with a far greater impact on the outcomes for the women of Monto and their peers than the man who took credit for closing it down. From the political to the personal, they stood together and alone to disrupt the controls they were subjected to and resisted the violence they experienced through building kindness and community. Many women worked tirelessly to support poorer women, especially those in the sex trade. Many of their actions helped, many of them caused harm, but it was the combination of their efforts that meant that by the time Duff arrived on the scene it was a swift finale to Monto's time on the stage. Below is a far-too-brief list of some of these advocates and adversaries. It is far from complete and is not inclusive of all the enormity of women's work that has improved their status. We must also reflect on the loss of knowledge of the actions of those we will never know, such as the efforts from those in the trade themselves and working-class women.

Alexandra College: An early adopter of the 'housing first' model that has shown success in tackling homelessness today, the school provided housing for those in the tenements and tried to address the roots of poverty for Dublin's inner-city residents.

Bridget Burke: Established Townsend Street Penitents for fallen women, which was filled with women from Monto.

Josephine Butler: Opposed the CDA and its forced examinations and drew attention to poverty and violence against women; she also helped to raise the age of consent from 13 to 16. She became the leader of the Ladies National Association in England in order to fight these laws. Josephine also nurtured dying women in their last moments in her own home and set up refuges specifically for women in the sex trade. She was religiously opposed to sex outside of marriage but felt that the law was not the right tool to tackle this moral issue, and she knew any law regulating sex would lead to targeting women, including forced examinations to 'prove' virginity. Josephine rigorously challenged the double standards of sexual purity for men and women.

Arabella Denny: Used her wealth to improve the conditions at the Foundling Hospital, saving the lives of many abandoned infants. As a result of seeing the hardship women faced, especially those in prostitution, she founded the first Magdalene asylum in Ireland in 1766. On Leeson Street, it offered a refuge to those in prostitution and set in motion a relationship that would exist for centuries. The refuge was for 'newly fallen women'; their names were taken from them as they entered, and they were considered cleansed and reborn through being bestowed with a religious name.

Anna Haslam: Established the Dublin Women's Suffrage Society in 1876, understanding that health was intimately connected with political representation.

Ellice Hopkins: Established the White Cross Vigilance Association, which operated in Monto from 1885 to 1910. Male volunteers patrolled the streets at night-time and had no hesitation in shining torches in clients' faces, bullying them into giving them their names, or bringing brothel owners to court.

Irish Women's Reform League: Opened a café and recreation centre for women, giving those working on the streets a space to drop in and access shelter and support.

Irish Workhouse Association: Attempted to bring in reforms and encourage democratic access to reform attempts, with large female participation.

Kathleen Lynn: One of the first female doctors in Ireland, Kathleen developed community care programmes to help those in need, especially children in poverty, many of whom had been born with syphilis. She co-founded the first children's hospital, St Ultan's, as she was so moved by the plight of poor children in the inner city. She was also a fellow of the Royal College of Surgeons and played a key role in the Easter Rising. Recently, there was a campaign to name the new national children's hospital after her but it was unsuccessful despite her years of hard work in improving conditions for inner-city children.

Florence Nightingale: Known mainly for her work nursing injured soldiers, Florence also publicly opposed the CDA. However, this was not for the same reasons as Josephine Butler – she blamed prostitutes for spreading disease because they were morally corrupt and therefore morally contagious as well as physically contagious. At a time when many nurses were from the lower classes and often supplemented their income through selling sex, Florence wanted stricter enforcement of anti-prostitution laws to protect the soldiers she nursed. She also established nursing training schools, whose graduates worked in workhouse infirmaries. Her designs for hospitals were implemented across the globe.

Christabel Pankhurst: Connected women's suffrage to class and prostitution and encouraged open conversations around sexual health and the status of poorer women.

Gladys Maud Sandes: Born in Dublin, at the age of 25 she became surgical registrar at the South London Hospital for Women and the London Lock Hospital. Her work with women impacted her deeply and changed how she pioneered care for vulnerable children, particularly children who were victims of sexual assault.

Marie Stopes: Established the first family planning clinic in Britain and first wildly popular sex education guide in Ireland, *Married Love*. This pamphlet allowed Irish women to practise safer birth control methods and saved countless lives.

Isabella Tod: Opposed the CDA and called attention to how they were punishing women, not men, and that women were suffering from venereal disease at an epidemic rate. She also advocated for increased education for women and campaigned for the ability for women to own property.

Mary Wollstonecraft: An early feminist advocate, Mary highlighted the hypocrisy and class structure of the medical field, as she remarked 'everything appeared to be conducted for the accommodation of the medical men and their pupils who came to make experiments on the poor, for the benefit of the rich'. Her work led to better patient advocacy and women's participation in politics.

Elizabeth Wolstenholme: Co-founded the Ladies National Association with Josephine Butler to campaign for the repeal of the CDA, saving the women of Monto from the fate of their Cork and Kildare peers.

The efforts of these women were accompanied by the Midnight Mission in the late 1890s. Based at 81 Mecklenburgh Street, the mission differed to the White Cross approach by having two women operate a drop-in centre, providing tea and chats for the women who would swing by, perhaps on their way to or from Bella Cohen's brothel next door.

Across Dublin, community groups set up by women for women offered information on employment and a space to socialise and find support. Many records and personal stories of these groups have been lost, and historian Maria Luddy laments the loss of this knowledge of community:

We know little about these societies. What relationships, for example, existed between the members of these organisations? What function did they serve in a woman's life? How did they shape women's experiences, and had their philosophy any impact on society?

The value of these spaces for groups who experience oppression, violence and marginalisation can be enormous and can play a vital role in creating positive experiences in a woman's life. They can also provide a space for autonomy and agency when the woman might not have much power or freedom outside the group. We know how much support groups can help in times of crisis, such as the Covid-19 pandemic, or poverty, where women's support groups work together in building resilience, providing support in uncertain times, and a sense of empowerment, which can offset the negative impacts of social isolation such as poor mental health and stigma.

While these activists and groups disrupted the status quo on a political level, the women of Monto looked after each other on a personal level and disrupted the violence experienced in life by nurturing each other in hard times and when one of them passed away.

In 1880s London, Marie Jean Kelly perished at the hands of Jack the Ripper and became just another 'Ripper victim'. Resisting this erasure, her friends and colleagues covered her casket in wreaths, and as a community of women, clients, drinking colleagues and friends, they gave her a proper send-off as Marie Jean, reclaiming her identity beyond 'murdered prostitute'. The women of Monto did the same, showing dignity and respect to their peers in life and in death.

Historian Patricia Lysaght gives us an idea of how the dying person was looked after by working-class communities like Monto who worked in shifts to ensure the person was never alone or left to suffer:

[They were] made as comfortable as possible in bed, and a strict vigil was kept by day and by night to ease the dying person. Food, of course, was at a minimum, but drinks were the order of the day. While the patient was conscious this was an easy matter, but when unconsciousness set in, drinks – usually of water, milk and water, brandy and water, or whiskey and water – were given to the patient with a spoon. As was often the case, the dying person sweated a lot and this was eased by applying a damp cloth or sponge to the forehead and face.

The Monto cross became an integral part of this loving care, as Martin explains:

When my mother's granny died in 1917, the priest refused to come and give her the last rites. He refused to bless her when she was dying, so someone on my father's side made a cross to go over that woman's bed. When she died it was loaned out to other families who had prostitutes who had a priest that wouldn't come to. It was on the wall of our parlour in our house in Cabra West for years. I never knew what it was. When my parents died, one of my sisters got that cross. She gave it to me with the story, and I loaned it to Terry Fagan's Museum, and I gave him the story.

The Monto cross, which brought comfort to so many and is hung up in Martin Coffey's living room in Cabra after its time in Monto came to an end.

Last rites are a religious ritual to cleanse the soul to assist the person with their ascension to heaven. Being refused this is a huge snub that, to believers, could condemn their soul, causing great distress to a dying person. The Monto cross helped these women to engage with religion on their terms, and the community of women ushered the woman into eternal rest without the humiliation of being refused the last rites by a priest from a patriarchal organisation. Instead of accepting rejection, they made their own rituals and gave respect and love to the person. This gentle care was a final exercise of agency in a final situation, when they may have had little opportunity to do so before. They were surrounded by people who didn't look down on them at their most vulnerable, and they passed away with the last memory of being with their community and where they called home. Dignity in death was a final act of resistance to the patriarchal violence that had led them to their end.

Planning a wake was taken seriously in Monto – important enough that Monto residents would bring the bodies of their loved ones back from the workhouse hospital if they had passed away there to wake them at home. While the men remained silent and sad, the women treated the occasion as a joyous celebration, drinking tea and playing games. Tommy 'Duckegg' Kirwan remembers a game that the women loved: 'if there was a policeman at the corner you had to go down and call him a name and *run back* into the wake'. It seems that they used the occasion to shake the controls over them and challenge those who normally were to be avoided. It was a safe way to express a sense of frustration at the death of yet another woman of Monto and rebel against the police.

Taken just as seriously was the funeral itself. It was another way to offer kindness and dignity to the deceased. If the deceased had no money, the other women would organise a collection amongst themselves and neighbours to pay for the funeral and even food for any family left behind. Seeing another opportunity to rebel, women also used the funeral to drink alcohol without men making them unwelcome in the pub. If they were able to set up camp there, they were hard to get rid of. One funeral driver had to wrestle the women out of the pub to get them to go home, so keen were they to make the most of a day off from restrictive social and gender norms.

The extravagant funeral tradition had been set in motion by Monto's first madam, Moll Hall, and her long-time friend Peg Plunkett, aka Margaret Leeson. Glamorous high-class madam Moll moved to Monto in the late 18th century and, whether she intended to or not, put it on the map as a growing red-light area. However, her shine and health soon faded and the debts racked up. Debt collectors were just as ruthless as madams, and they had no qualms about kicking in her door and taking everything of value, leaving her a broken and dying woman on the floor. When Peg heard about her fate, she organised an over-the-top funeral to restore some honour to Moll and make a statement. Moll's funeral had six coaches, her girls dressed in fine black attire to loudly mourn her, and Peg arranged cake, wine, tobacco and alcohol to be served on the furniture she also supplied.

A bold, unapologetic headstone was paid for by Peg for Moll's grave in St Anne's graveyard in South Dublin, which read:

Here lies honest MOLL HALL,
Who once had a great call,
And a fig for you all.
She departed this Life the 22nd of July, Anno Domini
1792, in the 49th year of her Age; and in remembrance
of her many Virtues, for she was in the actual
Possession of all but ONE, and how many great Ones
Retain that alone; her steadfast Friend and Compeer,
Margaret Leeson, of Pitt-street Nunnery, caused
this Stone, after being at the expense of her Wake
and Funeral, and many Masses for her Soul's Repose,
to be placed over her.
Requiscat in Pace

Alas, this graveyard near Tallaght is mostly in decay, with the church crumbled into scattered rocks and many inscriptions removed by weather and time, consigning Moll to history.

Peg did not follow suit, dying in poverty and having a simple funeral and grave at St James's churchyard, paid for by former clients. The last words of the legendary woman who started life as Margaret Leeson and who died as Pimpin Peg Plunkett were sombre yet defiant:

All Nature's works, now from before me fly,
Live not like Leeson, – but like Leeson die.

The appetite for loud, unapologetic funerals continued through Monto, even if others made their distaste clear. In the 1920s this defiance was present in the funeral of a woman called Mary, as described by Frank Duff:

In Glasnevin Cemetery we met Father Flanaghan at another funeral. When he saw our incredibly diversified and almost weird assortment coming along, he nearly dropped. I have seen ultra-startled looks on people's faces on several occasions; and that was certainly one of them.

Many of the women of Monto were buried in paupers' graves in Glasnevin when they passed away, their bodies brought there by a coalman and his horse and cart, which was dubbed a Dublin Corporation ambulance. Annie Carroll has a grave and head-stone in Glasnevin, while her mother, Margaret Carroll, spent her life in Canada after her release from prison for murder. Annie Meehan, once a pregnant child bride, later a glamorous, brutal madam, now rests in a grave in Glasnevin since her death on 21 August 1933. May Oblong passed away a year later in 1934. Becky Cooper was the last Monto madam to die, spending her remaining years until her death in 1949 in her Dublin Corpora-tion flat in Liberty House, which had replaced the old crumbling buildings of Monto. Mrs Dunleavy, the midwife of Monto, passed away in the 1960s.

The paupers' grave in Glasnevin has around 4,000 bodies in it, mainly those from the inner city who couldn't afford their own graves. It hit the headlines in 2017 when Glasnevin Trust revealed plans to build a car park and chapel over it. The chapel was proposed to honour the 1916 Easter Rising heroes, yet many of those buried in the paupers' grave played a role in the Rising, acknowledged or not. This plan faced pushback and was quietly abandoned.

Resistance and rebellion were not just reserved for death, however. Women used the workhouse system to their advantage in their survival. They could come in for a few days or leave chil-dren in the system, sometimes viewing the workhouse as a respite from whatever they were going through, with no plans to give up selling sex when they left. As is still the case now, some of the more desperate committed crimes to be imprisoned, which meant a roof over their heads and some food. But if they weren't looking to be imprisoned, they protested as much as they could. Magistrates remarked that the women could turn violent and refuse to cooperate. The geography of Monto was another deterrent for conducting arrests. The labyrinth of laneways was useful not just for robbing clients, but also for evading police efforts to raid or arrest the women. Even if the police did manage to successfully track down their targets, getting them back to the station was a whole other story. They could count on being attacked with any object to hand by those who didn't approve of their peers being arrested.

Many women from Monto who were convicted in the courts were given a choice between going to Mountjoy Prison or the laundries, and many chose prison because they knew they might never come out of the laundries. This shows that, even though conditions in the prison were extremely difficult, the women must have been aware of some of the horrors of the laundries, even at this early point in time. Many more women would see these horrors until the last laundries closed in the 1990s.

In the workhouse, rebellion from inmates and women deemed to be troublesome was not tolerated well. The culprits were deprived of rations, stripped and isolated in refractory wards, with no contact permitted with the rest of the residents. In some incidents, teenage girls teamed up together to take on the staff, necessitating police intervention. They could be punished by being sent to the refractory ward for days at a time, and in some cases the girls were sent to prison – the South Dublin Union sent almost 500 girls to Mountjoy Prison over the course of 11 years. After their release, some ended up in Monto and some ended up back in the workhouse as they had few other options – the rebellions gave the workhouse girls the reputation of being difficult to manage, making them less attractive to employers. Riots and rebellions became a feature in the South Dublin workhouse, with records showing riots from 1857 to 1862, with some girls leaving and coming back on a frequent basis, only too happy to rejoin the rioters. The girls also showed a sense of agency in how they rebelled against the prescribed uniform of the workhouse. They adjusted their uniforms, styled their hair how they wanted and refused to wear hats, which caused frustration amongst the staff. Multiple efforts to quash the girls' rebellious spirits failed.

In 1847, most children in the workhouse were aged around 15, making them adults as Monto emerged in the 1860s or the mothers of those who found their way to Monto a little later.

During the fight for independence, Monto was frequented by revolutionaries planning the Easter Rising; the women passed information from their British clients to Irish freedom fighters, and shebeens and brothels became safe houses for revolutionaries and weapons. Pearl was told by her grandfather that her great-grandmother Annie Meehan deliberately sent girls who had syphilis to

British soldiers for free. Many of the women married Irish soldiers and sheltered them while playing an active role as intelligence agents, with IRA leader Dan Breen remarking, 'The lady prostitutes used to pinch the guns and ammunition from the auxiliaries or Tans at night then leave them for us at Phil Shanahan's public house.'

The women also resisted the stigma from other patients while being treated for venereal disease. One of the lock doctors noted that the contempt shown by the medical staff towards the women resulted in violent pushback and awakened a 'fierce spirit of resistance' in them. One lock hospital matron in Manchester was found drinking with the women in their brothels when they were outside the lock, as well as drinking with them in the kitchen of the lock when they came in as patients.

Pearl's great-great-grandmother helped the women that worked for her to avoid the lock at the end of their days:

> There was this story in my family that a lot of the girls became quite unwell with syphilis, and they were taken up to Portrane, which was a mental institution. Some of them were older women who just had no way of looking after themselves, they were vulnerable, with what we'd probably see now as special needs. And so they were sent up there, almost like a modern-day retirement home. I suppose to me I always thought it sounded horrific until I started looking into it and realising that was quite humane, as they would have ended up in the lock hospital or the streets otherwise.

Stigma and rejection were not always calmly accepted, and women found ways to rebel or live outside a system determined to control them through culture, law or religion. Luddy notes that many women changed their names often to elude the authorities and moved around to evade arrest or to start again on new terms. The use of language is another way the women rebelled in Monto. While others called it the Digs or the Kips, the residents called Monto 'the Village', making it a place of support, community and home, as Martin explains:

> The Monto to me was very much like a small village, because we all came from the same area. It was only when I talked to others about different stories about my parents that they told me their families knew mine, there's connections everywhere and even in some of the photographs they would say 'that's my dad eating off your family's table'. So, to me it was a village within Dublin.

Creating their own community was a way to escape judgement from the outside world and to survive amongst like-minded people who *got* it and offered support instead of stigma. One social reformer remarked of these communities: 'On her soul lay the knowledge of the *horror* of respectable society towards what she had become and the *attraction* of the fellowship of those who would receive her freely.' Many of those in Monto were teenagers and young women and bonded over the same shared interests as their peers outside the sex trade. They had negative times, of course, but they also enjoyed shopping together for clothes they may never have been able to access otherwise, a sense of freedom that may not have been present in a restrictive family or in environments like the workhouse – and certainly not in the laundries. They could meet men that they some- times went on to marry and form a network of friends in similar circumstances to support them in hard times. They may also have been able to explore their sexuality in a way that wasn't safe to do at home, whether that sex was with clients or colleagues. If they were able to move to the position of madam, they had access to wealth beyond their wildest dreams when growing up. Monto was a space where exploitation was common, but it could also be a space of liberation and a pathway to a better life. This whirlwind of circumstance, violence and potential brought the women of Monto together to survive and even thrive as a community.

Modern research shows that residents of red-light districts are more annoyed at the secondary effects of the sex trade, such as alcohol use and unsavoury men making the area feel unsafe, rather than merely blaming the women themselves. The locals in Monto viewed the women as people to help, not judge:

> We'd pass them standing on the street corners and they would say hello to us, we would say hello, they weren't bad women. They had to live like everyone else. You got nothing for nothing, they had to pay for everything like everyone else I suppose.

Paddy McCormack, who grew up in Monto, supports this view: 'They weren't bad girls; they were unfortunate girls.' Because they did not face judgement from the everyday residents of Monto, they were able to build an inclusive space where they could access community support in a variety of ways. This support was immensely important for surviving tough times and influenced the women's ability to live life on their own terms, within the confines of poverty and the madams' controls. Local women also stepped in if they saw a woman on the streets being mistreated, as resident Diana Preston recalls:

> My mother, she feared no man. Well, this day I was going up to the yard to my mother in Purdon Street and, as I turned into the lane off Purdon Street, there was this man punching one of the girls around. I called for my mother and when she came down the lane she had this big sweeping brush in her hand. She charged at him with the brush and beat him around the place with it, telling him, 'There's no need to hit her like that!'

Sometimes survival was as simple as being allowed to come into the warmth of someone's home or hallway and dry off wet clothes while being warmed by a cup of tea and kindness. Elizabeth 'Blue-bell' Murphy, who grew up in Monto, stated no one was ever alone and that, given the choice, she would prefer to go back to living in a close-knit community like Monto because the community spirit was so nurturing.

Martin Coffey's story of the life of a young woman called Ginger Kate highlights how this acceptance could literally mean life or death. Kindness was present even in the most extreme poverty and cramped living conditions:

My granny married and moved into No. 11 Elliott Place. The front parlour was about a foot longer than a single bed and no wider than a double bed; they couldn't get a double bed in because it would take up too much space. So there was a single bed that my grandmother and her husband slept in. My mother, her sister, and her brother slept on a foldout armchair in the corner. A fireplace in it, they did all the cooking on the fire. They sat on the bed to have their dinner.

There was a prostitute called Ginger Kate, maybe late twenties or early thirties, who used to sleep on the floor at the top of the stairs every night. My grandfather said to my granny, 'Jesus, we can't leave her there, for God's sake the poor woman, bring her in, bring her in.' So, she came and lived in that small room and she lived under the small kitchen table. During the day she would look after my mother and her siblings, while my granny went out working cleaning houses up on Mountjoy Square and my granddad went down the docks looking for work. When they came in, she'd go out on the game at night.

When women who worked in the brothels became pregnant, many ended up sleeping rough in the hallways of tenements in the area and were looked after by local women who helped to deliver their babies and even sometimes brought them up as their own. These children were known as 'Monto babies', and Martin Coffey remembers the families of Monto treated them with kindness, knowing the desperation of the mothers and the harshness of the orphanages.

> My mother played in the streets with many of these children and sat next to them in school. Her own mother often '*took in*' some of these children while their mothers were in prison and the children would all cuddle up together in the same bed each night, sleeping on a sack filled with straw.

Part of being a good Catholic was looking after each other, and tenement life meant a communal life and making sure everyone had enough to survive. The families who took in the children gave them the family surname. Many of the birth mothers had first-hand experience of the harshness of the workhouse, so they preferred to leave their babies in the community that had shown them kindness than at the workhouse. If they didn't give up their babies, they could end up in a mother and baby home or separated from their child and locked up in the Sean McDermott Street Laundry. It was an act of survival rather than one of callous abandonment. Gemma Dunleavy shares with us how the Granny Dunleavy carried out her work of helping the women give birth:

> I remember the stories of me auntie saying that a knock would come on the door at all hours of the night. Grandad used to be going mad because sometimes he was woken up at 4:00 in the morning to the bedsheets getting whipped off the bed trying to get as many sheets as possible. She always had sheets on the go, washing and drying them and she didn't have any washer-dryer. She stood up to the madams and the bully boys in order to help the women of Monto deliver their

babies. She wasn't even five feet four tall but was strong and determined to help the women. She wouldn't ever have a new baby not having clean sheets.

Many of the women selling sex who became mothers gave up their babies, but some did not and tried to manage selling sex and parenthood. Sometimes they got enough money to get out of Monto for good, and sometimes their child became another Monto baby. Pearl Brock's great-great-grandmother Annie Meehan took in young women that arrived in Dublin already pregnant. These women were vulnerable to being exploited or being sent to a laundry, so Annie had her bully boys hang around the train station to find them, and she offered them jobs as nannies rather than have them end up in the laundries:

> They were nannying for her children and for other family members. Because my grandmother would say that 'ah they'd left their husbands behind'. They were looked after, they were given a decent wage, room and board. One of the things that I remember asking my granny about was what happened to them when they had their babies. My granny said she always believed that the girls were sent to America with their babies and given fake marriage certs, telling them to say that the husbands had died in the war, so that they could avoid the stigma of being an unmarried mother. Ah, she was really a powerhouse in looking after the girls.

Martin's great-grandmother did the same for women that were trying to leave the trade. Pearl also remembers her granny talking about Annie's acts of kindness towards the women, in particular one who had a physical disability and felt it hindered her ability to attract clients:

The girl said, 'Nobody wants me, I'm of no use, I don't make money, I'm this, that, and the other.' And Annie said, 'You're valuable, this is how much,' and gave her this fur collar. And seemingly it was from her wedding dress, a little white rabbit fur collar on her wedding dress. Now the girl probably sold it or whatever, but it made her feel special. My great-grandfather replaced it for her, and now I have it.

Those who were in demand could find their fortunes changed for the worse in an instant, but madams like Annie stepped in to help some of them, as Pearl recounts:

There was one story of one of the girls who worked for another madam, and she was seen as hot property because she never got pregnant. And two madams were actually fighting over her. One of them threw scalding oil or something over the other one and the girl herself got burned on the hands. And she was one of the ones that Annie Meehan took in and got her sent off to a man who had a big house and was looking for a young bride. He had lots of kids because his wife had died and didn't want any more. There just seemed to be something about Annie where she was cognitive of the hardships, she just seemed to have something in her that was kind; she was like a little woman on a mission.

The Meehans had properties around Dublin and Wicklow and used them to make money from the women not only through sex, but also through housekeeping work, as Pearl describes:

Some of the women had already had their faces slashed, making them no good for the sex trade as they would be unable to draw in clients. They would send them off to these houses and they'd work as housekeepers, just to keep them safe. And it was weird because I remember saying to my granny, 'How do you tell a prostitute what to do?' And my granny said you had to remember that they owned them. She said you might not like hearing this, but it was like slavery, it was like these girls had nothing else, they couldn't do anything else for themselves. She said you might not like hearing that because you want to romanticise it, but these women were owned. So, if there were girls that were of high value it was cheaper or better to send them off down the country for a few months and put them in service. It was also a way to clear up any diseases because they'd clear up for a couple of months and then they'd come back, and they'd be grand. It sounds bad because they didn't get paid, but they got room and board. My granny said a lot of them would be jumping at it because it was a chance to go and just kind of be, to not have to sell sex and just to get a break.

Everyday community life in Monto also involved chatting with neighbours on the doorsteps as they waited for trade, and if the women had extra cash, they would buy clothes, shoes or treats for the children, endearing them further to the Monto community. They would also ask the local children to run errands, such as buying alcohol or cigarettes, and give them a few pennies – which could mean the difference between a good meal or going hungry. Tommy 'Duckegg' Kirwan remembers the kindness of the women:

But the girls were very good, they were generous. They were very fond of kids. If you went for a message for them, you'd get thruppence or sixpence. If they seen a kid running around in his bare feet they'd bring him into Bretts' and buy him a pair of runners . . . the girls were generous.

253

The women did not allow the local children to see too much and encouraged them to go home if they were working. Monto resident Billy Dunleavy remembers the women fondly:

> If they saw any of the children coming along the street where they were working, they would say, 'Go home, boy,' and they would give them a penny or two pennies. They would not allow them down while they were bargaining with the men in the street. Ah, be God, they were gentle girls, kind-hearted too, they were. It was sad to see the way the madams treated them.

Terry highlights how the women would support others in Monto even if they hadn't much themselves. One former resident, Georgie Smith, was saved from having to pawn his families' clothes by a woman known as Belfast Bella:

> Belfast Bella said, 'What are you up to?' He says, 'I'm going to pawn my grandmother's shawl.' And she said, 'Look, stand there,' goes over to the other girls working in the lane, got a shilling each off of them and gave it to him to bring back the shawl, and said, 'The winter is coming, your granny is going to need it.'

If the rent money for the neighbouring families was a little short, they clubbed together to help out, often without the family even knowing – it was just something that had to be done. Empty sugar bags were used to collect contributions across the community, and they also supported each other to pay fines to keep themselves out of prison, or shared the details of doctors who could help them with abortions or ailments. Similarly, in London they had little, but they shared money, clothes and tips for attracting the best clients and helped each other look their best.

The women of Monto knew the stories of surviving the Famine and knew the vital lifeline of other women sharing their food or giving them whatever support they could, no matter how small. The earlier women of Monto may have experienced the Famine directly and taken that sense of communal survival into the brothel. That community spirit passed on to the women who grew up in Monto who treated the working girls well. This could be as small as giving the women a cup of tea in a jam jar called 'tenement china', and this simple act of kindness was always appreciated, with one woman receiving her tea with a cry of 'The blessing of God on you. Ah my life on you, girl'. Many families also left out coats and sacks for the women to cover themselves with if they had to sleep on the streets or in tenement hallways.

Woman cleaning cup in her yard, keeping the tenement dirt at bay.

Alcohol was also shared, as were pots of cooked food such as boiled cabbage. William Logan, on his travels around Victorian British red-light districts, noted that the women were 'very free with intoxicating liquors' in order to keep their neighbours onside. Most Victorian upper-class societies preferred for women selling sex to be as invisible as possible, but in Monto, they were not only seen but also welcomed into community life. This welcome was important not in terms of survival but in terms of self-esteem, as people who experience marginalisation and exclusion can have poorer mental health as they face extra hurdles and an increased risk of violence.

Tommy 'Duckegg' Kirwan, who lived next door to madam Polly Butler, remembers the madams often helping those in need:

> Now May Oblong, she'd see you down-and-out and she'd help you. She had a big heart. [. . .] If you hadn't any food she'd give it to you on the slate but she wouldn't charge you a lot of money for it, instead of going to these money lenders.

While May Oblong may have been generous to kids and the community, the madams were often resented because they were seen as taking advantage of the women, with May Oblong also having a reputation for slashing the women's faces. The madams did employ people to clean their brothels, so they provided an essential source of income for many locals. However, the locals who took those jobs faced stigma from the community, as resident Chrissie Ryan recalls:

> They were called 'brothel washers'. I only heard the word on the street when I was a bit older. I heard one woman shouting at another, 'Go on now and give yourself a good wash you brothel washer.' The women in those days could cut a person in two with their tongues. They had no time for those that lived off the poor women.

Tommy 'Duckegg' Kirwan's mother was one of these 'brothel washers' as she needed the money to survive.

In the Famine, those who took advantage of others' distress, as well as those who lived well while others struggled to survive, were resented. If this feeling was widespread in the countryside, it must have been intensified if the person you viewed as taking advantage was living next door and probably owned your building too. It also combined with having to bring children in at night-time to protect them from seeing the goings-on. Community spirit was strong in Monto, and since sitting outside talking to each other while the children played had to be curtailed, it must have bred resentment.

The local people knew the hardships the women faced in the laundries and supported them to leave if they could. In an interview for the *Dublin Inquirer*, two Monto residents, Tony and Betty Dunleavy, shared their experience of helping a young woman who had attempted to escape the Sean McDermott Street Laundry but became entangled in barbed wire. Freeing her, they took her in, fed her and, most importantly, hid her as they knew a search party would be out looking for her:

> I could see their determination, the nuns. This was the money aspect. Here was a slave worker that earned [money] for them. . . . We felt that we'd done a good thing, Betty and I, . . . that we'd done the humane thing.

The sensing of this unnamed fear continued through to Gemma's childhood where she used to attend mass in the laundries' chapel:

> It was the most eerie feeling I've ever had in my life, especially being there as a kid, and when I was there as a kid, I never liked it. I'd say to me Ma, please don't bring us to mass, I don't want to go to mass, and I loved mass. When I

was younger I was a little Bible basher, but I didn't like going there. I just did not like it. It was mad because, like, I didn't know what was going on back then. I just knew if you were bold you got put in there.

The community spirit of Monto was also found in the Curragh Wrens, the women who lived together outside the Curragh army barracks. They also shared their money and minded each other's children, not just for altruistic principles, but for survival. If the women couldn't go into the barracks, they couldn't earn money, so it was in all their best interests to get on well together and support each other. They also provided emotional support for one another in tough times, helping with folk cures for venereal disease and support after sexual violence.

We have lost so much knowledge of how the women of Monto kept each other safe through community, but we know that mutual aid in marginalised communities such as Monto is essential for survival. Sophie, a sex worker who has worked on the streets of Dublin, highlights how those selling sex look out for each other, reminding us that the sense of community built up in Monto has continued today:

Even in the worst of circumstances, if one of the women was out and clearly not in a condition to be able to work, we'd all have a whip around and we'd all give her money so that she didn't have to work. There was that care for each other which makes life a lot easier and a lot less lonely, especially when you're in really difficult times. We looked after each other without even saying anything. Like, if you'd been out and you knew you had enough money and you could make more if you stuck around a bit longer, but you noticed one of the other girls hadn't got a single job yet, you might just leave, just say nothing but you'll leave so that she can pick up the next job.

Izzy also shares how community helped them keep safer when they were involved in sex work:

> I had a need and desire for a connection, for an understanding from other people who understood the situation I was in, who understood the reason that I was going into sex work or doing sex work. And I found a lot of strength in that and I found a sense of community at a time when none of us had a community around. So it was so, so good for me to be able to meet those people even virtually at that time – I found it incredibly empowering. I was also aware of the dangers of sex work and the things that could go wrong, and things did go wrong and things did nearly go wrong on multiple occasions, but it was because of the community and the connections that I had created online that I knew what to look out for. I knew what red flags to watch for, I knew how to try to keep myself safe, I knew how to report content that was reposted without my consent. All those little tips and tricks aren't available as general knowledge for people who aren't . . . in the sex work community. Everyone that I spoke to, that I DM or texted, always had like a little piece of information or a tip to give. They always had something, they never ignored me. I don't think I ever had a text ignored by a sex worker when I was asking for advice or asking for help.

Nowadays, rebellion and resistance come in many forms, such as the *Sex Workers' Opera*, using songs and performances by sex workers to highlight the realities of their lives. In 2023 the first Red Umbrella Film Festival was held in Dublin, which featured films made by sex workers. Another form of resistance to violence is the Ugly Mugs initiative, operating as a way for sex workers to warn each other of violent clients and keep each other safe.

Resistance is found in colour and fabric too. From Monto to *Mean Girls*, pink has been associated with femininity and used as a colour of resistance. The 1860s mauveine decade of Monto resurfaced and reconfigured itself in the decade of millennial pink, the 2010s. This bright shade of pink became associated with feminism, popularity, sexuality, girl-bossing, ironic cuteness and online community. It has been interpreted as feminine, erotic, childish, kitsch, sophisticated and transgressive, showing us how the femininity of the colour pink and all its shades is still subject to dismissal or used in resistance. In India today, gangs of women strolling around in pink might be part of the Gubai Gang, a female collective that threatens violence towards abusive husbands and isn't shy about following through on their threats. Protesters on the 2017 Women's March on Washington DC donned a pink hat with ears, called it the pussy hat, and used it to make a collective visual impact on marches. Pink made its biggest splash this decade with the 2023 juggernaut that was *Barbie*, a movie that harnessed the power of pink to spread its message of feminism – or, as a more cynical mind might think, get social media users to do its marketing for it through user-generated viral memes. Whatever the reason, the result was groups of women bringing family and friends along to see it and spending time thinking about gender norms and feminism via an accessible pop culture format, united in pink.

Frank Duff might have hammered in the last nail, but it came down to the formidable May Oblong to make Monto's last stand.

In Monto's last days, May, nicknamed the Pink Leroy by Duff, turned up to a meeting with Duff, a priest called Father Mackey, and his gang of volunteers and priests to discuss closing down her operations. Despite her advanced age of being in her late sixties, May flexed her sartorial muscles to make a statement about her power and bow out in style:

She drove up to that place in an opulent-looking equipage, an affair like a brougham [a carriage with the driver outside and customer enclosed], with a high-stepping horse and a liveried driver. She did not own such an outfit, so presumably it was hired for the occasion. She descended from it, a commanding figure – she was about six feet in height, expensively yet quietly and tastefully dressed . . .

May played a verbal game of cat and mouse with them for four long hours, telling them that they didn't know anything about the ways of men and Monto, and did it in such a clever way that Duff felt he was facing defeat and was left scrambling:

She treated us as four naughty boys. [. . .] Oh! She was making a proper fool of us. [. . .] She was one of the worst elements in the whole place.

Eventually, Father Mackey lost his cool and shouted her into submission. Humbled, she agreed to forgive the debts of the women and close up shop. Duff delightedly remarked that

The Pink Leroy that finished up the session was a very chastened person from her who opened it. She who had entered like a supercilious lion went out gentle as a lamb with mint sauce.

Sadly, we will never know what May said to them or what exactly was so powerful about the priest's speech that took the wind out of her sails. Her fierce reputation may have meant some choice words, but Duff, through his lack of note taking, ensured they are lost to history.

CHAPTER 18

ETHICAL REMEMBRANCE

Today, we can walk on the same cobblestones of Monto as the women in this book. While people drive over them in cars now, they are still the very same cobblestones the jarveys raced down as they delivered customers to the flash houses. On his tour, Terry tells his tales of personally saving those cobblestones from Dublin City Council, who tried to remove them for use elsewhere in the city, while his tour guests follow him on those same streets today. The remains of the laundry still dominate Railway Street – still standing, still closed off, still foreboding, its cross a stern reminder of what could happen if you were not a good Catholic woman.

The Monto area is still very multicultural, with a bricolage of accents heard on the wind as Terry's born-and-bred Monto accent regales his audience in front of the former entrance to Madam Oblong's shop. One solitary house on Beaver Street is the only dwelling left. The area is now totally revamped, with a park, a museum, modern flat complexes and smaller council homes from the 1930s and 1940s. Its winding laneways that bordered crumbling tenements and two-story houses with open door policies are consigned to the past. Dismantled and discarded, Monto is almost invisible, remaining only in these few physical spaces and the artefacts held by Terry and the rest of the descendants.

But Monto is not just physical. Monto is in the blood of its descendants. It is political, social, cultural, genetic, medical, traumatic and feminist. It's a way to think about similar issues today, so perhaps the suffering that was common in Monto can be prevented from happening again – not through violence or speaking over people, but by listening with compassion and working equally to make women safer.

As discussed in Chapter 12, the women of Monto, like their peers across the British Empire, were experimented on, eventually leading to the invention of the modern treatment for syphilis. The experiments they were subjected to, potentially unknowingly and non-consensually, sparked a chain of events that led to the modern-day healthcare system in the UK and even to chemotherapy, used to treat cancer today. The dissections that they were often subjected to in death, under Irish law, informed the world of anatomy and improved medical knowledge. Their bodies saved millions from painful deaths. They also played a role in the fight for Irish independence and left their mark on the pages of literature, on the music and art worlds, and on feminism.

Are these dramatic claims? Well, yes – but they are also true.

In 1911, there was a substantial shift in the number of admissions to the Westmoreland Lock Hospital. This was not only due to Monto's general decline, but also because it was the year that Salvarsan was invented by Paul Ehrlich. While not a cure for syphilis, it relieved symptoms extremely well and allowed sufferers to take medicine at home instead of needing a bed in the lock for months. Salvarsan kept the troops on the battlefield instead of in the hospital, ensuring enough manpower to win wars.

Ehrlich became known as the father of chemotherapy, but this accolade would not have been possible without the experimentation on women in the sex trade. Perhaps, neither would the Nobel Prize awarded to Alexander Fleming in 1945, who discovered penicillin, which replaced Salvarsan. The first use of penicillin against syphilis in 1943 saved millions of lives in World War II that would have been felled by the brothel, not the battlefield. Professor Robert M. Kaplin believes that syphilis has not just impacted the field of medicine but has also changed the course of history and had one of the greatest influences of any illness. While a bold claim, it is likely an accurate one, since syphilis has made its way into the 21st century despite our best efforts to eradicate it.

Due to being more likely to end up in workhouses and other institutions, the women of Monto were more likely to be subject to the enforcement of the Anatomy Act, which mandated that paupers and those in receipt of relief should repay their debts by the use of their corpse for dissection by surgeons in order to understand the body's internal anatomy. Historian Anne Hanley also claims that because of the advances in medicine and science as a result of the experimentation on the women of the lock, the foundations for the modern-day National Health Service (NHS) were laid, showing the strength of their impact decades later.

The women of the lock and Monto have shaped the course of history. But we have learned from them without acknowledging them. It wasn't just the madams who got rich off the women: it was also the doctors who experimented on them without their consent or knowledge. Wealth wasn't just monetary: being seen to campaign for the improvement of the poor unfortunates of the lower classes was a way to access upper- and middle-class social capital. Dr Chaplin from both the Westmoreland and Kildare Lock Hospitals and Dr Richard Carmichael from the Westmoreland Lock held the post of president of the Royal College of Surgeons in Ireland, enjoying a high level of respect and status personally and professionally. Men such as Dr Richard Carmichael had buildings named after them, while Monto's buildings were consigned to history as well as the rubbish dump.

The fact that the women of the lock were subject to experimentation is part of the far-too-long history of the state inflicting harm on women in Ireland. Over 23,000 babies and young children were subjected to vaccine trials in mother and baby homes. As with the lock many records for these children were not available and survivors faced a hard battle to find the truth and still do today. In the 1940s, yet another medical violation became part of women's lives with symphysiotomy. Over 40 years, 1,500 women in Ireland were left with lifelong pain and complications from doctors sawing their pelvic bones during childbirth without their knowledge or consent. Women have also shared their experiences of finding out they had been given a 'husband stitch' after childbirth without their consent. This stitch 'tightened' the vagina for the man's pleasure but left the woman with debilitating pain amongst other disabling effects.

Things have not been much better outside of Ireland. In Tuskegee, Alabama, a number of working-class Black men were told they did not have syphilis when they in fact *did* in order to 'study' how the disease developed. They did not receive medication and it was passed to their wives, who gave birth to dozens of stillborn babies because of congenital syphilis. Over 100 of the men died as a result of their infection. To add more salt to this gaping wound inflicted by state and medical cruelty, this study ran from 1932 to 1972 but penicillin, the modern treatment for syphilis, had been invented and was available ten years after the start of this study – it was still carried on for an extra 30 years of racially fuelled violation. The racism and classism of the agencies involved allowed them to see the participants as less worthy of human rights – they targeted those they knew they could get away with treating brutally and fatally.

The plight of the women in the lock also cemented the beginnings of organised feminism in Ireland. Women came together to protest the CDA, advocating for sexual health and the safety and protection of women selling sex. Groups such as the Ladies National Association, Cumann na dTeachtaire, Irish Women's

Suffrage and Local Government Association, and the Irish Women's Franchise League worked together to resist the extension and continuation of the acts in the face of stark oppression. The mobilisation of women's groups against the CDA led them to campaign further on knowledge about sexual health and sowed the seeds of political participation as they connected bodily autonomy and poverty with the right-to-vote campaign. The women of Monto made sacrifices, and they deserve to be acknowledged. How do we pay tribute to those confined to these institutions or who succumbed to violence?

One way we can honour them is to embody what Irish people have practised for centuries: Machnamh. A compassionate concept, Machnamh means reflection, meditation, thought and contemplation, allowing for a multitude of narratives to be heard and for remembrance to be thoughtful and ethical. The women of Monto were many things, and were victims and perpetrators of violence, but they were as human as anyone else, and their lives ultimately changed the lives that came after them.

Because of the fight by Aboriginal people, we can also look to Australia for an example of Machnamh and ethical remembrance.

In the early 20th century, between 1908 and 1919, 800 Aboriginal men, women and children were transported to a lock hospital in Port Hedland, Western Australia, in chains on the excuse of treating venereal disease. Numbers vary, but between 20 per cent and 40 per cent of this group died there and were buried in unmarked graves. The building was later used as a nursing home, with the mortuary turned into a storeroom. Records were barely kept and little survived. Like the women of Westmoreland Lock in Dublin, the inmates were blamed for spreading the disease, and they were also subjected to experimental medical procedures, using mercury injections that had devastating side effects. Just as the women under the CDA were forced into these institutions because they were the wrong kind of woman, the Aboriginals were forced in because they were the wrong kind of race. This institution was described as a space of 'misery, horror unalleviated, and tombs of the living dead', created by white settlers solely for the Aboriginals.

Due to grassroots efforts, the lock hospitals were registered as protected areas under the 1986 Aboriginal Heritage Act, meaning that they have been preserved and memorials can be built while the truth is further uncovered. Kathleen Musulin, a great-granddaughter of one of the women buried at the lock hospital in Port Hedland, explains why lock hospitals need to be talked about and kept alive in oral traditions:

> It's important, not only for myself, but it's important for my children and grandchildren to know what happened to their ancestors. It's important for other families because of the trauma and the hurt that we have suffered, knowing what happened to our ancestors and the horrific things that were done to them.

Some parts of the building complex still exist today, and there are calls to excavate the bodies and uncover what was done to these people.

Back in Ireland, for those women that ended their Monto experience confined in the Sean McDermott Street Laundry and died there, there is a plot in Glasnevin Cemetery. However, the Justice for Magdalenes Research group has found the names of women unaccounted for, raising questions about who is really buried in this plot and where the missing women are.

A ground radar scan of the Sean McDermott Street Laundry was done in the 1990s, with no bodies found. But in 1993 in High Park in Drumcondra, where many women of Monto ended up, there was a different result. A mass grave was discovered when the site was being developed. Out of 133 women originally identified, only 75 death certificates were available. The nuns did not even know who was truly buried there, while being quite happy to sell off the land for millions. Instead of allowing the bodies to be examined, they cremated them quickly and buried them in a mass grave in Glasnevin Cemetery.

While shocking, burial on property grounds appears to have been common practice in at least a few Catholic institutions, with survivors of Bessborough House in Cork calling for the investigation of its grounds for the unmarked graves of children. The graves of the nuns and the women who died behind their walls were kept separate, for fear of contamination even in death.

The sheer violence perpetrated on those contained within these institutions is slowly coming to light, despite resistance and silence from the orders that ran them. As we continue to uncover mass graves and more injustices and violations in Ireland, the more we should recognise the need to protect the most marginalised in our communities today. An entire chapter of the McAleese Report on the laundries discusses the issue of deaths, burials and exhumations, but books upon books could, and should, be written about what's missing. Even in 2024, victims of these institutions still have to fight to receive justice, remorse, recognition and compensation.

We can also learn from the example set by over a hundred volunteers in a tiny sliver of the metropolis that is London. Before its closure in 1853, the Crossbones graveyard in London was the final resting place of 15,000 paupers, many of them sex workers and single mothers. They had been forgotten about until the graveyard was uncovered during excavations for the London Underground in 1996. Volunteers John Constable and Katy Nicholls worked for decades to restore the graveyard as a space to remember the outcast dead. Monthly vigils at 7 p.m. on the twenty-third of the month have been held since 2004, and a group

called Friends of Crossbones continues the graveyard's maintenance and memory. Now, it is filled with trinkets, flowers, art,
poems and ribbons galore.

Jennifer Cooper has been volunteering at Crossbones for
over 15 years and has been crucial in its transformation from
a neglected, overgrown wasteland to a space of remembrance
for the people who ended up there. She became involved when
she felt connected with the spiritual activism of the vigils, but
she also had a personal connection to the site through her
grandparents:

> When they wanted to get married, nobody approved of
> them because Nanny was too low down the social scale
> and Granddad was too Catholic. So they did what every-
> body did, they ran away. Where they ran to was what
> they always called the outlaw borough, Southwark. They
> married in a church that was just round the corner from
> where Crossbones is now. So I feel very much, for me, that
> *this* is *my* place of the ancestors.

Understanding the horrors that the graveyard's inhabitants must
have endured, Jennifer recounts one case that highlights the hardship of survival in the 19th century:

> The Museum of London was allowed to conduct a two-week
> dig and they took away 148 skeletons. One of those skele-
> tons was from the 1850s, and her skull showed she was a
> teenager aged between 16 and 19. Syphilitic lesions were
> burned into her very skull. According to medical research,
> she was not born with syphilis, but she was reinfected
> constantly with syphilis from the age of about six. That
> one skull is so descriptive of the type of life of the people
> who lived around Crossbones. Southwark was one of the

very poorest areas of London; it must have literally been like the Wild West.

Southwark also had a lock hospital – in fact, it was the very first lock hospital built, dating from the 12th century. Treating the lepers that gave the hospital its original nickname, Southwark Lock closed in 1760 but its name lived on in the London Lock Hospital, which would go on to play its part in the development of syphilis treatment and the regulation of the sex trade.

Jennifer's style of activism is inclusive and religion-free, and the Machnamh of Crossbones offers us a way to think about how we honour people, especially the 'wrong' kind of people:

> With the vigil we're not just remembering people. We honour the outcast. That's the outcast in the outside world, but of course, it honours the outcast within us as well. We've all got our secret places that we don't want to show anybody. The things that we don't like about ourselves. And so the difference is the honouring, as opposed to just creating a physical space. The difference between remembering and memorialising is that in remembering we put them back together again. We turn them into people. We remember that they are people with lives and they're not just a massive, scrabbling misery. They would have been vibrant. I'm a South London girl. I know Southwark, it's loud even now. The vigil says that transformation is possible. Crossbones Garden itself is the physical manifestation of that. However long it takes, however hard the work, transformation is possible.

In her seventies and widowed now, Jennifer finds peace in reflecting on what it means to be connected to others, even after death, in a place as special as Crossbones:

Everything in Crossbones is not only exactly what it is, but it also holds a deeper meaning. My son is dead, and now his photograph hangs on the gates. He smiles into Crossbones and for me that is an image of the Paradise Garden, heaven. In eternity, we are never separate, so I practise being eternal by sitting with my back to the gates underneath my Gary's photograph and we both smile for eternity into the Paradise Garden.

Machnamh is a way to free people's truth and knowledge and remove it from the confinement of institutional walls, official records or solely the mouths of others outside the community itself. This way of remembrance and honouring is a way of keeping people and history alive. Terry's weekly tour through Monto honours the women without sensationalising them, and in 2023 artist Ruby Wallis combined St Bridget's Day with a feminist walking tour of Monto. These tours offer glimpses into the reality behind the headlines.

Another example of ethical remembrance can be seen in the International Day to End Violence Against Sex Workers, which is held on 17 December. This was created by sex workers to call for legal change and remembrance of sex workers who died by violence and as a way to draw attention to the violence committed against them, including exclusion and stigma. In Dublin, candlelit vigils have been held by Sex Workers Alliance Ireland (SWAI) outside the Dáil, with the names of murdered sex workers in Ireland read out and their lives remembered.

Sophie, who helped organise the Red Umbrella Film Festival, feels it is an important day on many levels:

There's other days like the International Sex Workers' Day and there's Sex Worker Pride Day, but I've never had much interest in marking or celebrating those days. But December seventeenth is important for me and it's because it's community-focused and it's a day of remembrance. I've lost a lot of friends over the years that died way too young, that should never have died in the ways that they did. But it's also a day to rally and come out and demand more for ourselves. And that's really important to me, you know – we can stand outside the Dáil or outside the Department of Justice and say what's happening to us is wrong, what you're doing to us is wrong. And we've lost too many of our community already to this. And those people should never be forgotten, you know. That's part of what a community is for me; community has a memory, you know. And we need to keep that alive. And those people are part of that memory, so yeah, it's really important to me.

The people of SWAI held a banner-making workshop in December 2023 to use art to express their concerns, frustrations, resistance and fears. This artistic approach allows for the building of community and a communal way to honour those who have lost their lives to violence. As SWAI's coordinator Mardi Kennedy outlined at this event, it's a difficult but important day to mark:

It's a really hard time. Are we only going to be remembered and marked if we are dead? Are we only going to care about people when they have been murdered? Still, it's important for us to mark the day because there isn't going to be anyone else doing it. There isn't going to be anyone else pointing out the variety of violence that sex workers face. For an organisation like SWAI, I feel our role is to highlight how the law is damaging and highlight that there's an alternate narrative to what exists in law and in policies. It's highlighting the varieties of violence that sex workers face. The only thing you'll ever hear about is violence from clients. But they also face the violence of lack of resources, violence of poverty, violence of the law, violence of the gardaí, the violence of stigma, and so on. It's our role to highlight the voices of sex workers. It's a sex-worker-led date – it isn't highlighted or marked by organisations who support the law and oppose sex workers' rights.

Ethical remembrance means learning from the mistakes of the past so the *people* of the present and future don't have to suffer in the same way. The women incarcerated in institutions such as the Magdalene Laundries had been silenced and ignored for so long that the survivors feared, understandably, that they would not be listened to when they had a chance to contribute to the McAleese Report into the abuses of the laundries. The women submitted almost 800 pages of testimony – it must have been unimaginably difficult to relive, write down and expose their deepest pain to others. Retelling personal stories of violence can be very traumatising, and fear is magnified to an undefinable level when the person is vulnerable in front of the entire country, including the people who have loudly stated that you are not to be believed.

Hands surely trembling and hearts beating fast, they did it anyway.

Only for not a single sorrowful word to be quoted in the report in the end.

The survivors had also met with the Department of Justice and Equality – face to face with the people who had the power to endorse their stories or dismiss them and side with their torturers. We can only begin to glimpse the inner work it took to remain calm, to speak even if their voices trembled, and to share what they may have never shared publicly about acts of vicious cruelty meted out to them, often over decades.

This is clearly not acceptable as this approach puts barriers in the way of hearing the experiences of the person who suffered. It affords status to the staff and officials and none to the person with the lived experience; their knowledge is dismissed while official knowledge from those with power over them is judged to be correct, because these people were 'correct'. This is another form of trauma, and ethical remembrance needs to be conscious of not retraumatising those sharing their stories.

A more recent review shows an almost identical absence. The 2017 Criminal Law (Sexual Offences) Act adopted the Nordic model of addressing the sale of sex, which is to criminalise the buyer and prosecute sex workers working together under the same roof. This act came with the provision that it would be reviewed after three years. In 2020, the review was commissioned and it was estimated to take three months to complete. An open submission invited written statements, and some meetings were held with charities, researchers, trafficking victims and sex workers. However, as of December 2024, it is not complete or public yet; Covid and personnel changes have delayed the report's completion. Linda Kavanagh from SWAI highlights the frustration felt about this process:

> I don't know how a researcher is supposed to pick up the notes of a different person and be able to intercept them accurately. Rightly or wrongly, they didn't record the interviews we gave. They did take notes, but they didn't record them. So, all that knowledge is lost, and whatever relationship there was between the people who met is gone. The Minister for Justice refuses to meet with us and we don't get responses to our concerns over this process. People didn't feel listened to – it's a really terrible process. But yet we are supposed to trust this process?

When exploring something, as well as looking at what we know, it's also important to ask – what don't we know? Whose voices are missing, and why? The stories of the women in Monto tell us what the sex trade can and did look like, and as Monto was like other red-light districts, both then and now, we can learn many lessons from the women. How they lived their lives was often sad, often liberating, often violent, often boring, often happy, often destructive, but they were still people who deserve to be remembered as whole people, not just a 'prostitute' or a 'fallen woman', or a 'poor unfortunate'.

While May Oblong was ultimately unsuccessful in preventing Monto's demise, Monto has stayed alive in the blood of its descendants. Paula and Pearl tell us what it's like to be tied so intimately to Monto through their ancestors.

Paula is a poet and has used her heritage to help guide her work as she untangles her family history:

The complexity of the area is important to understand, and that I would not have any judgement on my ancestors nor of anyone in that area. I wouldn't judge them by my own feminist ideology of today. I wouldn't be here if it wasn't for my ancestors; I only appreciate them. It's complex when it's family history. It's not remote, it's immediate, and you have lived it. It's been epigenetically transferred through your body as well.

My grandfather Wattie taught me to read and write and used to say to me, 'You take after my mother,' who was Anna Meehan. Her head was always stuck in a book. I see her, she lives in me, in my bones, in my being. And I experience that information emotionally. In the life of an artist, the relationship between art and trauma plays a huge role. In fact, in my new book I start with a piece called 'Sister Trauma'. I personified trauma as a sister who sits with me when I make the work and she guides me. And in fact, when I started writing, I didn't know what I was channelling but I was still chasing what I'm chasing now in some kind of real way. It was still coming through me, all the complexities of those family histories, even though I wasn't aware of so much of it. So I'm interested in how that works on a community level, because I have watched each generation having to come to terms with what was handed on. Now, sometimes very important values were handed on in that community which I embrace and I'm full of admiration for. But I also see addiction handed on, all kinds of dysfunction also handed on. We need to ask how communities ameliorate these destabilising issues on a bigger scale than the individual. It's a more complex idea that these diverse communities create incredible creative energy that often, along with trauma, moves through the generations till it finds its moment of expression. So that would be my way of embodying trauma and living it out, by trying not to pass it on, deal with my own shite and to put out into the world stuff I think people could use as tools.

Pearl works as a therapist and feels that her connection to Monto through Anna/Annie Meehan influences the approach she takes with her clients today:

I work with sex workers now and a lot of them love their work, really enjoy their work, very happy doing it. They love when they hear I'm the great-great-granddaughter of a madam, and we sometimes have conversations about how the sex trade has changed since then or stayed the same. But it just makes me wonder about the difference, the story, the shame; there's so much that comes up for me when I start thinking about it. And how close I am to it. I remember my supervisor telling me there's a titanium core that's running through me, and it spells acceptance right through it. She said you just are the epitome of unconditional positive regard. And I just, I remember crying when she said that to me. I said, 'Well I know where I come from.' I like the idea of being different. I love the phrase 'understanding differently', and I kind of like to think that that's where it came from. And maybe that's what makes me work better with my clients, that I have a broader spectrum to dig from. Working with sex workers, I'm in awe of the resilience they have. Meeting someone where they are instead of where you want them to be, and not white-washing things.

I was talking to one of my colleagues here about this and she asked me how I felt about sharing all this in public, and I said, 'Well, honestly, a lot of it is factual stuff that is out there in the public already. I'm just putting more of a little personal spin on it.' For me it's all about the story. I think these are just stories that need to be told. This is part of my heritage, it's part of my history, and it's part of why I'm here, and maybe it is why I'm resilient and able to work with anyone. You know, I stand on the shoulders of giants in lots of ways; there's a lot of resilience and a lot of strong women in our family and in Monto. Women who went too soon. Women who didn't get to tell their stories. And I'm just hoping that through this book we can share their stories.

Monto's spirit is experienced in an uncannily similiar way by Gemma, who was not aware of Pearl or her answer before sharing how Monto lives on in her:

I've known a real strong line of resilience and backbone in the women in the Dunleavy side of our family. To know that we're from someone who was for women's rights, back when they didn't even know it as womens rights. She was just fighting for justice, and all the women in our family have a real strong sense of justice in them. When I found out about her, it just made sense. I got goosebumps reading some of the stories about her – I could see me, my niece, or auntie in her actions. I think when you have that much fight in you, it's going to pass down. Your kids are going to have it. A toughness roughness.

You know what is magic? The journalist Una Mullally used a term to describe me, and I've never heard something so spot on to describe me. She said that I had armoured tenderness and when I think of that, I think of every woman in my family and especially Granny Dunleavy because of being a hard nut to crack, but once you do, there's so much love.

I remember one day walking out of dance class having a feeling that I hoped the Granny Dunleavy would be fucking proud that her granddaughter is walking on the same streets she did, but now it's because she's coming out of a dance class that our parents could afford for her, all because of how she shouted at the fancy men and madams and did what she did. It would be something she could only dream of doing, something for leisure, And here I am on those exact same cobblestones. You kind of have to honour that, because in those moments I see us as one and not just me and her – I see us all as one. When looking into the history of the Monto and my family, I started seeing this common denominator. I call it the spirit of the Monto. I would find it in different places, might be in people, it might be in an idea, it might be in a song, it might be in an image that I see. It was more prominent in women and it was a real strong sense of justice, and a fight.

Gemma continued the Granny Dunleavy's legacy by campaigning for abortion rights successfully in 2018, following her maternal linage in advocating for a fairer society for all women. The last minute uncovering of some of Gemma Dunleavy's history reminds us of the value of talking to family and noting their stories. We can now honour the Granny Dunleavy as one of Ireland's first known sex educators, pro-choice feminists and midwives. Imagine what other knowledge about our heritage is there, waiting for someone to ask those questions of their family. I can only encourage you to take this step, given the magic that Gemma's involvement demonstrates.

One solid way to bring Machnamh to Monto would be to support the establishment of a north-inner-city folklore museum in the last remaining house in Monto, as Terry wants to see. The museum could display the Monto cross used by the women, and numerous artefacts could be gathered together to help us understand and remember the realities of Monto, from the joy to the heartbreak and everything in between. Terry has recordings of the elderly neighbours he learned his Monto tales from, and to hear their history, in their own words, accents and tone, is not only a democratic way to learn, but also an ethical one that centres the people themselves. Community-led, the space would offer a way to connect the past with the present and honour the people of Monto. To make this a reality will be a huge mountain to climb, but all mountains can be climbed with support.

CHAPTER 19

CONCLUSION

Monto leaves us with more questions than answers. This book has explored many aspects of the culture of Monto, from life to death, but what else do we not know?

We don't know the women's inner lives, their sense of self or sense of humour. Who were they beyond the label of 'poor unfortunate'? What brought them joy? What roles did they play in peer support? What skills did they have for entertaining their clients? How much power and choice did they have in their day-to-day lives? How did they understand sexual violence, power dynamics, consent, pleasure, pregnancy and contraception? If they survived Monto, how did they think about their experiences? Did they tell people about their time there, or did it become a secret to keep for life? We know that sex workers are stigmatised by many of the general population, but what we don't have is enough information on how the women of Monto responded to that stigma. Did they accept it or challenge it? Did they feel shame or a sense of exclusion, and how did this impact them?

And what happens if we can't find an answer? Do we just give up on piecing together these parts of Irish history, of women's history? How can we analyse class and power effectively without being able to learn about the personal impacts of poverty, abuse, lack of employment or education, and intergenerational hunger and trauma? How do we build a comprehensive understanding of trauma that includes the experiences of sex workers, prostitutes and trafficking victims? If there is a gap in knowledge or understanding, how is it acknowledged and how is access to the creation of knowledge granted or refused? What happens to those not in positions of power because of exclusion and stigma? Do we look at *why* we can't find an answer?

We can reflect on these questions and take them with us as we explore how to support sex workers, prostitutes, prostituted people and trafficking victims today. There are various legal approaches to the sex trade that support or clash with differing feminist ideologies, with the voices of those who have spent time as a sex worker, prostitute or trafficking victim heard to varying degrees. The sex trade takes multiple forms, from strippers to cam girls to porn stars and many more. Rather than viewing it in terms of solely exploitation or solely empowerment, we can look at a micro narrative where many different experiences are heard, whether they support or challenge our personal beliefs. Sex work is not a singular thing; neither is prostitution or trafficking; and they exist in differing legal limbos, enforced on whims and morals, some of which are racist, misogynistic and classist. Singular analyses of such complex topics can mean missing out on fully understanding the needs of the people in these positions, and therefore miss out on building survivor-led resources that offer trauma-informed, judgement-free support that meets the person where they are. Regardless of ideology, there is a human behind the label, and they deserve to be treated with respect and empathy the same as anyone else.

We now have a better understanding of some of the legacy of traumatic events such as the Famine or the Troubles, and that trauma can be intergenerational, but we also need to understand how trauma interacts with poverty, class, violence, gender, sex, death, institutionalisation, capitalism, selling sex and exclusion. Nuance allows us to humanise people and build a better world where no one is in the sex trade unless they want to be, and where those who are in the sex trade are supported without judgement, regardless of why they are there.

Some stories are more accepted by society, and stories about sex were not welcome in many parts of Irish society post Famine and especially after the establishment of the Irish Free State, when the Catholic Church and the state joined forces in adopting a conservative sexual morality. This strict categorisation of 'good' women and 'bad' women had an iron grip on Irish society throughout the 20th century that continues to a lesser extent today. This stranglehold contributed to the same culture in which the deaths of women and teenagers such as Ann Lovett, Savita Halappanavar and countless others, are needlessly lost. The public shaming of women who have any connection to sex or nudity is now recognised as part of the spectrum of sexual violence, but it is too late for women like Dara Quigley. Dara had nude images of her leaked by a garda in 2017; Dara later died by suicide a few days after learning these images were viewed over 100,000 times. The guard did not face prosecution for his actions and resigned. Dara was an activist who had written about the need for garda accountability and social justice for all. Dara's mother Aileen has campaigned on behalf of her daughter to change the circumstances so that no one else has to suffer like Dara did. Accountability needs to be genuine and widespread, as Aileen explains the impact that this violation of Dara has had on her family:

A therapist explained that Dara's death and the revelation of the video was like an emotional bomb going off in the middle of our family group. A bomb created by the Gardaí and online participants and dropped by GSOC. All of us were severely injured by it. We had wounds and emotional shrapnel that had penetrated our psychic selves. So we were too hurt to take care of each other and withdrew from each other to attempt to heal. At the time it made little sense. Looking back now I can see how accurate it was.

This change to a healthier, safer world involves a cultural shift across all of society, and that involves facing some harsh truths about the roles we can all play in contributing to the harm victims experience, as Aileen urges us to consider:

On whom do you place the blame?

Dara for putting herself in such a vulnerable position in the first place?

The Garda who gratuitously and deliberately shared what should have been a confidential and protected film of a vulnerable woman? Who started this snowball rolling?

Facebook, which allowed the film to be shared thousands of times on its platform over the four days from Friday to Monday. Facebook which allowed the film to be copied off its platform on to other sites and platforms?

The people who shared the video to others, spreading it further, raising the profile of it, so that it appeared again and again in others' Facebook feeds and Google searches?

The people who named Dara, the people who made shaming comments, the others who pitied her? The ones who changed the speed of the video and added music, dehumanising her further.

The sites that picked up the video from Facebook, making it no longer a local phenomenon, but international, attracting yet more commentary?

Garda management who only asked Facebook to take it down because that's where it originally appeared online?

Where should blame have been placed? A collective responsibility, shared by many, but borne by none.

So much pain has simmered under the surface as women suffered in silence, still impacted by their ancestors' trauma and the Irish state's attitudes and actions. Feminist microhistories can help us piece together this fragmented violence and allow us to understand what happened and how we can prevent it happening again.

Monto was a physical space, but it was also a liminal space where more than one thing was true at the same time. It was a world within a world, visible yet hidden, a family space while also a hedonistic sex space, and a space of exploitation while also a space to find freedom. Time went by as fast as an Irish jig for visitors, but time froze for those subjected to sexual violence. For many, Monto was a place of liberation, personal freedom and increased opportunity, but it was simultaneously a traumatic one that led to early deaths for the most marginalised. Its inhabitants may have been there briefly or for decades, but all left their mark on the collective consciousness of women in Ireland even today.

Monto was said to end on 12 March 1925. But this closure wasn't the end of selling sex in Dublin, or in Monto itself. We owe it to the people involved to listen to them and to look at the person behind the label. When they were alive, the women of Monto may have been reduced to 'poor unfortunates' and stripped of their identities, but we remember them with Machnamh today.

And there is still a sense of *something* in the air in Monto, an alluring siren song that has persisted over the centuries. As Gemma Dunleavy says:

> Monto has an electricity to it – it's a place where the energy can be felt as you walk along those cobblestones even now, because they are the same stones the women walked on and my mother walked on and my granny walked on. There's something in these cobbles that has given us this grit. There is *life* there. Even when you're not aware of it, you're absorbing

it somehow. It doesn't just dissipate. It's going to come to the surface at some point, no matter when that is.

One hundred years after its purported closure, Monto is still seducing us with its legacies, secrets and twists, and refusal to behave.

ACKNOWLEDGEMENTS

For kindly trusting me with their personal, professional and academic knowledge, and for offering invaluable words of support, my everlasting gratitude is due to the incredible humans that are Pearl Brock, Paula Meehan, Terry Fagan, Martin Coffey, Gemma Dunleavy and her family, Sophie, Mardi Kennedy, Linda Kavanagh, Hirantha Periera, Jennifer Cooper, Lucy Smyth, Sarah McInerney, Izzy Tiernan, Carol Queen, Nina Hartley, Kelsey Obsession, Aileen Quigley, Adeline Berry, Susanna Riordan, Kevin C. Kearns and Elisa Donovan.

Recognition is also gratefully given to the centuries of known and unknown activists, writers, campaigners and advocates who have gone before us, as nothing we do now could have happened without those people taking chances and fighting for justice for women, often at great personal risk and cost. May you all get the flowers, celebration, love, rights and peace that you want, deserve, and are overdue.

Heartful thanks are also given to my editor Deirdre Nolan, who believed in me and this book from the very first sentence all those years ago at Clodagh Finn's book launch, and Lisa Gilmour at Eriu for the patience and support; Bonnier Books UK and Florence Philip in Publicity; and Gill Hess, particularly Simon Hess, Declan Heeney, Jacq Murphy, Helen McKean; Rosaleen Rodgers from Audiotrans. Thank you all for making this book happen.

For all those who have shared softness with me, given me a chance, shared a kind word, made me smile, or joined me for an adventure whether it was sensible or not, you've changed my life in immeasurable ways I never imagined. Special shout out to Bel Loh, my heart sister from across the world, a respite and a glimmer in human form, the kindest human I've ever met, and the reason I'm here today. Shivvy Hickey – the best hello I've ever heard from the most extraordinary, inspirational woman.

My heart is also full thanks to the magic of Helen Hughes, Rowan Holiday, Jean-Philippe Imbert, DCU SALIS, Sarah Sproule, Lu Burns, Ian Burns, Amanda Gareis, Rodge Mortis, Beth Kilkenny, Linnea Dunne, Grace Kelly, Jason Joseph, Dublin North West Repeal, Eimear McBride and the Lesbian Chickens, the Viva La Vulva Crew, Becky, Rachel Thompson, Arpita Chakraborty, Babs and Maureen, Jenn Machado Flynn, Charlotte Flynn, Angela Broderick, Alice Beck, Aoife Drury, Shawna Scott, Lennon and Co, Karl Melvin, Fai Monaghan, Sinead, Monika Kijewska, the Galway Sausages, the UCC EDI team, Nuala Finnegan, Céline Griffin, Tony Groves and the Tortoise Shack gang, Active* Consent, Mariah McPhail, Natia Tchumburidze, Thanya, the Elevate team, the Bumble bees, my Kens, Vicky Phelan, Lynn Comella, Morgana Muses, Caroline Whitston, Paula Smith, Jizz Lee, Shine Louise Houston, Michelle Heffernan, Laura Lee, Muireann O'Connell, Tara Flynn, Sophie Blakemore-Carson, Elaine Crowley, Rachel Dugan, Sybil Mulcahy, my Maneskin babies, Café Rea, Slow Roast, Kate Dawson, Grace Alice O'Shea, Nicola Fox Hamilton and everyone who has shared kind words of support and believed in me. Dolly Parton and Pedro Pascal – I hope you'd be proud.

Co-writing credit does of course need to go to Jolene, the cutest menace of a sausage dog who snoozed on my lap for the entirety of the writing process (until snack time), and our co-dependency is unapologetic and joyful. A.W.W.W., my heart dog.

Michael, infinite thanks are due for the kindness, the patience, the softness, the domesticity, the indulgence, the joy, the ridiculousness, the love, the belief, the tech support, the enabling, the travel guiding, the wine, the bougie evenings, the dragging me into the modern age, the future and for the space to be me. We made it to the next chapter – where to next? I did indeed marry well, and one day I'll fold a bedsheet the correct way, as a little treat.

IMAGE CREDITS

Page 32 – Annie Higgins, whose candlelight got her five years in prison alongside Margaret and Nannie.
Photo credit: Martin Coffey

Page 35 – Woman sleeping on the street; like many women of Monto, home was often the streets or a hallway if they were lucky.
Photo credit: Martin Coffey

Page 37 – Margaret Carroll, Martin Coffey's great-grandmother.
Photo credit: Martin Coffey

Page 46 – Pets were a common part of the soundscape of Monto.
Photo credit: Martin Coffey

Page 48 – Outdoor socialising was an integral part of Monto Life.
Photo credit: Martin Coffey

Page 49 – Women braving the elements in their shawls and coats, looking for business in Elliott Place. Note the boarded up windows to block out the sights and sounds of the sex trade for the families who lived side by side with the women.
Photo credit: Terry Fagan

Page 56– Annie Carroll with her friend Mary Vincent. Mary was found abandoned on a road in Phibsborough as a baby, and later sold sex in Monto to survive. Annie supported her to leave.
Photo credit: Martin Coffey

Page 63 – Monto homes were decorated from floor to ceiling as a point of pride.
Photo credit: Martin Coffey

Page 64 – Annie Meehan – married at 13, a mother at 14, a madam and the great-great grandmother of Pearl and great-grandmother of Paula.
Photo credit: Pearl Brock

Page 65 – Charles Meehan, notorious gangster and husband of Annie Meehan, and great-great-grandfather of Pearl and great-grandfather of Paula.
Photo credit: Pearl Brock

Page 92 – Bella Cohen was rumoured to specialise in the wilder side of sexual services in Monto.
Photo credit: Lafayette Photographers

Page 101 – Annie Meehan's opera glasses, now belonging to Pearl.
Photo credit: Pearl Brock

Page 109 – Becky Cooper, one of the most successful madams of Monto and the last surviving madam by 1949.
Photo credit: Terry Fagan

Page 115 – Aprons were a sartorial staple in Monto.
Photo credit: Martin Coffey

Page 116 – Cardigans kept the chills away as the women went about their business; Monto resident Dennis Farrell's sister Julia is in the middle.
Photo credit: Martin Coffey

Page 117 – Julia Farrell, standing on the same streets she used to work on.
Photo credit: Martin Coffey

Page 131 – Then, as now, alcohol was a common feature of daily life for many.
Photo credit: Martin Coffey

Page 139 – Mrs Dunleavy, the most well known and well respected midwife of Monto.
Photo credit: Terry Fagan

Page 140 – Mrs Dunleavy had no problem standing up to madams and the bullies in order to help the women with birth.
Photo credit:Terry Fagan

Page 205 – Terry made his way into the tunnels at long last.
Photo credit: Terry Fagan

Page 209 – Prison mugshot of Margaret Carroll, great-grandmother of Martin Coffey.
Photo credit: Martin Coffey

Page 210 – Prison mugshot of Nannie McLoughlin, great-grandaunt of Martin Coffey.
Photo credit: Martin Coffey

Page 240 – The Monto cross, which brought comfort to so many and is hung up in Martin Coffey's living room in Cabra after its time in Monto came to an end.
Photo credit: Martin Coffey

Page 255 – Woman cleaning cup in her yard, keeping the tenement dirt at bay.
Photo credit: Martin Coffey

Further Reading

- Coffey, Martin. *What's Your Name Again?* No listed publisher, n.d.
- Curtis, Maurice. *To Hell or Monto.* The History Press, 2015
- Duff, Frank. *Miracles on Tap.* Montfort Publications, 1989
- Duff, Frank. *Frank Duff In His Own Words.* Concilium Legionis Mariae, n.d.
- Fagan, Terry. *Monto: Madams, Murder and Black Coddle.* North Inner City Folklore Project, 2000
- Finnegan, John. *The Story of Monto: Account of Dublin's Notorious Red Light District.* Mercier Press, 1978
- Finnegan, John. *Honour Bright and Nighttown.* Elo Publications, 1995
- Kearns, Kevin C. *Dublin Tenement Life: An Oral History.* Gill, 2006
- Kearns, Kevin C. *The Legendary 'Lugs' Branigan – Ireland's Most Famed Garda.* Gill, 2014
- Kearns, Kevin C. *Working Class Heroines: The Extraordinary Women of Dublin's Tenements.* Gill, 2018
- Kearns, Kevin C. *In Our Day: An Oral History of Dublin's Bygone Days.* Gill, 2022
- Logan, William. *The Great Social Evil: Its Causes, Extent, Results, and Remedies.* Leopold Classic Library, 2016
- Luddy, Maria. *Prostitution and Irish Society, 1800–1940.* Cambridge University Press, 2007

- Luddy, Maria, and Murphy, Cliona (eds). *Women Surviving.* Littlehampton Book Services, 1990
- Mathers, Helen. *Josephine Butler.* The History Press, 2021
- McInerney, Sarah. *Where No One Can Hear You Scream: Murder and Assault in the Wicklow Mountains.* Gill, 2008
- Meehan, Paula. *The Solace of Artemis.* Dedalus Press, 2023
- O'Keeffe, Tadhg, and Ryan, Patrick. 'At the World's End: The Lost Landscape of Monto, Dublin's Notorious Red-light District', *Landscapes*, I, 21–38, 2009
- O'Keeffe, Tadhg, and Ryan, Patrick. 'Representing the imagination: a topographical history of Dublin's Monto from Ordnance Survey maps and related materials', in Adelman, Julia and Agnew, Éadaoin (eds). *Science and Technology in Nineteenth Century Ireland.* Four Courts Press, 2011
- Peakman, Julia. Peg Plunkett. QUERCUS, 2016
- Smith, Molly, and Mac, Juno. *Revolting Prostitutes.* Verso, 2020

**For a full bibliography and reference list, please visit
www.iamcarolinewest.com**